Dismantling White Privilege

Studies in the
Postmodern Theory of Education

Joe L. Kincheloe and Shirley R. Steinberg
General Editors

Vol. 73

PETER LANG
New York • Washington, D.C./Baltimore • Boston • Bern
Frankfurt am Main • Berlin • Brussels • Vienna • Oxford

Dismantling White Privilege

Pedagogy, Politics, and Whiteness

Edited by
Nelson M. Rodriguez
and Leila E. Villaverde

PETER LANG
New York • Washington, D.C./Baltimore • Boston • Bern
Frankfurt am Main • Berlin • Brussels • Vienna • Oxford

Library of Congress Cataloging-in-Publication Data

Dismantling white privilege: pedagogy, politics, and whiteness / [edited by]
Nelson M. Rodriguez and Leila E. Villaverde.
p. cm. — (Counterpoints; vol. 73)
1. Critical pedagogy—United States. 2. Whites—United States—Race identity.
3. Discrimination in education—United States. 4. Politics and education—
United States. I. Rodriguez, Nelson M. II. Villaverde, Leila E.
III. Series: Counterpoints (New York, N.Y.); vol. 73.
LC196.5.U6D57   370.11'5—dc21   98-16308
ISBN 0-8204-3917-7
ISSN 1058-1634

Die Deutsche Bibliothek-CIP-Einheitsaufnahme

Dismantling white privilege: pedagogy, politics, and whiteness / edited
by Nelson M. Rodriguez and Leila E. Villaverde.
–New York; Washington, D.C./Baltimore; Boston; Bern;
Frankfurt am Main; Berlin; Brussels; Vienna; Oxford: Lang.
(Counterpoints; Vol. 73)
ISBN 0-8204-3917-7

Cover design by Roymieco A. Carter

The paper in this book meets the guidelines for permanence and durability
of the Committee on Production Guidelines for Book Longevity
of the Council of Library Resources.

© 2000 Peter Lang Publishing, Inc., New York

Printed in the United States of America

For Our Loved Ones

Acknowledgments

We would like to express our deepest gratitude and appreciation to those that made the conception and execution of this book possible:

Joe L. Kincheloe and Shirley R. Steinberg, for suggesting this book's existence and incredible assistance, support, and encouragement throughout;

Roymieco Carter, for his patience and technical skills in typesetting, his support, and his artistic genius for the cover of the book;

The contributors, for their insights and cooperation;

And generally to all those individuals we've met along the way who have expressed a need for this scholastic endeavor.

Contents

PREFACE

Aaron David Gresson III

In the 1960s, a tremendous discourse or conversation burst forth from "the hood": the white man was a "blond blue-eyed devil." Associated largely with black militant groups like the Black Muslims, this notion resonated for many of us who have lived with white racism in the United States. Still, few blacks believe that whites are the anti-Christ. Even back then, it was evident that, ultimately, the pursuit of a better world order would not permit us to construct revolutionary racial identities through the demonizing of whites. We knew that, in the final analysis, it would be necessary to to construct identities that are inclusive and communal (Gresson 1977; 1978). Images such as "blond blue-eyed devil," while powerful at one level, failed to allow sufficient space for white identity enlargement or cross-racial coalitions based on humanistic values and principles.

White Studies has revealed a similar discursive dialectic and trajectory, from the incipient scholarly gaze upon "whiteness" as symbol and substance to recent understandings that it is complex, contradictory, and capable of transformation. In *Dismantling White Privilege: Pedagogy, Politics and Whiteness,* Leila Villaverde and Nelson Rodriguez and their authors present an imaginative and exciting continuance of what might be termed the recovery school within White Studies. Arguing that there is value in "whiteness" and that its "existential evils" can be transformed through emanicapatory critiques and campaigns, the essays in this work avoid the temptation to essentialize "white identity." By initiating specific critiques of "white privilege," these authors point to the need to name and dismantle privilege in its various incarnations by resisting an all-encom-passing or totalistic condemnation of all forms of "white identity practice."

This is a necessary and complex task. It is necessary because of the inevitable temptation to fall back on soothing, self-enhancing collec-tive identities such as "white identity." This temptation is evident, for in-stance, by the numerous Internet sites inviting "whites" to re-identity . (One site sends forth its call back to whiteness by observing "a white person is anyone who might be recognized as such by the majority of other whites.") The task is complex because whites may move back and forth along the implied continuum of "whiteness", participating selectively in various "white projects." Failure to persist in the dismantling of whiteness even as one affirms "white identity" is potentially catastrophic.

But how does one dismantle a complex, deeply cherished struc-tural and cultural process? This is the emergent agenda of a critical white studies project; and *Dismantling White Privilege* is in forefront of this spe-cific project. This volume stands as an especially self-conscious advocate of specific critiques of "whiteness" and "white privilege" that invite read-ers to examine these dynamic forces in relational terms . One of its spe-cific strengths is the articulation of the need to grapple with individual biographies and specificied practices of white privilege in a dialectical manner, one sensitive to the limitations of earlier, important yet problem-atic "white studies projects." "Mapping whiteness" (Rodriguez 1998) is an important way of describing the "emotion work" - as we psychologists name it - that must take place in the dismantling of white privilege. The precise rationale for this orientation has been described by Nelson Rodriguez in his reflection on bell hooks's (1992) insightful discussion of the terrify-ing potentiality of whiteness. "In her specific discussion of whiteness as terror, hooks offers me a language with which to rethink my own personal understanding of and relationship to whiteness" (1998, 53).

In *Dismantling White Privilege*, the editors have collected a pow-erful set of essays that assist in the goal of transforming "white identities" through the deconstruction and reconstruction of white participation in the larger social order. Guided by their vision of the necessity for a non-alienative challenge to white preferential privilege, they invite the reader to gain languages and metaphors through which to re-live their own narra-tives as preludes to participation in the construction and practice of wider identities in a just and democratic society.

In recent years, teacher educators and research on professional development have come to a shared appreciation of the complex nature of identity development. In particular, they have identified the importance of the numerous factors facilitating professional growth. The common conclusion has been stated cogently by Goodson and Cole (1994, 91):

> As we followed the teachers [in their study of teacher development] through their transitional period, it became apparent that the process of redefining what it means to be a teacher and their developing sense of new professional identity were contextually dependent on their developing notion of professional community. This leads us to suspect that in order for teachers to have opportunities to realize their individually defined personal/professional potential, teaching and development need to be defined, intrepreted, and facilitated within a broader institutional context. When, in the context of professional developemt, the boundaries of a teacher's professional community are pushed back to encompass the entire workplace context and attention is paid to the micropolitical and contextual realities of school life, it seems to us that then teachers have a better chance of becoming truly empowered.

References

Goodson, I.F. and A. L. Cole, *Curriculum Inquiry*, 24:1 (1994), p. 91.

Gresson, Aaron D. (1995). *The Recovery of Race in America*. (Minneapolis: University of Minnesota Press).

Gresson, Aaron D. (1978). "Phenomenology and the rhetoric of identification: A neglected dimension of coalition comunication," *Communication Quarterly*, 26(4), pp. 14-23.

Gresson, Aaron D. (1977). "Minority Epistemology and the Rhetoric of Creation," *Philosophy and Rhetoric*, 10(4), pp. 244-262.

Rodriguez, N. (1998). "Emptying the Content of Whiteness: Toward an Understanding of the Relation Between Whiteness and Pedagogy." In Joe Kincheloe, Shirley Steinberg, Nelson Rodriguez, and Ronald Chennault (eds), *White Reign: Deploying Whiteness in America*. (New York: Saint Martin's Press).

CHAPTER ONE

Projects of Whiteness in a Critical Pedagogy
Nelson M. Rodriguez

A burgeoning discourse in academe loosely called "White studies" has added an important dimension to the continually developing conversations about and analyses of race.[1] Indeed, challenging the assumption that the study and analysis of race means only examining "people of color," many scholars are now investigating the historical and social construction of whiteness in an attempt to understand its multiple meanings and to consider how white identity has changed and been constructed, shaped, and appropriated historically. Within the context of White studies, even examining the phrase, "people of color," one soon happens upon a significant staple of thought within the field: Whiteness has historically been appropriated in unmarked ways by strategically maintaining as colorless *its* color (and hence its values, belief systems, privileges, histories, experiences and modes of operation) behind its constant constructions of otherness. In other words, everyone or everything else is "marked"; "whereas white is not anything really, not an identity, not a particularizing quality, because it is everything - white is no colour because it is all colours" (Dyer, 1988, p. 45). What results from the apparent colorlessness of whiteness is that it is seen, as Richard Dyer (1988) notes in his now well-known and highly cited essay, "White," "as a case of historical accident, rather than a characteristic cultural/historical construction, achieved through white domination" (p. 46).[2] The focus, then, of examining the historical and social construction of whiteness, as well as the attendant effects of that construction process, is one of the major projects currently shaping the many emerging texts on whiteness that, rather quickly, are helping to define a new field of study and research agenda.

In addition to analyzing whiteness from a social and historical perspective, another project within White studies wants to move beyond analyses and deconstructions of whiteness to the abolition of it.[3] For example, in their essay, "Toward a New Abolitionism: A *Race Traitor* Manifesto," the new abolitionists John Garvey and Noel Ignatiev (1997) offer us a sense of this shift in focus: "The 'social construction of whiteness' has become something of a catchphrase in the academy, although few have taken the next step. Indeed, we might say that until now, philosophers have merely interpreted the white race; the point, however, is to abolish it" (p. 346). Significantly implied in their proposal, Garvey and Ignatiev have equated whiteness *only* with domination and oppression. To further illustrate this point, let us glance at another explication of their proposal, one which is quite clear on the necessity that whiteness must be destroyed: They note that the point of their project is "to blow apart the social formation known as the white race, so that no one is 'white'" (p. 348). I will return later in this essay to a more in-depth discussion as well as critique of the new abolitionism. For now, however, it is important to keep in mind that White studies is made up of several projects, some of which are in political and theoretical opposition to each other.

An example of such opposition within the field might be seen by juxtaposing the new abolitionist project to that of a third, one which has especially been articulated by cultural and critical theorists such as Henry Giroux, Diane Jester, and George Yudice. That third project is the necessity *not* to abolish whiteness but instead to *rearticulate* it.[4] Those of us theorists working within this third project agree with the new abolitionists that whiteness has been and continues to be an oppressive force, even for Whites themselves. However, where we disagree is in how we must *respond* in the historical present to the knowledge, insights, and analyses that the first project - examining whiteness as a historical and social construction - has given us. Henry Giroux (1997b) captures and rightly critiques the political project that undergirds the new abolitionists as well as much of the recent scholarship on whiteness. It is important to cite him at length on this:

> Heavily indebted to the assumption that 'whiteness' is synonymous with domination, oppression and privilege, the critical project that largely informs the new scholarship on 'whiteness' rests on a singular assumption. Its primary aim is to unveil the rhetorical, political, cultural, and social mechanisms through which 'whiteness' is both invented and used to mask its power and privilege. The political thrust of such work seeks to abolish 'whiteness' as a racial category and marker of identity. . . . While the recent scholarship on 'whiteness' has provided an im-

portant theoretical service for broadening the debate on race and racism, it is crucial for cultural workers and educators to recognize the limits of this work and begin to move beyond the current impasse of reducing 'whiteness' exclusively to forms of exploitation and domination. (pp. 382-383)

I agree with Giroux that the counter-political project of rearticulating whiteness provides more opportunity for white students to respond to the legacy of white supremacy by instilling in them a sense of hope and purpose that they can use *their own whiteness* to undermine and/or challenge that legacy. This approach to dealing with the "whiteness as domination" problem strikes me as far more hopeful, progressive and positive than telling Whites that, because whiteness is intertwined with domination, they must therefore in wholesale fashion disavow their whiteness.

In this essay, I want to examine in more detail the three different projects of whiteness thus far outlined. Additionally, I will consider how the discourse of whiteness might intersect with the field of critical pedagogy, in particular how such an intersection might play itself out within the specific discursive context of multiculturalism. Concerning the former, my aim is to introduce the unacquainted reader to some of the primary or recurring themes, as well as newly emerging forms of thought, within the rapidly evolving field of White studies. Because of limited space, however, I will offer the reader an introduction to the vast literature on whiteness primarily by referencing for further reading those edited texts, single-authored books, and numerous essays in academic journals that have taken up the topic of whiteness. In terms of the second objective, my intention is to imagine, through the intersection of White studies with critical pedagogy, the possible contours, purposes, and meanings of a "pedagogy of whiteness" within the context of multicultural education. It is important, I argue, to bring the often absent politics of whiteness into the discourse of multicultural education.[5] From this perspective, and more to the point, with respect to a critical understanding of race, racism, and race relations, multicultural education must begin and end with the question of whiteness. Here, I agree with historian David Roeidger's (1994) assertion that "if it does not involve a critique of whiteness, the questioning of racism often proves shallow and limited" (p. 13). Bringing whiteness *inside* multiculturalism no longer enables the latter to remain exclusively focused on the "Other" as well as continue to be devoid of critical analyses of whiteness as an invisible norm, that is, as "an unchanging and unproblematic location, a position from which all other identities come to be marked by their difference" (Bonnett, 1996, p. 146).

Whiteness and the Concept/Social Construction of Race

The interest in examining the "centeredness of whiteness" has been partly fueled by the impact of deconstructionist theories upon the contemporary social sciences.[6] Further, deconstructionism has actually helped spawn the field of White studies itself. As Alastair Bonnett (1996) notes:

> [One] . . . stimulus for 'White studies' has been the impact of deconstructionist theories and themes upon contemporary social science. Indeed, by exposing the reliance of 'what is centered' upon 'what is marginalized', deconstructionism has provided a specific analytical praxis and intellectual climate that has enabled and encouraged researchers to start interrogating the 'centre' of a number of different social arenas. Thus masculinity is being unpacked in gender studies, heterosexuality opened out in research on sexuality, and Whiteness coming under examination in 'race' studies. (p. 147)

Coined by Jacques Derrida, one project of "deconstruction" has been to examine and critique the hierarchical ordering of Western thought. Barbara Johnson (1981), in her "Translator's Introduction" to Derrida's *Dissemination*, describes Derrida's argument that Western thought has consistently been structured around dichotomies such as "good vs. evil, being vs. nothingness, presence vs. absence, truth vs. error, identity vs. difference, mind vs. matter, man vs. woman, life vs. death, nature vs. culture, speech vs. writing" (p. viii). However, as Johnson (1981) further notes:

> The second term in each pair is considered the negative, corrupt, undesirable version of the first, a fall away from it. Hence, absence is the lack of presence, evil is the fall from good, error is a distortion of truth, etc. In other words, the two terms are not simply opposed in their meanings, but are arranged in a hierarchical order which gives the first term *priority*, in both the temporal and qualitative sense of the word. In general, what these hierarchical oppositions do is to privilege unity, identity, immediacy, and temporal and spatial *presentness* over distance, difference, dissimulation, and deferment. (p. viii)

Appropriating, then, Derrida's concern with and critique of privileged signifiers, White studies wants to examine the signifier of whiteness. In doing so, it wishes in part to challenge and/or undo the representations, values, experiences, and knowledges of the "Other" that have come to seem "lesser" or "different" or "deviant" as a result of being positioned in the "second seat," as it were, of a socially constructed polarity where whiteness has been situated as the "normal" and "natural" and therefore, privileged, signifier. But whiteness is hardly normal and natural. Instead, it is a social construction, and it is this recognition/assertion which has generated unswerving investigations into the project of examining whiteness *as a social construction*. It is this central focus of White studies that gives it its originality. As Bonnett (1996) explains: "White attitudes and behaviour have long been seen as a valid and important subject within 'race' research. The importance of the new 'White studies' lies not in the originality of its object of study but in its attempt to treat that object as a historically mutable social construction" (pp. 152-153).[7] Before examining some of the different theoretical angles by which scholars have approached the social construction of whiteness, it is important to briefly pause and consider the concept of race itself from a critical perspective, that is, also as an historical and social construction. Indeed, arguing that whiteness, in particular, is to be understood as a construction is to make the same argument for our understanding of the concept of race, more generally.

Drawing on their landmark text, *Racial Formation in the United States: From the 1960s to the 1990s* (1994), I agree with Michael Omi and Howard Winant that race is a concept linked directly to evolving sociopolitical and historical processes and, thus, does not refer *in any essential or biological way* to different human bodies.[8] As Omi and Winant (1994) note, race "signifies and symbolizes social conflicts and interests by referring to different types of human bodies" (p. 55). From this perspective, the meaning and significance of race changes over space and time, rendering it "an unstable and 'decentered' complex of social meanings constantly being transformed by political struggle" (Omi & Winant, 1994, p. 55). Which is to say that race is *not* a natural, fixed phenomenon but rather a social construct whose one constant or guarantee is its changing significance and effects given its evolving historical interaction and intersection with the political. By "the political" I mean, using Omi and Winant's terminology, the different and competing *racial projects* of a given historical moment, and how these racial projects find expression and work pedagogically at the institutional and cultural levels and at the level of the everyday. Omi and Winant (1994) explain that "*A racial project is simultaneously an interpretation, representation, or explanation of racial dynamics, and an effort to reorganize and redistribute resources along particular racial lines.* Racial projects connect what race *means* in a particular discursive practice and the ways in which both social structures and everyday experiences are racially *organized*, based upon that meaning" (p. 56). The significance, then, of these racial projects is that they give meaning and substance to the concept of race itself during any given historical period. Racial projects, in other words, are directly linked to, what Omi and Winant (1994) term, *racial formation*, "the sociohistorical process by which racial categories are created, inhabited, transformed, and destroyed" (p. 55). The process of racial formation, thus, necessarily entails power, conflict, and interest. How, for example, the racial category of whiteness in the late twentieth century gets created, inhabited, and/or is made to signify has much to do with that category's "entanglements" or deployment within the competing political/ racialized discourses (or projects) about whiteness occurring at any particular historical moment.

With this understanding of race as a social construction immersed in political struggle, scholars, activists, and cultural workers are now critically examining whiteness as a social construction. The critical gaze has been *extended* from an exclusive focus on the "Other" to an inclusion of whiteness itself. One important argument undergirding this gesture of extension is that Whites too are a racialized group, an important point that is often either absent from white consciousness or not critically understood. As Roediger (1994) explains, "Whites are assumed not to 'have race,' though they might be racists. Many of the most critical advances of recent scholarship on the social construction of race have come precisely because writers have challenged the assumption that we only need to explain why people come to be considered Black, Asian, Native American or Hispanic and not attend to what Theodore Allen has marvelously termed the 'invention of the white race'" (p. 12). This significant shift, then, has led to a variety of questions and concerns regarding the social construction of whiteness. These questions include, but are not limited to, the following: What have the *effects* been of whiteness as a social construction?; How and where has whiteness been *deployed* and for what purposes?; How can whiteness be *understood or defined*?; and What should we *do* about whiteness? Drawing briefly on a few representative texts within the field of White studies, it is important for both conceptual and pedagogical purposes to review how particular theorists working within this field have specifically engaged these questions.

Arguably, extending the critical gaze, by examining the social construction of whiteness, has been more fully developed within particular academic areas than in others. One such area is historical studies on whiteness.[9] Indeed, several single-authored texts have currently "begun to map out the salience of whiteness to the formation of nationhood, class, and empire in the United States and in the European colonial enterprise" (Frankenberg, 1997, p. 2). One of the stakes at issue in some of these historical discourses on whiteness is to focus not on how Whites and white culture have been influenced by Blacks and black culture, which represents the important bulk of work by previous historians of race. Rather, the theoretical gaze has shifted so as to examine historically the relationship between the construction of white identity and such matters as power, oppression and domination, representation, and "the politics of gaining privilege."

An example of such historical work can be found in the publication by Noel Ignatiev (1995), *How the Irish Became White*. Here, Ignatiev argues that the Catholic Irish, once the victims of discrimination in Ireland under the Protestant Ascendancy, became "white" in America by supporting and participating in a variety of practices that helped them to overcome anti-Irish prejudice and therefore be admitted to the "privileges of whiteness" at the expense of Afro-Americans. Ignatiev (1997) notes, for example, that "over here [in America] the Irish became 'whites,' by gaining the right to vote while free Negroes were losing it, by supporting the Democratic Party (the party of the slaveholders), and by preventing free Afro-Americans from competing with them for jobs" (p. 608). Regarding the intersection between race and labor, David Roediger (1994) also makes a similar point about the Irish in *Towards the Abolition of Whiteness*. Detailing, for example, the way the Irish performed musical skits "in which blacks were depicted as overly sexualized, lazy, ill-disciplined beings," Roediger argues that one effect of these performances was to picture Blacks as nonproductive, undesirable workers (Hyde, 1995, p. 93). Thus, "becoming white fit hand in glove with becoming desirable labor" (Hyde, 1995, p. 93). One important insight to be gained from Ignatiev's and Roediger's historical analyses is that identity formation has much to do with engaging in complex sets of political practices, ones that contribute to defining and delimiting the parameters of particular identities themselves. In other words, the Irish, in these cases, perform certain practices within particular social, historical, and political contexts which not only reshape their sense of self, but also (re)shape their relations with others. From this perspective, then, one important contribution of historical analyses of whiteness for other academic fields concerned with taking up the topic is examining "how whiteness is performed by subjects, whether in daily life, in film, in literature, or in the academic corpus" (Frankenberg, 1997, p. 3).

Certainly, much other work on whiteness takes up in one way or another the politics of *performing* whiteness. This body of work, however, stems not from one disciplinary location; rather, it comes out of a diverse range of fields within the humanities and social sciences.[10] Ruth

Frankenberg's (1993) publication, *White Women, Race Matters: The Social Construction of Whiteness*, is an example of such work, and it has, as Alastair Bonnett (1996) rightly points out, "rapidly established itself as a distinct, and recognized, trajectory within 'White Studies'" (p. 148). By investigating through interviews how race shapes the lives of white women, in particular a group of white female residents of California, Frankenberg's study has provided much understanding not only of whiteness as a concept but also of how we should respond to (our own) whiteness.[11] For example, in "naming" whiteness, that is, in providing an understanding of its multiple meanings, Frankenberg (1993) defines/describes whiteness as follows:

> Whiteness . . . has a set of linked dimensions. First, whiteness is a location of structural advantage, of race privilege. Second, it is a 'standpoint,' a place from which white people look at ourselves, at others, and at society. Third, 'whiteness' refers to a set of cultural practices that are usually unmarked and unnamed. (p. 1)

Embedded in each of these definitions is the notion of *performance* and its relation to questions of whiteness. For example, understanding whiteness as "a location of structural advantage" is to think through how Whites live out (i.e. perform) their whiteness from a privileged position in the web of reality. How do their performances, specifically in relation to minorities, differ based on the *degree of awareness* of their overall structural advantage in terms of race privilege? Similarly, understanding whiteness as a "standpoint" from which Whites examine themselves, others, and society also registers the connection between whiteness and performance. Indeed, depending on their *place of mind*, Whites "perform" the act of viewing differently. How do white people, for example, with a critical awareness of themselves as racialized, engage in viewing performances that are markedly different from those viewing performances by Whites who lack such a critical consciousness about themselves? Finally, understanding whiteness as "cultural practices that are usually unmarked" is to consider such practices not only in a performative sense, but also in terms of how they are shot through with whiteness. In other words, how do Whites perform (in) cultural practices that are themselves punctuated by whiteness but not named, understood, or characterized as such? As an example, how does the white, gay male body in the recent outpouring of queer films perform unwittingly particular cultural practices that reinscribe hegemonic forms of whiteness?[12] How can the (white and gay) audiences of these films, as well as those who produce and act in them, mark or name the whiteness etched in these cultural practices as they are manifested in the new queer cinema? From this perspective, this act of marking whiteness can be understood as the counter-performance par excellence undergirding the project behind White studies.

For example, continuing with the third dimension - whiteness as an invisible or unmarked category - Frankenberg (1993) additionally notes that,

> naming 'whiteness' displaces it from the unmarked, unnamed status that is itself an effect of its dominance. Among the effects on white people both of race privilege and of the dominance of whiteness are their seeming normativity, their structured invisibility. (p. 6)

Linking whiteness to race privilege and its structured invisibility is an important *counter-discursive marking* of whiteness. Such a move to mark or name whiteness has become especially important in light of contemporary articulations and celebrations of "color blindness." With this latter discourse, we are told that all people are the same under the skin and that we all have the same equal chances of making it. Therefore, the "logic" continues, if a minority person fails to achieve, then the blame lies *solely* with the individual. However, what is the discourse of color blindness but nothing more than a neoconservative right-wing racial project committed to dismantling important rights discourse as well as "preferential" programs like affirmative action. Indeed, color-blind discourse is not a racial project of benignly looking past race to the person under the skin motif. Instead, it is a project set up to "protect" white privilege and power by, as educational theorist Peter McLaren (1997) notes, permitting "white people to construct ideologies that help them to avoid the issue of racial inequality while simultaneously benefiting from it" (p. 262). In other words, the rhetoric of color blindness enables Whites to erase from consciousness not only the history of racism and how that history plays itself out economically, politically, socially, and culturally in the present; such an insidious discourse also dissuades both the individual and institutions from engaging in antiracist strategies for dismantling white privilege and for reworking the terrain of whiteness. Given the racial project of color blindness, then, it is fitting that part of the project behind the investigation of whiteness as a social construction should be to *mark* the invisibility of whiteness and white privilege. Indeed, as Ruth Frankenberg (1993) rightly and eloquently notes, "To speak of whiteness is, I think, to assign *everyone* a place in the relations of racism" (p. 6).

If Frankenberg's study enables whiteness to come into clearer focus by providing a better sense of its complex meanings, her study also, in its own way, provides an answer to what we must *do* with whiteness. Her proposal partly stems from her focus on the "politics of experience." That is, having analyzed how thirty individual white women think through race, Frankenberg emerges quite hopeful that, through the process of "naming whiteness," white people can begin to see it at work in their own day-to-day lives and experiences and therefore be in a position to begin the quite arduous task of living out their whiteness progressively. Thus, there is a strong sense in Frankenberg's work that the existence of *viable* forms of whiteness is not only a possibility, but also should be seen as an important goal in our theorizations about whiteness. "By examining and naming the terrain of whiteness," explains Frankenberg (1993), "it may, I think, be possible to generate or work toward antiracist forms of whiteness, or at least toward antiracist strategies for reworking the terrain of whiteness" (p. 7). This enterprise of naming whiteness so that it can be reworked so that anti-racist forms of whiteness can develop is, or at least seems to be, in opposition to the theoretical and politically active work of the new abolitionists. Also known as "race traitors," and heralding the slogan "treason to whiteness is loyalty to humanity," the new abolitionists are not for reinventing whiteness but instead are for its abolishment or destruction. It is to this second project of whiteness to which we now turn.

"Now You See It, Now You Shouldn't": Race Visibility, Race "Erasure"

Undergirding the new abolitionist project is a philosophy about race that oddly enough shares some similarity with the discourse of color blindness, at least in this regard: That race as a defining category of identity can be undone, nullified, or erased. Significantly, though, the new abolitionists arrive at such a proposition about the white race through a historical, theoretical, and political lens that is quite absent from essential "sameness" or color-blind discourse. Indeed, whereas the latter engages in the "double move toward 'color evasiveness' and 'power evasiveness,'" that is, refuses to see and engage with race, racism, and race relations, both past and present, the former does just the opposite (Frankenberg, 1993, p.14). And for this reason, the new abolitionists have been an extremely important force in challenging the "rightful" dominance of both whiteness and white privilege. Yet any discourse that proposes the erasure of race, white or otherwise, is, in my view, wrongheaded and misguided for at least three reasons:

First, any project that proposes the destruction of (the white) race seems unwilling to acknowledge or to take seriously the *embeddedness* of race in culture, social relations, and at an institutional level. In other words, the important insight that race *is* a social construction, a process that has taken place over a long period of time and under varied and changing political circumstances, seems not to play a significant enough role in the proposal by the new abolitionists about what should be done to or with whiteness. As Winant (1997) notes, "Despite their explicit adherence to a 'social construction' model of race, theorists of the new abolitionist project do not take that insight as seriously as they should" (p. 48).

Second, though the new abolitionist project is articulating itself as a radical position, how is it that such a project can actually aid in the encouragement of a celebration and "discursive maneuvering" of race erasure? In other words, by seeming part of a broader movement in the United States that wishes to do away with race, the irony of the race traitor position is that it might strengthen the erroneous notion that race does not matter. From this perspective, how does the apparently radical position of renouncing white racial identity actually complement conservative support for denying the relevance of race in contemporary American society? Put another way: How does the notion of the abolition of whiteness provide Whites with a position not only to deny the relevance of race, but also to deny the existence of white privilege? It's no doubt, then, that minorities would look to the race traitor position with possible apprehension or agitation. As Peter McLaren (1997) remarks, "from the perspective of some people of color, offering the choice to white people of opting out of their whiteness could seem to set up an easy path for those who don't want to assume responsibility for their privilege as white people. Indeed, there is certainly cause for concern" (p. 275). Before further examining the problems associated with the race traitor position, let us first briefly look at a conservative argument advocating the elimination of race consciousness. My intention here is to emphasize the following broad point: *Any* theoretical and political efforts aimed at the abolishment of race run the risk of downplaying and not seeing just how deeply lodged race is at all levels of American life.

An example of such a theoretical blindspot, especially around questions of whiteness, can be seen in a recent article by Jim Sleeper (1997) titled, "Toward an End of Blackness: An Argument for the Surrender of Race Consciousness." Here, Sleeper calls for transcending racial identity. As he explains:

The problem is not that racism has grown stronger; it is that American civic life has become weaker - and not primarily because of racism. If we find it difficult to say that a black person's color isn't important, that is because we no longer know how to say that being an 'American' is important - important enough to transcend racial identity in a classroom, in a jury room, or at the polls. . . .The most that blacks can expect of us is that we will embrace and judge blacks - and let ourselves in turn be embraced and judged by them - as individual fellow participants in our common national experiment. (pp. 36 & 44)

What are the implications or consequences of surrendering racial identity to one of national identity? I take it that such a change in focus allows whiteness itself to remain unproblematized and uninterrogated, and to continue on with its "naturalized" status. That is, whether Sleeper recognizes it or not, such a shift turns out, in actuality, to be a strategy of "exnomination." John Fiske (1996) explains this strategy as follows: "exnomination is the means by which whiteness avoids being named and thus keeps itself out of the field of interrogation and therefore off the agenda for change" (p. 42). Indeed, the process of renouncing racial consciousness for national consciousness can, and most likely will, fail to ask these basic but crucial questions: Which national identity are we surrendering to? Which national identity is being referenced? I would argue that the national identity to which Sleeper uncritically refers, as well as others who embrace his line of reasoning, is a national identity that is shot through with *white* values, *white* beliefs, *white* history, and *white* experience. Therefore, to erase race, as is proposed within the context of Sleeper's argument, is to call for a program of homogenization around whiteness itself. Indeed, such a shift would, especially within the workings of "official" public memory, downplay difference and particularity in favor of the rhetoric of a common (white) culture.[13]

Finally, returning more specifically to the new abolitionists, I am further apprehensive about their proposal for the following two reasons: First, I am concerned that their call for the destruction of the white race will *not* dismantle white solidarity, as they think it will, through acts of "race treason" on the part of Whites. In the highly politically racialized climate that in general characterizes the contemporary landscape in the United States, many Whites now believe that their whiteness is not only under attack, but also has become a liability, especially in the labor market. From this perspective, then, asking Whites to renounce their whiteness - because it represents nothing but negativity - will more than likely be seen by them as "insult to injury." That is, already angry, anxious, and threatened by the implications of their growing awareness of themselves as racialized, an awareness which has engendered an identity crisis for many Whites, the added gesture of white race treason will clearly signal to Whites that such an act is a form of punishment for having become aware of their whiteness. It is as if they are being told, "now you see it, now you shouldn't," *with no space in between for negotiating their identity otherwise.* In this context, it seems likely that white people will *rush to white solidarity* in the reactionary attempt to rewrite, however skewed, a white identity that is "non negative" as well as engage in racial logics that offer up a Disneyesque revisionism of cultural history (i.e. of the history of racism and of race relations in the United States). Indeed, because whiteness as it is propounded by the discourse of race treason is nothing but negative, many Whites will unfortunately respond to such a discourse not by developing solidarity with disenfranchised groups but, instead, by developing solidarity *in their whiteness.* This response no doubt would be a manifestation of, and connected to, a broader contemporary movement of, what Charles A. Gallagher (1994) has brilliantly labeled, "white reconstruction."[14]

Drawing on Annalee Newitz and Matthew Wray's (1997) crucial theoretical intervention, my second apprehension with the race traitor position is its tendency to overlook the *differences within whiteness*, thus engaging in reductive forms of analysis. Newitz and Wray (1997) argue that an unexplored domain within White studies is "white trash" identity, an identity that "is, in many ways, the white Other" (p. 168). The importance of white trash identity for White studies is, it challenges the pervasive notion within the field that whiteness is *exclusively* about domination. As Newitz and Wray (1997) explain:

> We are suggesting that an alternative and as yet unexplored way to deconstruct whiteness is to examine the differences within whiteness. We thus argue for the necessity of breaking down whiteness by examining how, for instance, discourses of differences among whites tend to de-stabilize and undermine any unified or essentialized notion of white identity as the primary locus of social privilege and power. (p. 169)

Highlighting the reductive problem of collapsing whiteness with domination is not the only challenge a white trash identity poses for White studies. Such an identity also challenges a related common sense assumption within the field: That whiteness is always an unmarked or invisible category.[15] That is, the "white" of white trash is indeed marked, and it is immediately registered as something other than a dominant form of whiteness. As Newitz and Wray (1997) note, "Unlike unmarked hegemonic forms of whiteness, the category white trash is marked as white from the outset. . . . The whiteness of 'white trash' signals something other than privilege and social power" (p. 169). By examining the relationship between race- and class-based forms of oppression, thus providing an important critical lens for appreciating the complexities and contradictions within whiteness, Newitz and Wray join an important and newly emerging theoretical and political project within White studies. To be sure, as a counter pedagogy to the insistence on equating whiteness *only* with domination, Newitz and Wray's discourse of white trash identity has become part of an emerging theoretical assemblage within White studies that wishes to argue for a more *dialectical* approach to the study of whiteness.[16] While this particular way of thinking about whiteness is still in its inchoate stages, one site from which to examine the efficacy of this emerging project of whiteness is education. In particular, I am interested in the following question: How might a pedagogy of whiteness committed to the notion of *rearticulating* whiteness provide multicultural education with a project that moves it beyond simply a disingenuous exercise in "cultural tourism"? I now examine this question by discussing the relationship among White studies, critical pedagogy, and multiculturalism.

The Politics of Rearticulating Whiteness in a Critical Pedagogy

One important and central tenet emerging from the complex and varied discourses associated with the term "critical pedagogy" has been the insistence that the enterprise of education should be linked to questions of social justice, that is, to the elimination of forms of *injustice*.[17] Indeed, educating students to analyze critically how oppression is structural, that is, how it is deeply embedded in the norms and practices of a well-intentioned liberal society, is crucial to the project of having them acquire languages of critique as well as languages of possibility.[18] In their essay (1996), "Context and Culture: What Is Critical Pedagogy?" Pepi Leistyna and Arlie Woodrum provide us with the radical democratic project underpinning the discourse of critical pedagogy:

> Critical Pedagogy . . . while widely misunderstood and misinterpreted, challenges us to recognize, engage, and critique (so as to transform) any existing undemocratic social practices and institutional structures that produce and sustain inequalities and oppressive social identities and relations. (p. 2)

Concerning our focus in this essay on whiteness, the discourse of critical pedagogy offers insight into the overall purpose of a pedagogy of whiteness.[19] That is, it is imperative that such a pedagogy invite (white) students to critically engage with inequality and asymmetrical relations of power so as to challenge and transform them. However, to do so they must encounter, be challenged by, and negotiate with the discourse of race *as a social, historical, and political construction.* Significantly, though, such an encounter must also include the study of the social construction of whiteness.

Within the context of multiculturalism, this translates in part into a pedagogy that asks students to challenge forms of multicultural education that are disengaged from questions of power, access, oppression, and domination.[20] From this perspective, then, rather than calling for an end to or destruction of race, be it in the form of a race traitor manifesto or in the discourse of color blindness, educators and other cultural workers, as Henry Giroux (1997a) rightly points out, need to "fashion pedagogical practices that [both] take a detour through race . . . [and] address how Whiteness might be renegotiated as a productive force within a politics of difference linked to a radical democratic project" (p. 297). To be sure, analyzing race, and whiteness in particular, as part of a *critical* multicultural curriculum provides not only the important space for white students to understand the legacy of whiteness and how they *do* benefit in the present because of that legacy, as well as for imagining how whiteness itself "can be used as a condition for expanding the ideological and material realities of democratic public life" (Giroux, 1997a, p. 297); in addition, such a curriculum challenges an approach to multicultural education where "issues of cultural diversity are reduced to points of 'cultural enrichment' that can be extolled without upsetting the power of dominant groups" (Kincheloe and Steinberg, 1997, p. 17). To put it another way: By highlighting the necessary tension between understanding whiteness as oppression as well as thinking through its potentiality, such a dialectical approach to the study of whiteness pushes the boundaries of multicultural education not only by bringing whiteness inside multicultural education for critical analysis, but also by thinking through its potential as a progressive racial identity linked to a broader democratic project. The priority of this type of multiculturalism is not merely to celebrate racial difference; rather, such a critical multiculturalism wants to link, in this case, the question of race to a politics that challenges social inequality and cultural injustice. While certainly multicultural education can challenge racial injustice without taking up the issue of whiteness, I believe that bringing whiteness inside multiculturalism, in the dual sense described above, helps to *refine and extend* a multicultural education committed to the critical project of racial equality.

To summarize, then, the argument so far: A dialectical approach to the study of whiteness - that is, an approach that examines whiteness in relation to oppression and domination *and* as a viable, progressive, and contradictory category - pushes multicultural education in a more critical direction for the following two reasons. First, by making a critical interrogation of whiteness part of the discourse of mainstream (pluralist) multiculturalism, multicultural education must now face a subject which has typically, perhaps strategically, been excluded from our understanding of the concept of race, racial politics, and race relations. This is important, for leaving whiteness "untapped" is in part how it maintains its dominance. Second, so that bringing whiteness within multiculturalism does not end up reducing whiteness into domination, a dialectical approach to the study of whiteness challenges multicultural education to consider what whiteness can *do*. This, too, is important, for leaving whiteness with no project of possibility would be, as I have already argued, a pedagogical and political mistake. Indeed, with no project of possibility or hope white students are more likely either to experience their whiteness as immobilizing guilt or to create solidarity in their whiteness.

In addition to expanding the contemporary dialogue about multiculturalism in a more critical direction by inserting the politics of whiteness into multicultural discourse, a pedagogy of whiteness committed to a dialectical approach to the study of whiteness provides further insight for constructing a critical multicultural education. For example, the dual process described above of deconstructing *and* rearticulating whiteness simultaneously helps prevent Whites from *disingenuously* opting out of their whiteness. As Joe L. Kincheloe and Shirley R. Steinberg (1998) explain:

> Whites alone have the privilege of opting out of their racial identity, of proclaiming themselves as non-raced. No matter how vociferously they may renounce their whiteness, white people do not lose the power associated with being white. Such a reality renders many white renunciations disingenuous to some extent. It's as if some race traitors want to disconnect with all liabilities of whiteness (its association with racism and blandness) while maintaining all its assets (the privilege of not being black, Latino, or Native American). Such cold, self-interested realities will always be an impediment to wide scale efforts to forge new white identities. (p. 22)

As implied by Kincheloe and Steinberg, the process of rearticulating whiteness is just that: It is a process of reworking racial identity, not renouncing it. To rearticulate whiteness entails a sustained effort at living out one's whiteness progressively; to renounce whiteness is more akin to changing one's racial identity as one would his or her clothing. Henry Giroux (1997a) puts it succinctly when he says, "for progressive Whites, 'crossing over does not mean crossing out,' or renouncing Whiteness as a form of racial identity" (p. 299). This process of rearticulating whiteness, however, must occur alongside the process of deconstructing whiteness. That is, white students must engage in the process of identity formation by simultaneously critically examining whiteness in its historical, social, political, economic, and cultural contexts. Indeed, white students have to "learn to engage in a critical pedagogy of self-formation that allows them to cross racial lines not in order to become Black, but to begin to forge multiracial coalitions based on a critical engagement rather than a denial of 'Whiteness,'" (Giroux, 1997a, p. 299). Not disingenuously opting out of one's whiteness, then, entails going head-on with, while at the same time reworking one's, whiteness.

A dialectical approach to the study of whiteness also ensures that multicultural education, insofar as discussions of race are concerned, focuses on the serious issues that are linked to questions of race in contemporary American society. With mainstream pluralist multiculturalism's emphasis on and highlighting of racial difference, typically evaded are more pressing issues, such as racism, racial politics, and the relationship between race and the control and ownership of wealth in the United States. One can't help but conclude that pluralist multiculturalism is a hegemonic project that, in fact, helps reinscribe racial inequality by participating in a politics of evasion. As Kincheloe and Steinberg (1997) argue, "The hidden hegemonic curriculum of pluralist multiculturalism involves the promotion of a form of cultural tourism that fails to address or understand the harsh realities of race . . . subjugation" (p. 18). Within the context of multicultural education, however, deconstructing and rearticulating whiteness challenges the hegemony of pluralist multiculturalism in at least two significant ways. First, by bringing into multicultural education a critical analysis of whiteness, it becomes almost impossible not to discuss such matters as social inequality, exclusion, racism, and oppression as part of the story of whiteness. Indeed, raising questions about whiteness often leads to an understanding of it above and beyond simply highlighting it as another form of racial difference. Second, by discussing the politics of rearticulating whiteness, especially within the context of deconstructing it, serious racial concerns arise as white students are made aware of the issues at stake in living out their whiteness progressively in the name of racial justice. From this perspective, they are invited to consider what they can *do* with their whiteness in light of the broader project of expanding democratic possibilities.

Finally, a dialectical approach to the study of whiteness can challenge multicultural education by pushing it to probe the question of pedagogy outside the "precincts" of traditional classroom settings. Most often, pedagogical considerations remain within the realm of classroom teaching and learning. However important the latter, there are other public spheres, such as popular culture, where pedagogy takes place - indeed, where consciousness is constructed, identities are formed, and knowledge is produced. From this perspective, then, it might be more useful to extend the definition of pedagogy as follows: Pedagogy means "how, and in what context, we learn what we learn" (Leistyna and Woodrum, 1996, p. 4). With such a definition meaning multiple sites where "education" takes place, we are now in a better position to examine or ask questions about those multiple discourses outside of the traditional classroom setting that, in one way or another, attempt to fashion a particular pedagogy of whiteness. So, for example, in terms of popular culture, a dialectical approach to whiteness might engage in the processes of deconstruction and rearticulation by examining, on the one hand, how certain films reproduce the oppressive nature of whiteness by the very way in which they take up the topic. Here, I am reminded of a past student of mine, an African American woman, who, when asked by a white student why she did not want to see the movie, *Dangerous Minds*, responded by saying, "I'm not interested in seeing *another* movie about some white person who saves black people." On the other hand, however, how might certain films provide particular narratives about whiteness that link it to some kind of progressive identity and politics? What do these narratives look like? What forms will they take? And what type of pedagogy of rearticulation will they envision? By politicizing whiteness, then, through the twin operation of deconstruction and rearticulation, I am hopeful that white students will productively negotiate their identities and ideologies around the necessary tension between unsettlement, on the one hand, and political agency, on the other. Multicultural education is one site that proves to benefit from such a dialectical approach to the study of whiteness.

Notes

1. For articles announcing and formally making official the rise of White studies, see Liz McMillen, "Lifting the Veil from Whiteness: Growing Body of Scholarship Challenges a Racial 'Norm,'" *The Chronicle of Higher Education*, September 8, 1995, A23; and David W. Stowe, "Uncolored People: The Rise of Whiteness Studies," *Lingua Franca* 6, no. 6 (September/October 1996): 68-77. Scholarly journals devoting entire issues to the topic of whiteness include, K. Anthony Appiah, Henry Louis Gates, Jr., and Michael Colin Vazquez, eds., *Transition: The White Issue* 73 (1998); and Mike Hill, ed., *the minnesota review: The White Issue* 47 (1996).

2. A classic and pioneering work in contemporary White studies in marking the invisibility of whiteness is Richard Dyer's "White," *Screen* 29 (1988): 45-64. See also his more recent publication, *White* (New York: Routledge, 1997).

3. Examples of new abolitionist discourse can be found in Noel Ignatiev and John Garvey, eds., *Race Traitor* (New York: Routledge, 1996); and Danny Postel, "Race Traitor: An Interview with Noel Ignatiev, March 1996," *Z Magazine*, January 1997, 32-37. See also David Roediger, *Towards the Abolition of Whiteness* (London: Verso, 1994).

4. For a brilliant essay that challenges the notion of the abolition of whiteness, especially within the context of a discussion of pedagogy, see Henry A. Giroux, "Rewriting the Discourse of Racial Identity: Towards a Pedagogy and Politics of Whiteness," *Harvard Educational Review* 67, no. 2, (Summer 1997): 285-320. See also by Giroux the following two essays: "White Squall: Resistance and the Pedagogy of Whiteness," *Cultural Studies* 11 (1997): 376-389; and "Race, Pedagogy, and Whiteness in *Dangerous Minds*," *Cineaste* 22, no. 4, (1997): 46-49. Other work on rearticulating whiteness includes, Diana Jester, "Roast Beef and Reggae Music: The Passing of Whiteness," *New Formations*, no. 118, (Winter 1992): 106-121; and George Yudice, "Neither Impugning nor Disavowing Whiteness Does a Viable Politics Make: The Limits of Identity Politics," in Christopher Newfield and Ronald Strickland, eds., *After Political Correctness*. (Boulder: Westview Press, 1995): 255-281.

5. For a superb and brilliant discussion of a pedagogy of whiteness within the context of multicultural education, see Joe L. Kincheloe and Shirley R. Steinberg, *Changing Multiculturalism* (Philadelphia: Open University Press, 1997).

6. A useful discussion of the different factors influencing the growth of White studies can be found in Alastair Bonnett's essay, " 'White Studies': The Problems and Projects of a New Research Agenda," *Theory, Culture, and Society* 13, no. 2 (1996): 145-155.
7. An important contribution to White studies that exhumes a past tradition of thinking and writing by Blacks about whiteness can be found in David Roediger's important edited publication, *Black on White: Black Writers on What It Means to Be White*. (New York: Schocken Books, 1998).
8. Several important texts that discuss the social construction of race include, Michael Omi and Howard Winant's, *Racial Formation in the United States: From the 1960s to the 1990s*. (New York: Routledge, 1994); Howard Winant's, *Racial Conditions: Politics, Theory, Comparisons*. (Minneapolis: University of Minnesota Press, 1994); and Ruth Frankenberg's, *White Women, Race Matters: The Social Construction of Whiteness*. (Minneapolis: University of Minnesota Press, 1993).
9. Some representative examples of historical studies on whiteness include: Grace Elizabeth Hale, *Making Whiteness: The Culture of Segregation in the South, 1890-1940*. (New York: Pantheon Books, 1998); Noel Ignatiev, *How the Irish Became White*. (New York: Routledge, 1995); Theodore W. Allen, *The Invention of the White Race*. (New York and London: Verso, 1994); David Roediger, *Towards the Abolition of Whiteness*. (New York and London: Verso, 1994); Vron Ware, *Beyond the Pale: White Women, Racism, and History*. (New York and London: Verso, 1992); David Roediger, *The Wages of Whiteness: Race and the Making of the American Working Class*. (New York and London: Verso, 1991); Alexander Saxton, *The Rise and Fall of the White Republic*. (New York and London: Verso, 1990). See also Richard Delgado and Jean Stefancic, eds., *Critical White Studies: Looking Behind the Mirror*. (Philadelphia: Temple University Press, 1997); George Lipsitz, "The Possessive Investment in Whiteness: Racialized Social Democracy and the 'White' Problem in American Studies," *American Quarterly* 47, no. 3, (1995): 369-387. For a legal and historical viewpoint, see Ian F. Haney Lopez, *White by Law: The Legal Construction of Race*. (New York: New York University Press, 1996). From a literary and historical perspective, see Toni Morrison, *Playing in the Dark: Whiteness and the Literary Imagination*. (New York: Vintage Books, 1992).
10. Examples here include: Matt Wray and Annalee Newitz, eds., *White Trash: Race and Class in America*. (New York: Routledge, 1997); Ri-

chard Dyer, *White*. (New York: Routledge, 1997); Daniel Bernardi, ed., *The Birth of Whiteness: Race and the Emergence of U.S. Cinema*. (New Brunswick, New Jersey: Rutgers University Press, 1996); Fred Pfeil, *White Guys: Studies in Postmodern Domination & Difference*. (New York and London: Verso, 1995); Ruth Frankenberg, *White Women, Race Matters: The Social Construction of Whiteness*. (Minneapolis: University of Minnesota Press, 1993). See also the following academic articles: Thomas K. Nakayama and Robert L. Krizek, "Whiteness: A Strategic Rhetoric," *Quarterly Journal of Speech* 81 (1995): 291-309; John Gabriel, "What do you do when minority means you? *Falling Down* and the construction of 'whiteness,'" *Screen* 37, no. 2, (1996): 129-151; and Carrie Crenshaw, "Resisting Whiteness' Rhetorical Silence," *Western Journal of Communication* 61, no. 3 (Summer 1997): 253-278.

11. For other work discussing the relationship between whiteness and gender, see Peggy McIntosh, "White Privilege and Male Privilege: A Personal Account of Coming to See Correspondences through Work in Women's Studies," in Richard Delgado and Jean Stefancic, eds., *Critical White Studies: Looking Behind the Mirror*. (Philadelphia: Temple University Press, 1997): 291-299. See also Vron Ware, *Beyond the Pale: White Women, Racism, and History*. (New York and London: Verso, 1992).

12. See here Jose Esteban Munoz, "Dead White: Notes on the Whiteness of the New Queer Cinema," *GLQ: A Journal of Lesbian and Gay Studies* 4, no. 1, (1998): 127-138.

13. An important and critical discussion of the notion of a common culture is Donaldo Macedo's, *Literacies of Power: What Americans Are Not Allowed to Know*. (Boulder: Westview Press, 1994).

14. An examination of the process of white reconstruction, especially in higher education, can be found in Charles A. Gallagher's excellent essay, "White Reconstruction in the University," *Socialist Review* 94, nos. 1-2, (1995): 165-187.

15. For an important argument highlighting the increasing visibility of whiteness in contemporary politics, see Henry A. Giroux, *Channel Surfing: Race Talk and the Destruction of Today's Youth*. (New York: St. Martin's Press, 1997).

16. Examples of such writing include: Henry A. Giroux, "Rewriting the Discourse of Racial Identity: Towards a Pedagogy and Politics of Whiteness," *Harvard Educational Review* 67, no. 2, (Summer 1997): 285-

320; Matt Wray and Annalee Newitz, eds., *White Trash: Race and Class in America*. (New York: Routledge, 1997); Joe L. Kincheloe and Shirley R. Steinberg, *Changing Multiculturalism*. (Buckingham and Philadelphia: Open University Press, 1997); Joe L. Kincheloe, Shirley R. Steinberg, Nelson M. Rodriguez, and Ronald E. Chennault, eds., *White Reign: Deploying Whiteness in America*. (New York: St. Martin's Press, 1998). See also George Yudice, "Neither Impugning Nor Disavowing Whiteness Does a Viable Politics Make: The Limits of Identity Politics," in Christopher Newfield and Ronald Strickland, eds., *After Political Correctness*. (Boulder: Westview Press, 1995): 255-281.

17. For a useful introduction to the wide-ranging field of critical pedagogy, see Pepi Leistyna, Arlie Woodrum, and Stephen A. Sherblom, eds., *Breaking Free: The Transformative Power of Critical Pedagogy*. (Cambridge: Harvard Educational Review, 1996).

18. For an excellent discussion of the structural dimension of oppression as well as the many "faces" of oppression, see Iris Marion Young, *Justice and the Politics of Difference*. (Princeton, New Jersey: Princeton University Press, 1990). See also Nancy Fraser, *Justice Interruptus: Critical Reflections on the "Postsocialist" Condition*. (New York: Routledge, 1997).

19. For recent publications linking (critical) pedagogy to questions of whiteness, see Michelle Fine, Lois Weis, Linda C. Powell, and L. Mun Wong, eds., *Off White: Readings on Race, Power, and Society*. (New York: Routledge, 1997); Alice McIntyre, *Making Meaning of Whiteness: Exploring Racial Identity with White Teachers*. (Albany: State University of New York Press, 1997); Joe L. Kincheloe, Shirley R. Steinberg, Nelson M. Rodriguez, Ronald E. Chennault, *White Reign: Deploying Whiteness in America*. (New York: St Martin's Press, 1998); and Henry A. Giroux, *Channel Surfing: Race Talk and the Destruction of Today's Youth*. (New York: St. Martin's Press, 1997).

20. An excellent typology of the different types of multiculturalism is Joe L. Kincheloe and Shirley R. Steinberg's, *Changing Multiculturalism*. (Buckingham and Philadelphia: Open University Press, 1997). See also Peter McLaren, "White Terror and Oppositional Agency: Towards a Critical Multiculturalism," in David Theo Goldberg, ed., *Multiculturalism: A Critical Reader*. (Oxford UK & Cambridge USA: Blackwell Publishers, 1994).

References

Bonnett, A. (1996). White studies: The problems and projects of a new research agenda. *Theory, Culture & Society*, 13(2), 145-155.

Johnson, B. (1981). Translator's introduction. In J. Derrida, *Dissemination* (pp. vii-xxxiii). Chicago: The University of Chicago Press.

Dyer, R. (1988). White. *Screen*, 29, 45-64.

Fiske, J. (1996). *Media Matters: Race and Gender in U. S. Politics*. Minneapolis: University of Minnesota Press.

Frankenberg, R. (1997). Introduction: Local whitenesses, localizing whiteness. In R. Frankenberg (Ed.), *Displacing Whiteness: Essays in Social and Cultural Criticism* (pp. 1-33). Durham: Duke University Press.

Frankenberg, R. (1993). *White Women, Race Matters: The Social Construction of Whiteness*. Minneapolis: University of Minnesota Press.

Gallagher, C. A. (1994). White reconstruction in the university. *Socialist Review*, 94(1-2), 165-187.

Garvey, J. & Ignatiev, N. (1997). Toward a new abolitionism: A *Race Traitor* manifesto. In M. Hill (Ed.), *Whiteness: A Critical Reader* (pp. 346-349). New York: New York University Press.

Giroux, H. A. (1997a). Rewriting the discourse of racial identity: Towards a pedagogy and politics of whiteness. *Harvard Educational Review*, 67(2), 285-320.

Giroux, H. A. (1997b). White squall: Resistance and the pedagogy of whiteness. *Cultural Studies*, 11(3), 376-389.

Hyde, C. (1995). The meanings of whiteness. *Qualitative Sociology*, 18(1), 87-95.

Ignatiev, N. (1997). Treason to whiteness is loyalty to humanity: An interview with Noel Ignatiev of *Race Traitor* magazine. In Richard Delgado and Jean Stefancic (Eds.), *Critical White Studies: Looking Behind the Mirror* (pp. 607-612). Philadelphia: Temple University Press.

Ignatiev, N. (1995). *How the Irish Became White*. New York: Routledge.

Kincheloe, J. L. & Steinberg, S. R. (1998). Addressing the crisis of whiteness. In Joe L. Kincheloe, Shirley R. Steinberg, Nelson M. Rodriguez, & Ronald E. Chennault (Eds.), *White Reign: Deploying Whiteness in America* (pp. 9-44). New York: St. Martin's Press.

Kincheloe, J. L. & Steinberg, S. R. (1997). *Changing Multiculturalism*.

Buckingham and Philadelphia: Open University Press.

Leistyna, P. & Woodrum, A. (1996). Context and culture: What is critical pedagogy? In P. Leistyna, A. Woodrum, and S. A. Sherblom (Eds.), *Breaking Free: The Transformative Power of Critical Pedagogy* (pp. 1-7). Cambridge: Harvard Educational Review.

McLaren, P. (1997). *Revolutionary Multiculturalism: Pedagogies of Dissent for the New Millennium*. Boulder, Colorado: Westview Press.

Omi, M. & Winant, H. (1994). *Racial Formation in the United States: From the 1960s to the 1990s*. New York: Routledge.

Roediger, D. (1994). *Towards the Abolition of Whiteness: Essays on Race, Politics, and Working Class History*. London: Verso.

Sleeper, J. (1997, May). Toward an end of blackness: An argument for the surrender of race consciousness. *Harper's Magazine*, 294, 35-44.

Winant, H. (1994). *Racial Conditions: Politics, Theory, and Comparisons*. Minneapolis: University of Minnesota Press.

Wray, M. & Newitz, A. (Eds.). (1997). *White Trash: Race and Class in America*. New York: Routledge.

CHAPTER TWO

Virtual Shades of Pale:
Educational Technologies and the Electronic "Other"
Vicki K. Carter

Introduction

Virtual is an antonym for actual. In virtual reality the substance or effect of an experience has been copied or simulated, in essence constructing or constituting a reality based on the artificial and the hidden. Computer technology, for example, can create peripheral devices such as disks or memory without them physically existing, and for instructional purposes electronic microworlds and even imaginary students can be conjured up. In other words, a reality which substitutes imagery or representation for the world can be technologically constructed. Similarly, whiteness functions as a hidden construction through which the privilege of being white shapes experience and in which race can be ignored and white normative culture go unrecognized and unacknowledged. The qualities inherent in both virtual technologies and whiteness allow people to deny, ignore, or be oblivious about what is happening in the world, permitting them to substitute their own preferred version. In virtual worlds as in the physical and social worlds, nonwhites become the "Other." In computer-based instruction and in distance education, the Other becomes present in a virtual or electronic form but here, too, is surrounded and silenced by an elusive yet central white privilege.

When virtual worlds, such as those created via educational technologies, are juxtaposed upon pervasive but hidden cultural norms such as whiteness, the resulting educational experiences for nonwhites may easily become a complex double whammy-a permeating and potentially lethal combination of veiled, taken-for-granted cultural practices. This combination is then layered on a supposedly colorless, neutral, and seemingly impenetrable technological infrastructure, and instruction developed by an overwhelmingly white-and male- cadre of instructional designers, distance educators, and educational technologists .

Because something is invisible does not mean it is absent or non-existent. Technology, particularly when deployed through educational institutions, reinforces basic societal norms. The fact that something is not there or not seen hardly negates its power and may, instead, help to dramatically refine and consolidate it. The powerful assumptions of whiteness embedded in the narrative forms created by instructional designers and distance education curriculum planners cannot help but alienate and anger those who are ultimately marginalized, separated, and erased from those narratives. Toni Morrison's analysis of American literature speaks from just such a perspective. In her exploration of American literature, Morrison described the overwhelming absence of Afro-Americans from the text. In her assessment, this absence was both strategically and elaborately well planned, consequently making it an essentially unremarkable and uninteresting phenomenon. Rather, for Morrison, the more staggeringly interesting question concerned "What intellectual feats had to be performed by the author . . . to erase me from a society seething with my presence, and what effect has that performance had on the work?" (1988-89, p. 11).

This chapter attempts to illuminate the educational and cultural ramifications of whiteness as manifested in instructional systems and distance education texts and practice by first reviewing foundational concepts about whiteness as framed by Frankenberg (1993). Next, theory and practice in instructional systems and distance education are highlighted as well as multicultural issues within media-rich educational environments. Then, contemporary attitudes and viewpoints of educators toward technology are examined along with possible responses for educators concerned with the practice of a critical multiculturalism.

Foundational Concepts: Typologies of Multiculturalism

Recent writings on multiculturalism have focused attention on the concept of whiteness as one of the present-day discourses surrounding a multiracial society. For example, Ruth Frankenberg (1993) described multicultural discourse as pendulum-like shifts moving from difference as established by white Americans, to similarities between whites and non-whites, and back again to difference as redefined by people of color. These discourses or categories were defined by Frankenberg as, first, essentialist racism characterized by a hierarchical society based upon the alleged biological and genetic inferiority of people of color. This has been the dominant paradigm throughout U.S. history. A second discursive articulation, that of assimilationist multiculturalism (we are all the same under the skin), had its beginnings in the 1920s. In Frankenberg's view, this perspective was one of color/power evasiveness-or color-blindness-as the politically correct response to multicultural issues and questions. The third category, race cognizance, was a product of the U.S. civil rights movement which reestablished difference, but difference as recognized from the viewpoint of the Other. In other words, race cognizance was a cultural *divergence* in opposition to the cultural convergence of *assimilationism*.

In spite of these shifting paradigms and countless diversity initiatives within the United States, justice does not exist in a society structured via power and privilege. As multicultural discourses have mutated, their effects have been cumulative and competing rather than total shifts from one perspective to another. There has been minimal change in societys attitudes toward race, class, gender, and more subtle forms of othering ex'cept that essentialist racism has become highly obfuscated and codified. Assimilationist multiculturalism is now espoused as the norm. Race cognizance, while recognizing limitations of dialogue and understanding for people on the outside of a culture, often has the effect of turning history upside down and inside out-exoticizing and romanticizing the past in celebration of otherness. Furthermore, race cognizance (also described as left-essential or liberal multiculturalism) does not promote clarifying inquiry into the equivocal and paradoxical course of history. This form of multiculturalism contradicts, as well, the bona fide consequences of a reality which is historically *and* socially constructed, and molded by power and privilege.

In response to the challenge of whiteness, a subset of the educational and cultural worker community is attempting to research and practice a politically progressive form of multiculturalism and pedagogy, a critical form recognizing the nature of power and scrutinizing the various affiliations by which human beings define themselves. In a critical approach to creating and sustaining a pluralistic and democratic learning environment, educators and other workers hope to create spaces for difference and cognizance of race where power differentials and privileging of certain voices can be acknowledged and analyzed. One way to move forward a pedagogical agenda based on critical multiculturalism is to study whiteness as a positionality, in essence circumscribing whiteness in order to make visible what has been hidden and assumed.

*Theory and Practice of Educational Technologists
and Distance Educators*

Designers, programmers, and media developers emerge from fields of study based upon psychological and scientific models, models which value the objective, rational, instrumental, and empirical. Professionals in these fields have templates which describe for them what knowledge is. The products and educational modules they produce and deliver are often pre-scriptive, restrictive, and reductionist due in no small way to the culture they acquired within their areas of study and the training they received. In this recipe is found both a system of domination and a delimiting whiteness created via structures, standpoints, and unbounded cultural practices, the same kinds of practices described by Frankenberg (1993) and summarized earlier in the chapter. The discourse surrounding educational technology is management of systems, social engineering, standardization, efficiency, and effectiveness, all powerfully modern ways of shaping knowledge accompa-nied by the notion that technology, science, hardware, and software is neu-tral and democratic (Muffoletto, 1994). Techniques of instruction and educational methodologies control and manage "learning" in a way that is similar to the military-industrial complex's approach to managing soldiers and employees (Bowers, 1988; Wells, 1986). Two of the main purposes of system creation and design are to organize and control. An organizing and controlling system can and often does result in dehumanizing people and creating hierarchical privilege. Therefore, the unexamined and inherent trust and valorization of science and technology in conjunction with positivist thinking could, according to Yeaman (1994, p. 16), ultimately, create a utopian dream of navigating cyberspace and controlling all things by press-ing a few keys. Given these potential outcomes, how aware and concerned are distance educators, instructional designers, and educational technolo-gists about critical pedagogy, critical multiculturalism, and the powerful political nature of technological systems and their cultural practices? Well . . . at this point in time, not very.

Reflect, for example, on five distance education textbooks. In Moore's *Contemporary Issues in American Distance Education* (1990) there was a single mention (in reference to television courses) of ethnic minori-ties and socioeconomic levels of student populations as compared to an vast majority of Caucasian participants. In *The Virtual Classroom* (Hiltz, 1994), *Verduin and Clarks Distance Education: The Foundations of Effective Practice* (1991), and Anandam's *Transforming Teaching with*

Technology: Perspectives from Two-Year Colleges (1989) there were no references to marginalized groups except in the area of demographics and minority enrollment statistics. And although the authors purport to approach conferencing technologies specifically from a holistic viewpoint, the fifth textbook, *Classrooms with a Difference* (Burge & Roberts, 1993), this otherwise excellent book neither found nor confronted difference in multicultural terms.

Instructional systems texts and practices are similar to those of distance education. Models depicting linear transmission of information and a pervasive use of design approaches such as the military's. Instructional Systems Development format for building technology-based instruction are typical. The underlying precepts in most theory and practice within educational technology are that authors, teacher's and instructional designers, and their technologies and devices, are the dispensers of unequivocable, objective truth (Yeaman, 1994, p. 22). Basically, efficiency, progress, and outcomes take precedence over human interests. The overarching concepts of educational technologies and distance education are means for controlling the educational experience framing not only how education is accomplished but also how education is thought about (Muffoletto, 1994, p. 26). Knowledge and guidance for these educational experiences comes from the expert-the professional designer or developer. And so, if beliefs, attitudes, and behaviors are formed and reformed in educational environments, one weighty and immediate question involves whether machines, machine-like designs, and expert knowledge should become unconsidered sources of those beliefs and values, particularly for nonwhite students already immersed in education prepared by the oppressor and dominated by the interests, values, and ideology of the dominant culture (Gadotti, 1994, p. 51). Race, class, and gender issues disappear even more easily in instructional systems constructed by mostly white males, reflect the American/Western canon, and are packaged into requisite text and graphic formats that further limit diversity.

By breaking down processes into contained, manageable, detailed, isolated, and self-directed pieces, instructional systems and distance-education development mirror the rise of industrialization, subordinating the student to the process and, at times, helping to make the skills and even the presence of a classroom teacher unnecessary. Furthermore, although instructional designers list individualization as one of the principles of educational psychology and computerized instruction and acknowledge its importance for learning (Hannafin & Peck, 1988; Ross, 1984), due to the

all-encompassing nature of most instructional software and distance curricula design, individualization is limited to the confines and parameters of
each design. Only minimal adjustment is possible. Individualization for
instructional designers means adjusting the model for changing levels,
amounts, and speed of instruction. Designs that are flexible in these areas
are profoundly normative in others, heavily constrained by authorship, pack-
aging, framing, and authority as well as the time and expense involved in
their development. The costs involved in these forms of instruction require
a broad appeal and attraction of large audiences; in order to accomplish
these goals, race and difference disappear into electronic uniformity. These
global, model- and script-based forms of education directly contradict
Freire's (1970, 1990) condemnation of universalization of teaching material. Freire felt teaching resources should be regional or local and that
standardized material was saturated with acts of authority and ignorance of
difference.

Inherent in these instructional development models and philosophies are unambiguous messages of whiteness which do not bode well for
adoption of a critical multicultural agenda or examining whiteness as a
positionality and an unmarked cultural repertoire. Design of instruction
and curricula send out clear signals about what is to be learned, what behavior to emulate, and for whom instruction is meant. Traditional instructional design and development models do not provide for contextual construction of meaning, the validity of multiple perspectives, or the examination of the inherent biases found in homogenous design teams.

For example, instructional designers would benefit from Toni
Morrison's critique (Morrison, 1993, p. 67-69) of textual strategies and
linguistics. Morrison theorized that until recently writers of American fic-
tion, regardless of the ethnicity of the author, have assumed a white reader.
According to research in educational software, this is also the case except
that the user of the software is assumed to be male as well (Huff & Cooper,
1987). Like American literature, American software is often complicit in
acts of racism, classism, and misogyny. Morrison outlined six linguistic
strategies employed as recipes to portray and reference blacks in books for
and about white people. The following brief (see Morrison's *Playing in the
Dark* for more detail) commentary suggests the texts of technologically
mediated instruction mirror at least four of the six linguistic strategies
Morrison found in traditional American literature.

First of all, economy of stereotype is formidable in its presence in
educational software more often than not producing flat, weak, one-dimen-

sional images and representations. Second, color and other forms of coding along with stereotypical physical characteristics erase and displace (metonymic displacement as theorized by Morrison) nonwhite characters. The technique of metaphysical condensation, a third strategy, is excessively prevalent in educational software which has evolved collapsing persons into animals (1993, p. 68) into a mature art form. In effect, this condensing technique then precludes the possibility of a Habermasian notion of virtuous communicative action and creates an atmosphere where avoiding problems of inclusion and diversity is easily accomplished. And finally, dehistoricizing allegory is a very interesting concept relative to technology and the virtual. This tactic supplants *dis*closure with *fore*closure by magnifying difference so that the civilizing process becomes indefinite and history, as a process of becoming, is excluded from the literary encounter (p. 68). These linguistic strategies identified by Morrison via her study of literature are also plentiful in contemporary mediated texts, serving as totalizing discourses which conceal or forestall ongoing struggles over contested meanings between whites and nonwhites.

Although mainstream practice is overwhelmingly steeped in whiteness, practice within these fields is not hopeless in terms of the emergence of a critical multiculturalism. Some distance educators and instructional designers are aware of critical pedagogical concepts. Evans and Nation's *Reforming Open and Distance Education* (1993) contained a chapter on developing an equal opportunity plan for black and ethnic minorities; the plan, however, was designed with the British Open University, not a U.S. institution, in mind. In February 1994, the journal Educational Technology published a special issue (edited by Yeaman, Koetting, & Nichols) on critical theory and cultural analysis which investigated at length ethical and moral issues of educational technology and the fields relationship to social responsibility. And Hawkridge (1991), in his critical observation of distance education, has pointed out that two key values held by educational designers were 1) a division of teaching into design and execution phases, and 2) valuing knowledge produced and derived from theoretical sources versus knowledge stemming from practice or intuition. These held values, according to Hawkridge, conceal the intent to manage or control other people (1991, p. 107).

Unfortunately these reflective and self-critical viewpoints within the field of educational technology and distance education are not mainstream thinking, but are instead part of a smaller initiative toward critical pedagogy and educational reform. These practitioners acknowledge education mediated by technology and facilitated by instructional designs is far from benign or innocent, but rather can alter the identities and social realities of both learner and teacher. But most designs remain merely prescriptive. Designers take little responsibility for creating instruction that is permeable to nonwhites nor for taking ownership in the struggle for freedom and social justice. Fundamentally, instructional systems, educational technologies, and distance education are very powerful representations of the postmodern condition, coopting what have been traditionally espoused values in education-education as equally liberatory, empowering, and democratizing.

Attitudes and Viewpoints of Educators Toward Technology

According to Hess (1995) it is difficult if not impossible to plan curricula in public schools and higher education without at least considering diversity and the voices of marginalized groups-at least in the humanities. Hess, however, believes questions of bias and racism to be less common, as well as deemed theoretically uninteresting, in technical fields, however. Similarly uncommon was an examination of multiculturalism and whiteness/nonwhiteness in technologically mediated instructional environments. The lack of an awareness of the affects of whiteness within the fields of instructional systems and distance education is exacerbated by a lack of critique, absence of reflective practice, and sometimes a major phobia about technologically mediated education on the part of many educators, including even the subset of critical educators who are working toward changing pedagogies based on white cultural assumptions. The paucity of a critically reflective practice within these venues intensifies the effects of the forms of text produced by instructional designers and distance education curriculum development.

Should there be any doubt about how unimportant technologically mediated educational environments appear to be within the current discourse on critical pedagogy, a brief review of some of its language will be most convincing. Maxine Greene (1993) on pluralism, multiculturalism, and the expanding community stated it was clear that the more continuous and authentic personal encounters can be, the less likely it will be for categorizing and distancing to take place (p. 185). When she wrote of transformative pedagogy, hooks (1993) described classroom settings as places of transformation, talked of losing control in a classroom, spoke of spaces for constructive confrontation, learning, and hearing one another. She wrote of the sound of different voices and of making presences felt inside and outside the classroom. What and where are the inside and outside of a classroom when the learners are in computer labs working through instructional modules, completing lessons by correspondence, or engaged at home in tutorials delivered via the World Wide Web? How do you hear voices and make presences felt in these hyperreal or virtual learning situations?

Simon (1992) questioned at some length technology as a practice of semiotic production and as *poeisis*. Technology became a "mode of production, a way of organizing and regulating the bringing forth into presence of something previously without presence" (p. 42). In other words, technology could be viewed in cultural terms as related to what is able to be known. Simon even wrote specifically of teaching machines and the introduction of computers into the classroom, but referred to them as technicist approaches to teaching. And yet, after all his interrogation of technology and its effects, Simon remained throughout his work within the context of the traditional classroom, social relations in the classroom, trust and respect in the classroom, authority and identity politics in the classroom, space and time in the classroom, pedagogy in school, in hallways and at weekly class meetings. Simon failed to include technology itself as a location or a text and to critique that venue accordingly. What differences are there if the classroom does not exist and the physical identities of instructors and classmates are unknown? In such cases, what is able to be known and how is it brought forth?

Cherryholmes wrote of textual power and social change defining textual power as an "asymmetrical relationship between readers and texts wherein readers in experiencing texts, produce multiple readings, interpretations, and criticisms" (1988, p. 154). Discursive practices and texts necessarily, and sometimes violently, stipulated what was valuable, created typologies, and defined knowledge. Textual power reflected decisions and actions by individuals and groups and the social world made up of practices, discourses, and texts that could be leveraged by varying interpretations and criticisms. Although Cherryholmes specifically referred to textbooks, he also referred to texts and discursive practices, opening the door for viewing both technology and cyberspace as text. But once again, Cherryholmes's writing adhered to the paradigm of the traditional classroom, to classroom interactions, to written texts, and to publishing companies.

Kincheloe provided a critique of the electronic information tidal wave and hyperreality, stating that "class and racial inequalities are perpetrated by new technologies and at the same time rendered more impervious to exposure by the removal of those with limited access to information from those who produce it" (1993, p. 86). Kincheloe's analysis of the effect of image and the nature of today's information formats went further than Simon and Cherryholmes, but stopped short of engaging educational technologies contribution to class and racial inequalities. Within this book also was the assumption and continuation of the traditional classroom as the place into which people entered, where knowledge was mutually produced by student/teacher interaction, where a classroom culture existed, and within which the nature of interaction, participation, and learning was and should be examined. For example, a technique suggested by Kincheloe for improving teaching consisted of viewing and reflecting upon videotapes of teaching episodes; teaching strategies were then adjusted ad hoc in the classroom. If this is a good technique for improving traditional classroom teaching, what are the techniques and strategies for a critical pedagogy in the absence of a classroom or for a teacher who is separated by time and/or space from his or her students?

In many instances teachers dislike learning about technology and how to deal with it, sometimes to the point of near paralysis. Understanding the variety of technologically mediated learning environments requires an investment by teachers and often significant dependence upon technicians familiar with the intricacies of the hardware and software. Also, the fear teachers experience when confronting any paradigm shift (hooks, 1993) must be included as part of understanding teacher resistance to educational technologies. Too many teachers and faculty are true technophobes, willing (and hoping) to ride out this latest wave of educational technologies producing pedagogical disruption and change. After all, as Postman (1995) recently observed, many media solutions to the educational problem such as teaching machines and television have been touted as a cure-all for what ails schooling in America, but the cure never happened. This may indeed be the case again, but somehow it feels different today.

If, as bell hooks described, a valuable project would be to imagine and enact pedagogical practices that engage directly . . . the concern for interrogating biases in curricula that reinscribe systems of domination (1994, p. 10), then she must also consider those biases as already inscribed in technological systems of power and domination. Consider Hinksons (1995) critical evaluation of education and postmodernity, an evaluation describing the emergence of information and images constructed by technology as a central and profound communications medium. If media and mediated learning are assuming and transforming educational functions, by what means do students and learners comprehend a wider society? According to Hinkson, a lack of social space for relations constituted outside of those generated by high-tech means (p. 128) is one important missing element; another is essentialist conceptions of self, guided and formed through relations of self to other, where the Other is the fleeting image (p. 132) instead of a tangible relationship.

The above examples situated within critical pedagogy writings are a very small portion of volume after volume written about teaching and learning. The critical pedagogy literature as well as the traditional teaching/learning literature represents an all-pervasive assumption of the traditional classroom as *the* site of learning. In the meantime education at every level from kindergarten to workplace learning is becoming mediated. Colleges and universities have set goals for developing and putting in place major portions of the curriculum constituting basic degree requirements. Tutorials and texts ranging from learning songs and the alphabet to studying quantum physics are available on the World Wide Web. Schools offering instructional design, educational technology, and distance education programs are enjoying consistently increasing enrollments. Is anyone, whether from a critical pedagogy and multicultural perspective or not, looking at the classroom as defined by technology, within hyperreality, inside cyberspace? Lather asked how teachers with liberatory and emancipatory intentions created spaces for learners to acquire ownership by speaking and acting on their own behalf and how teachers helped breach the univocality of the message (1991, p. 137). Although Lather was not writing specifically about educational technologies, her words are full of meaning for teachers, instructors, and critical multicultural workers of all types who become involved in classrooms per se and in instructional systems and distance education. Critical educators must explore these new territories if they are to break the pattern of yet another controlling schema of interpretation (p. 137).

Critical Multicultural Responses to Whiteness

Does this critique of distance education and educational technologies imply that instructional designers and curriculum developers for distance education are evil, bad, incompetent, or thoughtless? Of course not. Like most Americans, instructional designers and distance educators have not examined their whiteness and other cultural assumptions critically. Although much continues to be written about the effect of technology and computers on society, social commentary often neglects to see the social within the technological. Virtual realities can be most effective in educational environments by, for example, providing exposure to racism or sexism in virtual worlds, which when experienced from the inside by a member of the majority population, might actually increase levels of tolerance in the majority of diffuse volatile societal situations (Kelly, 1995, p. 28). In this case, it is to be hoped that tolerance would be the minimum expectation, but even to achieve only that much, designers would have to be open to building these worlds, and teachers and students using their designs would have to critique them. What are some ways a critical multicultural agenda can be promoted? How can distance educators and instructional systems professionals respond to ongoing perpetuation of whiteness within their discipline?

Perhaps Habermas's theory of communicative action (Wells, 1986) is one way to think through educational technologies and their tendency to oppress. Do instructional designs achieve or attempt to achieve a space for authentic communication? Are the designs and the environment they create and support truthful and authentic forms of implicit and holistically structured knowledge? Is there an authentic form of dialogue in which basic elements intrinsically define one another? Are there ways to examine and analyze power and privilege, and create ways to acknowledge and eliminate them?

Other approaches, in addition to that of Habermas, would allow learners to shape their own messages by using sound, video, and multimedia technologies to create them. Another technique would be to think about Noddings's ethic of caring and attempt to step out of one's personal frame of reference and into the other's (1984, p. 25) or confer with people with different frames of reference about proposed designs and learning environments. People who design instruction should remember that the means are truly the ends. They must think about who speaks and who does not, who is privileged and who is not, and they must consider unintended and negative effects resulting from the implementation of any design. Classroom teachers must consider what systems are operating within their arenas and become as critically aware of what is inherent in educational technologies as they are about traditional textbooks and familiar media such as television and movies. Teachers must also take their observations, concerns, and criticisms back to distance educators and instructional designers and speak with them about the hegemonic worlds they have created. Distance educators and instructional systems professionals, steeped as they are in defining

standards and eliminating variation, must build upon the emerging awareness of their conscious and unconscious complicity in creating, recreating,
re-covering, and making invisible a place where whiteness is still firmly
established as the norm, the expected, and the desirable. Every educator
and cultural worker must consider the effects and impact of an unexamined
whiteness upon themselves and in their work. Quite simply, as Morrison
has asked, what does whiteness mean to the mind, imagination, and behavior of masters (1993, p. 12)?

Summary

As whiteness is starting to be examined and as a critical
multiculturalism begins to be introduced as practice into traditional classroom environments, some forms of whiteness have taken up residence in
spaces that are less easily critiqued. There is minimal recognition that computer networks and instructional materials delivered on computers and at a
distance are sites of cultural imperialism, recolonization, racism, patriarchy, or whiteness. In many cases these circumstances are unconsidered
and unintentional results of course material design and development framed
by the commanding subjectivity of "all-knowing" professional designers,
but they have the effect of exacerbating what is already a world actively
sustaining white hegemonic positionality. If a vision for a different future
is attainable, then social and physical realities of mediated education must
be recognized as significant factors which represent and order educational
processes. Educators, especially distance educators and instructional systems professionals who wish to alter the status quo, must become self-
aware and acknowledge the influences, both good and bad, of white culture
and white privilege. Teachers and cultural workers who hope to bring a
critical multicultural perspective to their practice must address an overwhelming focus on only the traditional classroom as the site of contestation, confrontation, dialogue, encounter, and struggle.

Simon (1992) described the importance of cultural dialogue and
how a shifting of the whole occurred when dynamics and power relations
changed in response to perspectives becoming reconstituted and transformed. As a caveat, Simon expressed concern about formalization of pluralism itself evolving into a version of apartheid, particularly in terms of
administrative tendencies "to essentialize and encrust certain phenomeno-
logical features of a culture as the key expressions through which cultural
borders are defined and diversity secured (p. 25). Simon's concerns point

out a framework within which instructional systems and distance education usually work-that is, administrative and discipline-defined borders and structures. Such a framework makes multiculturalism difficult enough without the culturally narrow format of mediated instructional materials and teaching/learning at a distance erasing most benefits of traditional dialogue and face-to-face interactions. If, in technologically mediated educational environments, apartheid and racism continue to flourish as they appear to be doing, this form of education must be even more carefully observed and critiqued. Can the fragmentation of time and space, the dehistoricizing properties stemming from virtuality, and the emerging self-questioning conscience of people who recognize whiteness as status and privilege become catalysts to integrate and include instead of continuing to tell a presumptive, incomplete, and monocultural story?

Learning as espoused by Freire (1970, 1990) is a form of knowledge acquisition in which learners develop a critical consciousness by constructing and problematizing their positionality in dialogue with others. Educational practitioners and cultural workers hoping to assist in the development of a Friereian critical consciousness must ask themselves whether all parties are present in the mediated forms of learning they use or are aware of, and whether full opportunity for dialogue exists as part of these products and the texts they have created. In computer-based or technologically assisted instruction, subjectivity can be virtual and Othering becomes electronic, but the consequences are just as dangerous, unjust, and alienating. These cultural and educational landscapes also require a critical interrogation of whiteness.

References

Anandam, K. (Ed.). (1989). Transforming teaching with technology: Perspectives from two-year colleges. McKinney, TX: Academic Computing Publications, Inc.

Bowers, C. (1988). The cultural dimensions of educational computing: Understanding the non-neutrality of technology. New York: Teachers College Press.

Burge, E., & Roberts, J. (1993). Classrooms with a difference. Toronto: OISE.

Cherryholmes, C. (1988). Power and criticism: Poststructural investigations in education. New York: Teachers College Press.

Evans, T., & Nation, D. (1993). Educational technologies: reforming open and distance education. In T. Evans & D. Nation (Eds.), Reforming Open and Distance Education: Critical Reflections from Practice (pp. 192-214). New York: St. Martins Press.

Frankenberg, R. (1993). White women, race matters: The social construction of whiteness. Minneapolis: University of Minnesota Press.

Freire, P. (1970). Pedagogy of the oppressed. New York: Continuum.

Freire, P. (1990). Education for critical consciousness. New York: Continuum.

Gadotti, M. (1994). Reading Paulo Friere. Albany, NY: State University of New York Press.

Greene, M. (1993). The passions of pluralism. In T. Perry & J. Fraser (Eds.), Freedoms Plow (pp. 185-196). New York: Routledge.

Habermas, J. (1984). The theory of communicative action: Vol. 1, Reason and the rationalization of society. (T. McCarthy, Trans.). Boston: Beacon Press.

Hannafin, M., & Peck, K. (1988). The design, development, and evaluation of instructional software. New York: Macmillan.

Hawkridge, D. (1991). Challenging educational technology. Educational Training and Technology International, 28 (2), 102-110.

Hess, D. J. (1995). Science & technology in a multicultural world: The cultural politics of facts and artifacts. New York: Columbia University Press.

Hiltz, S. (1994). The virtual classroom. Norwood, NJ: Ablex.

Hinkson, J. (1995). Lyotard, postmodernity, and education: A critical evaluation. In M. Peters (Ed.), Education and the Postmodern Condition (pp. 121-146). Westport, CT: Bergin & Garvey.

hooks, b. (1993). Transformative pedagogy and multiculturalism. In T. Perry & J. Fraser (Eds.), Freedoms Plow (pp. 91-97). New York: Routledge

hooks, b. (1994). Teaching to transgress. New York: Routledge.

Huff, C., & Cooper, J. (1987). Sex bias in educational software: The effect of designers stereotypes on the software they design. Journal of Applied Social Psychology, 17 (6), 519-532.

Kelly, R.V., Jr. (1995). Virtual culture, religion, and politics. Virtual Reality, 2 (4), 19-28.

Kincheloe, J. (1993). Toward a critical politics of teacher thinking. Westport, CT: Bergin & Garvey.

Lather, P. (1991). Getting smart: Feminist research and pedagogy with/in the postmodern. New York: Routledge.

Moore, M. (Ed.). (1990). Contemporary issues in American distance education. Oxford: Pergamon.

Morrison, T. (1993). Playing in the dark: Whiteness and the literary imagination. New York: Vintage Books.

Morrison, T. (1988-89, Winter). Unspeakable things unspoken: The Afro-American presence in American literature. Michigan Quarterly Review, 11.

Muffoletto, R. (1994). Technology and restructuring: Constructing a context. Educational Technology, 34 (2), 24-28.

Noddings, N. (1984). Caring: A feminine approach to ethics and moral education. Berkeley: University of California.

Postman, N. (1995, October 9). Education and technology: Virtual students, digital classroom. The Nation, 377-382.

Ross, S. (1984). Matching the lesson to the student. Alternative adaptive designs for individualized learning systems. Journal of Computer Based Instruction, 11, 42-48.

Simon, R. (1992). Teaching against the grain. New York: Bergin & Garvey.

Verduin, J., & Clark, T. (1991). Distance education: The foundations of effective practice. San Francisco: Jossey-Bass.

Wells, S. (1986). Jurgen Habermas, communicative competence, and the teaching of technical discourse. In C. Nelson. (Ed.), Theory in the classroom (pp. 245-269). Urbana, IL: University of Illinois Press.

Yeaman, A. (1994). Deconstructing modern educational technology. Educational Technology, 34 (2), 15-24.

Yeaman, A., Koetting, J., & Nichols, R. (Eds.). Critical theory, cultural analysis and the ethics of educational technology as social responsibility. Educational Technology, 34 (2), 5-72.

CHAPTER THREE

border crossing: The Act and Implications in the
Production of Art vis á vis Patriarchy and Whiteness

l e i l a   e .   v i l l a v e r d e

t h e   e x p a n s i v e n e s s   o f

                                                                        w

                                                                        h

                                                                        i

                                                                        t

                                                                        e

                                                                        n

                                                                        e

                                                                        s

                                                                        s

                                                                        &

                                                                    of

patriarchy

is redefined through border theory   &

illustrated via art...

```
whi      te      ness
      pa      tri      archy
```

pawhitritearchy:

the act
          of interrogating
patriarchy and whiteness to
redefine its core,
parameters, and boundaries
and to enact what is not yet.

patriarchy and whiteness have disseminated

particular standards for producing, judging, and

canonizing art . . .

BORDER THEORY

INVERTS...

TRANSFORMS...

. . . leaving an open space for possibility, in its

rearticulation and struggle over the present condition of

power asymmetries in any institution . . . .

PATRIARCHY: A systemic ideological apparatus which exerts power over women, men of color, and men who exercise alternative masculinities.

> The concept of patriarchy is important because it asserts that g e n d e r inequality is a pervasive feature of contemporary society. To invoke patriarchy is to problematize the social construction of gender and gender relations in a way that moves us to consider what constitutes a just and democratic academic curriculum, politics, and social consciousness.[1]

WHITENESS: Another systemic ideological apparatus that is used to normalize civility, instill rationality, erase emotion, erase difference, impose middle-class values and beliefs with an assumption of a heterosexual matrix. = *privilege*

"I find myself trying to understand how whiteness accrues privilege and status; gets itself surrounded by protective pillows of resources and/or benefits of the doubt; how whiteness repels gossip and voyeurism and instead demands dignity."[2]

These discourses have informed the production and legitimation of art throughout history. Works are canonized in the hope of preserving their creativity and uniqueness, to reinforce (solidify) their distance from outsider art: the art from nonwhite women and men. **Access is a threat to whiteness when whiteness requires the exportation (and denigration) of color.**3 The purpose of canonization is to create "the" standard for all art, attempting to retain the work's life long after its death, enstating an elite, incestuous circle of "fine art," demarcating high from low art and culture. Yet canonized art is threatened by the inherent dynamism of outsider art as a consequence of where it is created **(on/in/through the margin)** and its necessity to engage in continuous struggles with the canon for survival.

Historically speaking, when the third world artists borrow from the first world it has been called colonialism, but when the modernists borrowed from Africa, for example, it was an enrichment of the vocabulary of the fine arts.4

Whites and whiteness can no longer be exempted from the comprehensive racialization process that is the hallmark of U.S. history and social structure. 5

Modernism dictated and furthered notions of patriarchy and whiteness in the arts through its marriage to the scientific method, rationalism, and utopian aesthetics. Seeking **TRUTH** (objectivity, clarity, purity, reduction).

A principal attitude of modernism was to posit artworks as the products of an autonomous, disengaged form of labor and consumption, freed from normal social commerce by virtue of their status as objects designed for visual pleasure.6

The art history books chart the succession of
artists' contributions that maintained the status quo
despite intentions to somehow radicalize the
established canons. The art world was an incestuous
circle, internally criticizing itself, holding fast
to the myths of artist as genius and maintaining the
gap between artist and society. With the advent of
the civil rights movement, the art world took a turn
towards the political, allowing its boundaries to
become porous to the outside, turning its world
inside out. Even though whiteness and patriarchy are
still very strong discourses within the art world,
their power is decentralized due to the influx of
discourses and productions from men and women of
color, gays, and lesbians.

Dominant groups are now driving very carefully through a cultural terrain in which whiteness can no longer remain invisible as a racial, political, and historical construction. The privilege and practices of domination that underscore being white in America can no longer remain invisible through either an appeal to a universal norm or a refusal to explore how whiteness works to produce forms of "friendly" colonialism.[7]

Whiteness-visible whiteness, resurgent whiteness, whiteness as a color, whiteness as difference - this is what's new, and newly problematic, in the contemporary U.S....[8]

This gradual shift or mutation in the rigidly structured forms of modernist art has led not to another style, but to a fully transformed conception of art founded on alternate critical premises.[9]

Through the lens of critical theory, sections of
the art world have acquired a meta-awareness of
the systems which constructed the way it
operates, analyzing the hegemony of its ideology
and through this process hybridizing the very
nature of art, highlighting its
interdisciplinarity and its need for
contextualization.

ART IS A POLITICAL IDEOLOGY ADDRESSED
TO RELATIONS OF POWER...IT OCCURS IN
THE SOCIAL SITUATION, IS AN INTEGRAL
ELEMENT OF SOCIAL STRUCTURE, AND IS
MEDIATED AND DETERMINED BY SPECIFIC
AND DEFINABLE SOCIAL INSTITUTIONS...[10]

Feminist theory was instrumental in
questioning the construction of the canon,
pulled the shade up on the good old boys . . .
flagging the incongruencies of gender and
power hierarchies....

Postmodernism rolls around "structured by
time rather than form, concerned with
context instead of style, it uses memory,
research, confession, fiction-with irony,
whimsy, and disbelief. Subjective and
intimate, it blurs the boundaries between
the world and the self. It is about
identity and behavior."[11]

another ism, hardly......

postmodernism..... it's still in there

~~PATRIARCHY & POWER~~

                         whiteness and civility

        "Any critical postmodernist theory of patriarchy must
focus on the privilege men derive from their male power as
well as the oppression women experience in relation to it.
In this context the ways that power shapes gender
subjectivity becomes a central concern, as analysis focuses
on both the discursive and ideological dynamics of
patriarchal masculinity."12

A. **IMPERIALIZING POWERS**
B. LOCALIZING POWERS
        A. in the form of white supremacy, class elites and
patriarchy attempt to extend their influence as far as
possible over various societies, the tide of history,
social organizations, and individual consciousness.
                         B. on the other hand, in the form of
individuals or alignments of oppressed peoples the attempt
is to shape the immediate conditions of their everyday
lives.13

                    fix your attention on the relationship between the social domain

and the construction of subjectivity 14

...the institutional design of whiteness, like the production of all
colors, creates an organizational discourse of race and a
personal embodiment of race, affecting perceptions of Self and
Others, producing both individuals' sense of racial "identities"
and collective experiences of racial "tensions," even coalitions.15

With discourses of whiteness and patriarchy, undoubtedly there will be
asymmetrical power configurations. Within the art world these are used
as overarching barometers of success and validity....overtly otherizing
the Other, representing the Other as exotic, eccentric, not quite...
                    n e c e s s a r y...   safe
                                        at the
                                            margins
                                                for
                                                    whom...

During the 1970s and 1980s, a number of artists tried to
decenter language within the patriarchal order, exposing
the ways that images are culturally coded, and renegotiating
the position of women and minorities as "other" in
patriarchal culture.16

T H E N

    BACK L A S H

the system reverts on itself = CONTEMPORARY ART

content: political in nature, addresses issues of power, race, gender, class, sexual orientation, social justice, knowledge production, consciousness construction, and so on.

form: multiple, imaginative, performative

BORDER ART
IN PARTICULAR...

with its utilization of BORDER THEORY

TARGETS:

negotiation
inversion
transformation
risk
exchange
multiplicity
hybridity

...the reader [audience] of border [work] may experience a deterritorialization of signification; to read [experience, engage in] border text is to cross over into another set of referential codes.[17]

the border crosser is both 'self' and 'other'[18]

                double consciousness...

DiSplaceMeNt of time & s p a   c e [19]

is sedimented...

BAKHTIN'S(as border intellectual) ...notion of the dialogic: "as **rupture** of the one-dimensional text of bourgeois narrative, as a **carnivalesque** dispersal of the hegemonic order of a dominant culture."20

Border [text] offers a new knowledge: information about and understanding of the present to the past in terms of the possibilities of the future.21

...ADDRESSING POLITICS OF REPRESENTATION,
HUMAN RIGHTS,
EPISTEMOLOGY, INDIGENOUS KNOWLEDGE, AMBIGUITIES,
RESPONSIBILITY, APPROPRIATION, AESTHETICS, TEXTS,
MATERIALITY, MEMORY,
POWER RELATIONS &
MAXIMIZA T I O N O F S P A C E

interrogating the dynamics between artist &
audience, above all
inseminating high doses of
pedagogy into every and any exchange,
perception, internalization,

a   p
n   a
d   r
expression   a
                                                     l
                                                     l
                                                     e
                                                     l
                                                     e
                                                     d
                  with a critical postmodern theory

                                                of

                                                patriarchy

                                                and

                                                an

                                                unlearning

                                                of

                                                whiteness

t
h
e
n

THERE'S A BIRTH

that strides towards a
radical democracy
&
critical citizenry

*where power asymmetries are pliable

*access is made possible

*double consciousness is maximized/ lived not negated

*counterhegemonic struggles are pursued through a multiplicity of terrains both public and private

*pedagogy infects all

*agency is enacted and not just

discussed

...and what it boils down to is... the nuts and bolts of this

birth are:

4 CRUCIAL ELEMENTS:

*ART

*CRITICAL POSTMODERN THEORY OF PATRIACHY

*WHITENESS STUDIES

*PEDAGOGY

that speak to AND create

possibilities/potentialities

necessary for regotiating

social/power relations

and for   constructing a

critical consciousness

in the

mainstream.

End Notes

1. Kincheloe, J. L. (1997). Constructing a critical pedagogy of patriarchy: Thoughts on the crisis of masculinity. unpublished paper, p.4.

2. Fine, M. (1997). Witnessing Whiteness. In M. Fine, L. Weis, L.C. Powell, & L. Mun Wong (eds.), *Off white: Readings on race, power, and society.* New York: Routldge. (p.57).

3. Ibid; p.60.

4. Fusco, C. (1990). Sankofa & black audio film collective. In R. Ferguson, W. Olander, M. Tucker, & K. Fiss (eds.), *Discourses: Conversations in postmodern art and culture.* New York: The New Museum of Contemporary Art. (p.25).

5. Winant, H. (1997). Behind blue eyes: Whiteness and contemporary U.S. racial politics. In M. Fine, L. Weis, L.C. Powell, & L. Mun Wong (eds.), *Off white: Readings on race, power, and society.* New York: Routldge. (p.49).

6. Wallis, B. (1984). What's wrong with this picture? An introduction. In B. Wallis (ed.), *Art after modernism: Rethinking representation.* New York: The Museum of Contemporary Art. (p.xiii).

7. Giroux, H. A. (1994). Living dangerously: Identity politics and the new cultural racism. In H. A. Giroux & P. McLaren (eds.), *Between borders: Pedagogy and the politics of cultural studies.* New York: Routledge. (p.40). Giroux also credits Dyer 1988, hooks 1990, and Young 1990 as also taking up these issues.

8. Winant, H. (1997). Behind blue eyes: Whiteness and contemporary U.S. racial politics. In M. Fine, L. Weis, L.C. Powell, & L. Mun Wong (eds.), *Off white: Readings on race, power, and society.* New York: Routldge. (p.49).

9. Wallis, B. (1984). What's wrong with this picture? An introduction. In B. Wallis (ed.), *Art after modernism: Rethinking representation*. New York: The Museum of Contemporary Art. (p.xiii).

10. Linda Nochlin, quoted in the introduction to Duro, P. & Greenhalgh, M. (1994). *Essential art history*. London: Bloomsbury. (p.11).

11. Levin, K. (1988).*Beyond modernism: Essays on art from the 70's and 80's*. New York: Harper & Row. (p.7).

12. Kincheloe, J. L. (1997). Constructing a critical pedagogy of patriarchy: Thoughts on the crisis of masculinity. unpublished paper, p.16.

13. Ibid; p.17.

14. Ibid; 44.

15. Fine, M. (1997). Witnessing Whiteness. In M. Fine, L. Weis, L.C. Powell, & L. Mun Wong (Eds.), *Off white: Readings on race, power, and society*. New York: Routldge. (p.58).

16. Chadwick, W. (1990). *Women, art, and society*. London: Thames and Hudson Ltd. (p.356).

17. Hicks, E. (1991). *Border Writing: The multidimensional text*. Minnesota: University of Minnesota Press. (p.xxvi).

18. Ibid; p.xxvi.

19. Ibid; p.xxviii.

20. Ibid; p.xxviii.

21. Ibid; p.xxxi.

additional resource:

Taylor, M. C. & Saarinen, E. (1994). *Imagologies: Media philosophies.* New York: Routledge.

CHAPTER FOUR

"As if bereav'd of light":
Decoding Whiteness in My Academia
San Juanita Garza

How much more productive the last three years would have been if I had begun my excursion into academia with a more cognitive understanding of whiteness. I would have been better equipped to negotiate with professors, classmates, students. I would have known not to cringe when the postal worker greeted me with a bold, blazing "Hey Senorita!" my first week on this predominately white campus. And I would have known to give the country of my birth—the U.S.—before responding "Chicago" to my doctor's casual, perfectly innocuous question: "So, where ya from?"

He had to take a few seconds to locate Chicago on his mental map, and he was embarrassed at having his incorrect presumption exposed. Apparently it hadn't occurred to him that I could've been born in this country, and it hadn't occurred to me that he was presuming I was born in another country—all because of my name. Go figure.

My doctor and I had our little moment of awkwardness and embarrassment: he because he had made a mistake in his assumptions; me because I had not anticipated his assumptions and therefore could not avoid the embarrassing moment. However, we got through it. We chuckled about it. He offered a reasonable explanation: "Well, this is a large campus with a significant international student body," he said.

Though this embarrassing moment lasted but two minutes, the implications of our little exchange were very significant. My doctor and I took a few moments to learn about each other. We endeavored to under-

stand each other's process of reasoning, and that precious little time allowed each of us to become human beings in each other's eyes, instead of
just roles.

Had we not taken that time, had my doctor not attempted to make
himself understood, or had I not been open to his explanation, we would
have stayed in that uncomfortable place. We would not have made a connection that allowed us to move forward, together. Unfortunately, too many
of my professors and classmates were not willing to meet me somewhere,
and thus connections were not made, and thus disappointment pervades
many of my memories of graduate school.

Now, I'm not naive. Prior to my acceptance into graduate school I
had worked four years with the Chicago City Council. I know politics. I
understand racial and social divisions. I know where the class lines are
drawn, and how those distinctions manifest themselves in the little subtle
responses we all give to one another. I've had the waitress wait until my
food was cold before she served it to me. I've been overlooked for promo-
tions because (as one supervisor put it) "certain people don't think certain
people should get certain jobs." I'm a short, fat, Mexican-American woman
with stringy brown hair and thick-lensed glasses. Oh, and I'm a poet. Believe me, I know bigotry. I have lived with it all my life. I know there are
people in the world who wouldn't give me the time of day because of such
superficialities as hair color, or brand of gym shoe.

But I'm not writing about bigotry, I'm writing about whiteness.
And though whiteness, left unchecked, can and often does manifest itself
as bigotry, it is not the same. Unfortunately, trying to extract whiteness
from all the other quirks and tics people carry is a particularly difficult
task. Also unfortunate for me was my belated introduction to the concept
and culture of whiteness.

Though I grew up understanding that "white" people were not to
be trusted: "Always trust a black person before you trust a white person,"
my mother taught me, my experience with "white" people led me to a different perception of them. I went to a private, all-girl high school in a white
suburb of Chicago. While many of the white suburban girls were rude, I
didn't attribute their rudeness to their race; I attributed their rudeness to
their individual natures. I don't like to ascribe any attributes to any particular race. I don't like when it's done to me. But "whiteness," to me, and
contrary to popular belief, is not an attribute of any one particular race. I
think whiteness is an affliction all people in our society are capable of at
any given point in time. All too often, however, too many fellow Americans seem to unknowingly subscribe to it, and thus cause many others to

suffer from it on a daily basis. I use the word "suffer" because this is perhaps the greatest effect of whiteness: whiteness subjects others. It lords over others. It doesn't give others a chance to breathe, to grow, to prosper, to gather their bearings about a subject, a place, or a feeling. It defines others before offering others the opportunity to define themselves.

Naturally, I don't mean to dismiss the tendency toward whiteness in "white" people, I mean only that the tendency is one available to all peoples in our society. Because whiteness garners much of its potency from power, and from existing power structures, it is most blaringly evident in those interactions between groups with supposedly stark differences: Black/White; rich/poor; straight/gay and so on. The problem with thinking of whiteness as existing only in these dichotomies, however, is that no one is ever *merely* black or white, rich or poor, straight or gay. Each of us has ties to many different identities at every given moment. So, to ascribe "whiteness" only to people who are "white" would be to diminish the implications of whiteness solely to racism. Again, whiteness is not racism. And "white" people are not the only people who act out of whiteness. As a matter of fact, I've known white people who didn't ooze whiteness as much as some Hispanic or African American people I know. The point is that whiteness is not so much a thing or trait or attribute ascribable only to race or ethnicity as it seems to be *the compulsion to* ascribe things or traits or attributes to *different* races or ethnicities or ideologies or sexual preferences, and so on, or sometimes to the *seemingly* same race, ethnicity, ideology, sexual preference, and so on. And this compulsion is accommodated without much thought to the consequences *for the receiver* in the process. People who act out of whiteness do so with the surety of their own assumptions, and without a second thought to how others might or might not fit those assumptions.

Early in my last year of graduate school, I was invited to attend a Latina writers conference by a professor who teaches Latin American Studies. She knew I was a writer, and Hispanic, so she thought I would enjoy the conference. What she didn't know was that I don't identify myself as an "Hispanic" poet, or a Latina poet, a woman poet, a Midwest poet, a fat poet, or any other *kind* of poet. I am a poet. Period. Still, I hadn't been out of town in a while and the conference was free, so I went. Also, one of my favorite writers was going to be the keynote speaker. Now this writer happens to be Latina, and lesbian, but while I respect her self-identifications, I appreciate her writing for its many other qualities, as well as its political statements.

So, there we were at the Latina writers conference, with all the other Latina writers, artists, and scholars, many of whom took advantage of various panels to gripe about the "establishment," or to give voice to imagined episodes of bravado wherein they put "whitey" in their subjected "*lugares*." (I should note that many interesting and insightful discussions also took place.)

With great impatience and some anxiety (I am a bit shy), I waited in line to meet the keynote speaker. The line moved unbearably slowly, she chatted with every person she met, but still not slowly enough, for my turn was approaching and I couldn't think of a thing to say! I wanted to let her know what a tremendous impact her last book had had on me. I wanted to let her know that I felt more comfortable with my own heritage because of the openness and honesty of her work. I wanted to let her know. . .

"Hello," I stammered and held out my hand. She smiled, took my hand. "My name is Juanita, and I just wanted to. . ."

"*Hoowaneeta*," she corrected my pronunciation. I assumed she had misheard me, as I pronounce my name in a sort of Anglicized way: "Waneeta." I reintroduced myself: "My name is Juanita. . ."

"*Hoowaneeta*," she corrected my pronunciation. Again.

". . .I just wanted to let you know how much I enjoyed your last book. . ."

"*Muchas gracias*," she cut me off. I felt a lot of pressure to respond to her in Spanish—which I can do—but I thought to do so would be to compromise *my* sense of my identity to accommodate *her* sense of my identity.

Obviously, because of the situation, I couldn't question her compulsion to impose ethnicity as the primary component of my identity—and I wasn't afforded the luxury of informing her of the innumerable experiences wherein my ethnicity has been utilized as a weapon to bar me from certain opportunities. It is an unfortunate condition of my life that I have had to downplay—not deny, not dismiss—my ethnic background to overcome many prejudices. It is also an unfortunate condition of my life that I have had to prove my distinction from many stereotypes (that "fat people are lazy" or that "people with thick glasses are nerds" or that "poets are dreamers"—I can go on and on!) just to be allowed to do the things that so many others are allowed to do automatically, without question.

Because of the context, I didn't push back when this woman imposed her value system upon me. Instead, I smiled. And left. No connection. Hopefully, this experience serves to illustrate my point that "whiteness" is not idiosyncratic solely to white people. Hopefully, this experience also serves to illustrate a few other points about whiteness, specifically that "good intentions" do not necessarily good engagement strategies make, and that to sincerely respect difference we must all be willing to invest the time and effort in respecting others. To sincerely respect one another, we must be willing to engage with one another. We must recognize that respect for an other grows out of a relationship *with that other*, and to have a relationship with an other, one must know that other, not just assume that one knows that other because of one's assumptions.

All too often, as this instance illustrates, whiteness flourishes on the superficial level of appearances—it flourishes and it acts and when the response isn't what was expected, it reacts *with a vengeance*. Furthermore, whiteness seems to react with a vengeance because it doesn't know it has committed an offense. What was so wrong of the postman to acknowledge my "difference"? Why should that keynote speaker not have granted me the "freedom" to pronounce my name in Spanish? Well, who gave them the power to grant *me* something that belonged to me in the first place? Problem is, these people, who to me clearly exhibited whiteness, just could not fathom how they were offensive. They just don't know, and unfortunately probably aren't open to learning what they don't know. To them, they are doing the "right" thing. They are acknowledging difference—as they have learned to acknowledge difference: superficially.

As I've implied, most people like to link "whiteness" with racism, but it seems to me that whiteness isn't as aware of itself as racism is. While whiteness does discriminate, it doesn't seem to know its own biases well enough to reveal its logic or process of judgment. Ask a racist why they don't like someone and they'll be able to give you an answer. Even if the answer is disagreeable or offensive, it will be an answer. People who subscribe to whiteness, however, will most likely deny not liking that someone, or they will adhere steadfast to the party line of "everything's fine." Maybe, if they're creative, they might even turn the tables on the inquisitor with a line I frequently received from one of my professors: "Oh, you're being paranoid"—this from a man who found approximately 60 minutes (total) to "direct" my thesis in roughly 32 weeks of the academic year. Oh, sorry, that *is* the academic year.

Okay, I might be exaggerating, maybe we spent a bit more time together, but it's difficult to tally as he kept skipping our appointments. I would arrive at his office and wait, and wait, and wait. Then I would call his home, leave message after message on his answering machine, or talk with his wife, or his son. I would reschedule and reschedule, and wait and wait, until I finally stopped scheduling appointments and stopped seeking his input altogether, a development he actually noticed—ten days before my graduation. "You never come see me," he commented, actually lamented.

"You're never available," I responded.

"You should have called me at home," he chided.

"I did."

"Excuse me," he left me standing at the table, alone. Again.

I suspect if this man were asked if he "liked" me, he would commence a response with a list of all of my fine academic and poetic accomplishments. But, why then could he not find time to discuss my work with me? Why were my appointments apparently the most convenient appointments to miss? Why, after three years as my "advisor," would this man feel compelled to emphasize his role in my poetic development in his final evaluation of my work? ". . . its [sic] clear from her MFA thesis (which I directed) that [Ms. Garza]'s had a very productive writing year," he wrote. Obviously, he needed to claim some of my productivity as his own. Obviously, this man has some personal issues with which he must contend. And I write this with the knowledge of my experiences in graduate school fresh in my mind. And some rumors of his perceptions of me as well.

One rumor, which seems to be supported by his behavior, was that he felt intimidated by me. What exactly spurred that intimidation I never found out, but I'm certainly willing to conjecture (aren't we all?). Whiteness.

Exactly what whiteness is, is too complex to contain in a singular definition. When dealing with a *culture*, there are many variables to take into account, and the possibility of stepping into the quagmire of personal traits is anything but remote. On the one hand, my experiences with this professor have allowed me to develop a sense of his personal pathologies. I think he's a bit immature for his age. I also think he's possibly insecure about his talents as a writer and/or a teacher. (Most writers and/or teachers are insecure about their talents.) I also think he's a bit of a chauvinist. I feel very strongly that this man didn't find me pretty enough to fulfill his professional obligations to me. Can't prove it, but it sure feels that way. So, if all of these quirks are personal pathologies, where does whiteness fit into the equation?

I have included various instances from my excursion into academia to, hopefully, develop a theme of whiteness. Thus far, with the postman, the doctor, the keynote speaker, and the professor, one theme could be that whiteness has to do with perspective. These people made certain assumptions about me the moment they saw me. They created images of me based on their knowledge of the world, which knowledge did not expand to allow *me* to influence a perception *of me*. Naturally, we can only meet the world with whatever knowledge of the world we have accumulated at any given point in time. However, I would hope that our knowledge of the world is a dynamic, active archive of information and stimuli that receives some of its charm from the relationship we have with it, instead of thinking of knowledge as some kind of fixed stagnant thing. I would hope so, if for no other reason than a dynamic relationship will usually provide more impetus to greet the day than will a stagnant body.

No, about the only thing a stagnant body will inspire is fear. And I believe fear is one of the factors which spurs whiteness. More specifically, fear of the unknown, fear of the "other," spurs whiteness.

It is a curious word, "other." When used in cultural studies it is meant to denote those, well, other entities, forces, subjects outside the perspective of the subject. In layman's terms: it is the base or origin of a particular vantage point, kind of like a camera lens. Using one particular vantage point, a subject "sees" others. And those others are different because they are not the subject. Again, the models used to discuss various relations turn into a system of stark differences: subject and other; or you and I; or in or out, good or bad. The problem with these dichotomies, and probably where whiteness tends to nestle, is in the judgment of the "different" entity: the other. I suppose I'm thinking of whiteness as the way people respond to difference. With whiteness, people tend to judge others in the negative, rather than the positive. To make another analogy: take an orange. If we use the orange as the center of the fruit world, then an apple is not simply an apple but, rather, it is not an orange. The apple becomes the other. If we were to grant whiteness to oranges, then not only would the apple not be an orange, but it would also be "bad." It would be bad simply because it was not an orange, and because the orange would have deemed it "bad." And if the apple didn't like being deemed "bad," the orange would deem the apple "bad" and "obstinate." Or "troublesome." Or "problematic." Even "cute" and "sweet" and "interesting and rich" (the singular most prominent commentary my thesis "director" afforded my work) are products of whiteness, for whiteness often compels a judgment which uses the judge as the seat of objectivity while it fails to recognize the judge as this seat.

In other words, whiteness uses its own comfort as the measuring stick for how other people should live, think, work, play, feel, and so on. Whiteness says "you" are bad because "I" am uncomfortable with you—

only whiteness forgets that the reasoning employed is self-referential. What is most ironic about these types of interactions is that the other continually seeks a relationship with the subject even though the desire to have a relationship, historically, is one-sided. Whiteness doesn't allow itself to know the other, indeed, often doesn't need to know the other to exist.

The other, on the other hand, probably because it has inherited much of its identity from the subject, does need the subject to know itself: the beginning of self-identification comes from the other's position as an "other." It is interesting, and a bit sad, that I, for example, am referred to as "Hispanic" because the dominant culture in our society is "white." As the "other" in our society, to understand myself I must understand how the dominant culture understands "Hispanic" people. My self-identification owes much of its definition to how these "white" others view me. Whiteness, however, doesn't have to endure this process in its quest for self-identification. At least, it doesn't think it does. But, with the continuing self-identification and self-empowerment that many minorities in our culture are engaged in, whiteness has become an area of subjectivity with more finite boundaries. The dichotomy of "us" and "them" that was once merely accepted has given way to an examination of who "us" is. Our culture has already turned its inquiry to who "them" is, and much of that valuable work has allowed those others to focus their attention on those who would judge them; they, we, can turn to whiteness and ask "what are you about?"

Of course, with this inquiry comes the responsibility actually to endeavor to understand the subject. As shown in my experience with the Latina writer, whiteness doesn't just thrive in "white" people, and as we inquire after whiteness, we must take care not merely to judge "white" people for their differences from this newfound "us." We must not simply replace the white players with players of color in the hegemonic model, in the dichotomy of "us" and "them." We must recognize that polarized models in themselves construct this dichotomy and thus detract from our objectives of initiating a relationship of understanding and respect.

Now, I'm not saying that we should abolish judgment in our society, but shouldn't we be able to present our reasoning for the conclusions we reach? And if we want to share our reasoning, if we want others to abide by our reasoning, shouldn't that reasoning be sharable? Unlike oranges, which do not go around judging apples, people do judge other people—particularly if those "other" people are, well, apples and not oranges. But there are people in this world who mysteriously classify other people according to unnamed, unexamined, *undetermined* criteria, and, when called upon to express these criteria, they use the discomfiture of the moment as an excuse to label the inquirer after these criteria as "bad." My theory is that the inquirer is labeled bad because when people can't name their criteria, they feel stupid. So the person who made them feel stupid must be bad. What else could they be? They couldn't just be, golly gee, curious? They couldn't really want to understand? No! They're just plain old bad!

I know I have been dubbed all manner of negative misnomers because I had the audacity to want to comprehend something. Of a professor. In graduate school. Like, duh! And why was a curious, knowledge-seeking student straddled with these pejorative attributes? I suspect it was because these professors felt uncomfortable with their own knowledge and therefore felt intimidated by me, as my director—again this is a rumor—felt intimidated by me. Let's think about intimidation for a second.

The last time you felt intimidated, how did this intimidation feel? Were you scared? Did it seem like this other person was more "powerful" than you? That's what intimidation usually feels like to me. Intimidation makes me feel lesser than that other person. Whether the intimidation is physical or intellectual or artistic, when I feel *intimidated* it usually means I feel *inferior*. And if this professor felt intimidated by me, maybe that was his way of saying he felt inferior to me.

Oh, I know what you're thinking: 'inferior to me...' just who does this woman think she is? Well, I know who I am. I know where I've been, I know what I've done—I even know a bit of what I haven't done. And this scares people. It scares people because it is an indication not only of self-awareness, but also of self-reflection and self-criticism. I have ethics. I have standards. And as I strive to live up to my own code of behavior, I expect others to do the same for themselves. What I learned in graduate school is that many people don't evaluate the modes of behaviors in which they engage—they just do what they are accustomed to doing, or what they perceive they are "supposed" to do. And when they encounter people who question what is "supposed" to be done, those people are labeled troublemakers, naysayers, dumb, stupid, bad, or whatever other kind of judgment whiteness can muster to shift responsibility away from itself. This type of reaction to discomfiture doesn't encourage a relationship with an other, but rather, secures one's positionality over and above the other, or imposes an identity and/or value system upon the other that the other may not need or want—a rather sad and dangerous scenario, particularly when one is involved in the enterprise of fostering knowledge in those others.

The end result is a power game wherein the student will always be the loser because all the student will have learned is that he or she is powerless, and, because they didn't play by the teacher's unexpressed rules, they'll probably get a bad grade to boot!

For example, I remember an exchange in my (other) poetry workshop. The professor this time—a Jewish lesbian—was making reference to "some Hispanic poet." She was scribbling something on the board, then stopped, stammering. "Oh, what is her name?" (the Hispanic poet) when suddenly her eyes opened wide. Of course! The answer must have shot across her mind like a meteor. "Juanita! You know, that Hispanic poet, what's her name?" (Understand, gentle reader, that I have never specifically studied "Hispanic" poetry; have never aligned myself with an established "Hispanic" aesthetic—if there is such a thing; and, again, I don't identify myself as an "Hispanic" poet, or any other *kind* of poet.) The first thing that went through my mind was "Now is this a Chicago Hispanic poet? A South Side Chicago Hispanic poet? A North side Chicago Hispanic poet? Is this Hispanic poet from the West Coast? The Midwest, the South? A confessional poet? A narrative poet? An "experimental" poet? I need something more to go on than just 'Hispanic poet'!" Naturally, I didn't voice this little mental screening process, though it no doubt influenced my response:

"I left my Hispanic poet index at home," I muttered.

She was not amused.

I wish I could say that, like my doctor and I, this professor and I were able to move forward from this uncomfortable place. Unfortunately, that would be a blaring falsehood. I had many problems with this professor. Before I continue, however, I want to make a few things as clear as possible. I mention above that this professor is a Jewish lesbian not because I care that she is a Jewish lesbian, but because *she* cares that she is known as a Jewish lesbian. Obviously, cultural and sexual identities are important to her. They are not to me. (I would rather my poetry be known for its depth of thought, its insight, its frivolity, its technical prowess with the language.) I could have lived my entire life without knowing she was Jewish or lesbian and I would still have felt that she was a pushy, presumptuous, kinetic little fireball with some serious self-doubts. Any teacher who conducts a class with an iron fist despite her entire class's vehement cries of distress has got some problems. (I'm talking poetry here, folks, not brain surgery.)

Having a wee bit of teaching experience under my belt, I acknowledge that occasionally a student or two will feel overwhelmed. But you talk to those students, you haul them into your office, and you ask questions. You determine problem areas. You listen and coax and explain, and if necessary, you adapt, you change to accommodate *learning,* not your own ego. You don't dismiss a troubled student, particularly when they are actively seeking assistance.

I could not understand this professor's responses to my work. Time after time, she expressed her confusion—but never expressed any grounds for that confusion. I didn't know what was confusing to her. I didn't understand how my images didn't add up to any kind of sense to her. I had no clue as to how we kept missing each other, how my words held no meaning for her whatsoever. So, on my own initiative, I went to her office to discuss my poetry. I tried to explain my concerns. After several attempts—and several dismissals—I finally blurted out in exasperation: "I feel you don't understand my work!" (Poetry, like all art forms, is very subjective and I wanted to make sure we were at least reading the same book, if not the same page.)

"Of course I understand your work," she protested. "And I'm the greatest supporter of your work," she declared—just before she literally, albeit gently, shoved me out of her office. This encounter took place midsemester.

When she returned my portfolio at the end of the semester, she sat stoically behind her desk, hands clasped into a tight little knot, a self assured little smirk perched on her thin lips, and stated: "The bottom line here is that I simply didn't understand your work."

Dismissed! Don't let the door smack your behind on your way out!

How is a student supposed to "learn" from someone who doesn't try to reach her? Who doesn't even attempt to create a meeting ground?

If I sound bitter, the reason should be obvious. I tried. I tried and tried and tried to work with this professor. And all of my attempts were met with dismissals and/or lies. I felt betrayed. I felt unknown. And worse of all, for a long time, I felt as if I was unworthy of being known, of attracting some little modicum of attention from a person whose chosen profession it was to help students understand and achieve at least a little of their potential.

As I stated earlier, whiteness isn't as aware of itself, its logic, its process of reasoning as racism is. I don't think this professor was being racist. I don't think she was being mean. I think she was scared of realizing that her value system didn't fit into my work. I think she feared that what she had to offer me was a body of knowledge that I neither wanted nor could make any use of. And this is one of the consequences of viewing knowledge solely as a stagnant "body" of information: sometimes the buyer isn't in the market for that particular body of information. I expected graduate school, metaphorically, to take me onto the superhighway of poetry. Instead, it took me for a Sunday drive through the white, middle-class countryside—then found fault with me for being unsatisfied with the great expanse of dandelions, wild grass, and the occasional ruddy apple lying hopelessly upon the worn path.

This is not to say that I find these kinds of excursions unsatisfying in and of themselves, quite the contrary. I love to admire nature. I love being engaged with nature. I love feeling the spreading warmth of sun on my skin. But, like the black child in William Blake's poem ("The Little Black Boy"), graduate school has left me feeling empty: "as if bereav'd of light."

I chose this little part of Blake's poem as my title because of the dual implications of the word "bereaved" and the metaphorical implications of "light." During Blake's lifetime, the word "bereaved" meant deprived of something precious, especially by force. Hence, when used in the line: "White as an angel is the English child,/But I am black, as if bereav'd of light," bereaved means deprived. The little black boy is deprived of light. In the poem, "light" is both the physical (sunlight) and the metaphorical (God's love). Thus, in the poem, the little black boy is deprived of both sunlight and God's love—because he is black.

How this line is appropriate to my attempt to decode whiteness in my experience of academia is both physical and metaphorical as well. Very often, contemporary metaphorical models liken knowledge to "light." To "know" something is to be able to retrieve that something from the murk of swirling impulses in our brains. "I saw the light" is a common expression implying a way out of the darkness of mis- or nonunderstanding. Well, I now "know" something which has caused me grief and/or bereavement: whiteness. Whiteness, literally speaking, is the opposite of darkness, it is "light." So, my reinscription of this line, "as if bereav'd of light" means, to me, to have been deprived of knowledge, and to have been made to suffer the loss of a loved one (to be "bereaved") by whiteness. The loved one in this case being that part of me which always loved to learn, which always believed in education—which always sought the "light" of knowledge.

"White as an angel is the English child/But I am black, as if bereav'd of light," the line goes, and its construction sets up a comparison of two unlike entities: the white English child and the black child. Similarly, in graduate school, I found myself labeled as "different" because of my name. Because of my skin color. Because of my urban background. Because of these superficial distinctions, I was the aberration. I wanted to *learn* something, and simply because I questioned and strove to understand, I was the mistake, the rabble-rouser, the troublemaker, the "difficult" student.

And I earned these labels because of whiteness. I was different, not because I *am* different, but because my academia viewed me that way. From their perspective, from their position of power, they determined what the central definition of "graduate student" meant. Apparently, it meant a meek, mild, unquestioning person from a (predominantly) white, middle-class suburban background, preferably with Ivy League credentials. Of course, they probably would not agree with me. Of course, no teacher likes to think of him or herself as a power tyrant who stifles their own students. Furthermore, no teacher who does feel compelled to exert their authority in a classroom feels he or she does so *out of fear*. I doubt many teachers/professors *feel* they are intellectually intimidated by their students, even if they actually *are* intellectually intimidated by their students.

Because of whiteness, because I didn't have at my disposal a cognitive understanding of whiteness, I didn't know how to negotiate with these professors and many of my classmates. I couldn't come up with other, more effective strategies to engage with these arbiters of "rightness." After many feeble attempts, and horrendous defeats—yes, I do think of graduate school as a war—I withdrew. I stopped writing poetry. I stopped enrolling in poetry workshops (except for my last semester, which was a requirement I tried desperately to get out of, and which was basically a 16-week Juanita blood bath!). I stopped enrolling in classes in English altogether. Fortunately, a class in critical pedagogy introduced me to the various paradigmatic approaches to teaching—and I learned that I wasn't "wrong," that respecting a student, even a "difficult" one, isn't a bad way to go about teaching. I learned that truly to teach, one must allow the student to question, and judge, and disagree. Students must be given the space to grapple with information, and they must be given the opportunity to disagree with the teacher without fear of retribution. We can't all think alike. We can't all see everything the same way. But if teachers do their jobs well, their students will see something. And that something will not only be their own powerlessness in the academic power structure.

My last semester as a teaching assistant, I taught an introduction to poetry-writing class. From the first day, I was straightforward with my students about my expectations, about my objectives, about my methodologies. I even shared my work with them—I not only showed it to them, I criticized it. I evaluated it according to the criteria I employed to criticize their work. I invited them to criticize it, to discuss it, to not like it if they didn't like it. I gave them the opportunity to exercise their burgeoning critiquing skills, with my work as the object of that criticism, so they would learn to trust their perceptions even if their perceptions didn't mesh with mine.

Near the end of the semester, one student saw fit to offer this bit of advice: "You shouldn't let students know you and your work," he said.

"Why not?"

"Because then they can judge you."

"They're going to do that anyway, Danny." I responded. "I'd rather supply them with my criteria than have them come up with criteria that have nothing to do with me or with what I want to accomplish." This student and I had had many conversations about his work, and the class. His classmates viewed him as "different" and thus could not value his participation. I tried to recognize his contribution to the class, and took great pains to explain his thoughtful and valuable insights, and so he and I had developed a nice rapport with one another.

"I see your logic," he smiled. "But you have to really know your stuff, then."

"Does it seem like I don't?" I smiled. I didn't want him to distance his pedagogical concerns from the object of his insights, namely me.

"Oh no, you know what you're doing," he said.

"Yeah, I guess I'm pretty confident. But not stoic, I hope."

"No, you're not closed off. If you were, I wouldn't feel comfortable telling you this." First he chuckled, then I chuckled. We both knew how much effort I had taken to engage with my students. I held my required office hours, but I also encouraged appointments outside those office hours. I instituted an open, out-of-class poetry discussion on the weekends. I invited my students to various poetry readings about campus.

"You know," I began. "I do know what I want to teach my class. I know this is an introductory course and I hope that it will provide a good foundation for everyone to use to build on. But it's not just about poetry, you know."

"Oh, I know that. This class has already made me look at things, art, people, school, differently."

"Thank you. That's nice to hear," I said. "So, do you feel you know what you're doing? Now? After being in my class all these weeks?"

He pondered his response for a moment, then sort of nodded. "Does it seem like I don't?" he grinned.

"Oh no," I smiled. "You've come a long way."

"Yeah," he nodded more confidently. "And I don't even fully understand it—yet. I have a feeling this class is going to affect my life for a long time to come."

After he left, I realized that that class would affect my life for a long time to come. Being a teacher, being an effective teacher, does change a person, for in teaching someone else, one learns as well. The trick is to allow oneself to see how one is affecting students.

I have a friend who has been teaching in Chicago for several years. When I read a draft of this essay to her, she chided me with: "Oh, you can't let your students run your life. You can't give them that kind of attention all the time. It will burn you out."

"But isn't giving attention to students part of the job?" I asked. "Aren't we supposed to help them?"

"Help them yes, but you can't expect to have a profound impact on everyone!"

Having a scant two years of teaching experience under my belt, I know she's right. I haven't had a profound impact on every student. But I've wanted to. And for those students who were open to a profound impact, even if they didn't know it of themselves, they got one.

As for whiteness, my friend told me she was taking a class, for the first time in several years. The class was in Latin literature, a specialty of hers. The teacher wouldn't veer from the text or the syllabus or the lesson plan. She also wouldn't hear the input of her Hispanic students, who knew the myth written about in the story being discussed. They tried to explain to her that the story had incorrectly recorded a very important detail in the myth. The teacher would not listen, though, even closed down the discussion. "Oh, she was an idiot!" my friend exclaimed.

I thought it odd that a teacher who had just chided me for wanting to listen to my students, to pay attention to their perceptions, to inspire their engagement with the material would call someone who didn't do these things an idiot. But then I remembered that everyone is susceptible to whiteness. As a teacher, I'm sure my friend is far more open with her students than she claims—that's the kind of person she is. But she also is far more experienced a teacher than I am and her friendship with me compels her to help me avoid the pratfalls of teaching. She doesn't know me as a teacher, so she treats me as an "inexperienced teacher," a role which I must accept because I am an inexperienced teacher. But I'm not a bad teacher. I'm not an ineffective teacher. I'm not overly involved in my student's lives. My friend doesn't know these things though, and she imposes her definition of inexperienced teacher upon me because she doesn't know how I fill the role of "inexperienced teacher." She just assumes I'm "bad." She just used whiteness to maintain her authority as the "experienced" teacher in our relationship.

What she doesn't realize is that, now that I know about whiteness, I won't be a victim of it anymore. She could have learned something from me, but whiteness kept *her* from growing. I can see the whiteness at work in her experience with that "idiot" teacher. And I can see whiteness at work in our exchange as well.

Something she can't do.

CHAPTER FIVE

Where's My Body and What's On It?
Theoretical Twists on Notions of Race and Sexuality
Laurie Fuller

I have been wondering about my body, my "white female" body. I have been wondering if there is a way to think about race, whiteness specifically, that undoes current ways of using race theoretically as well as a way that undoes the current uses of the term "race" to imply "people of color." Such an implication often leaves whiteness absent from theorizing about race, which can normalize whiteness as just human (meaning not "raced"). Not only is whiteness normalized in discussions of race, but also many of the current constructions of race have roots in biological differences, implying that race is fixed, a constant unchanging genetic aspect of a person. So, in response to such constructions, I am interested in analyzing how whiteness gets theorized and trying to re-theorize the construction of whiteness for the purpose of undoing the fixity of whiteness as natural and normative, as the point "from which we tend to identify difference" (Carby, 1992, p. 193). Thus, I will theorize whiteness and work to denaturalize it and make it visible in the theories of race I discuss.

I have been wondering about my body, not just my "white female" body, but my "white female queer" body. Because of my focus on the relationality of identity positionings, I believe there may be ways that some theorizations of identity positionings, like the performativity of sex/gender/sexuality, might be useful for thinking about other identity positionings, like social constructions of race, including whiteness. Notions of performativity may be a way to challenge understanding race as fixed. My specific understandings of performance come from queer theory's challenges to the construction of sexuality, including the work of Anzaldúa (1987); Bad Object-Choices (1991); Butler (1990); Crimp (1987); and Phalen (1993). Using these notions of performance and transposing them onto notions of the social construction of race, I hope to create a disruption that could reconceptualize whiteness as some sort of performance, not as just the natural way of being human. Moreover, identity positionings, like "white" and "queer," refer both to the context in which these positionings are mobilized and also to the process of mobilization. They are not fixed positionings but refer to the social acts and performances that enact and improvise on existing practices of race and sexuality. These social acts and performances constitute relationships between self and other in and through the repetition of race, gender, class, sexuality and so on.

This essay will investigate current constructions of whiteness in cultural studies to contextualize my investigation of the social constructions of whiteness. My focus is on the meanings and usefulness of insisting on the relationality between performativity of sexuality and performativity of race. Toward this end, then, I analyze Judith Butler's (1990) conceptualization of sex/gender/sexuality and performance (from the field of queer theory) and transpose those conceptualizations onto notions of constructions of race. Butler's theoretical constructions of sexuality point out the contextual constraints on sexuality and explore how agency might be located within understandings of sexuality. To disrupt the discourses of race, I transpose notions of performativity from queer theory into constructions of race and discuss the possibilities of "dragging" race. This is a transposition and disruption because drag can no longer mean exactly the same thing after its use in the context of race and vice versa. Moreover, conceptions of race are related to those of sex/gender/sexuality through the transposition and disruption. Thus a relationship among aspects of queer theory and critical race theory is created through the concept of dragging race. As an example of the performativity of race, I provide a reading of an episode of the television program *Northern Exposure*. As a representation of social life, media provide a space to enact performances and to analyze them. I will use the television show to illustrate some complex notions of whiteness and performance and discuss what performances of whiteness(es), parodic and comical performances, might look like in the context of the episode's theme: white healing stories.

The Visibility and Invisibility of Whiteness

In order to delineate constructions of whiteness, I take as my jumping-off point current theories in cultural studies. I begin with a focus on constructions of whiteness working to "to make visible what is rendered invisible when viewed as the normative state of existence" (Carby, 1992, p. 193). Too often constructions of race have focused on notions of difference, specifically difference from the normalcy of whiteness. So I will outline some constructions of whiteness as a framework for theorizing relationality between race, gender, and sexuality. I concentrate on notions of whiteness put forth and understood by some theorists of philosophy, history, media studies, and sociology—Marilyn Frye, Vron Ware, Richard Dyer, Ruth Frankenberg—who focus specifically on whiteness. Using only theorists who position themselves as "white," however, may seem problematic given the normalcy of whiteness. As a "white," I want to research how theorists who position themselves *as* "white" struggle to conceptualize whiteness as something other than the normal, natural way of being human for "white" people. Additionally, each of these theorists comes to their discussion from a different theoretical background as well as with different approaches to conceptualize whiteness. Frye is contextualized in feminist coalition struggles, Ware is tracing feminist histories of whiteness, Dyer is analyzing representations of whiteness in film, and Frankenberg interviews "white women" and analyzes their understandings of whiteness. Each theorist emphasizes very different conceptions of whiteness, in part because they have different methodologies and assumptions. However, their different points of view provide a starting point from which I will discuss whiteness and the performativity of race.

As a "feminist" and an instructor in Women's Studies, I start with Marilyn Frye and her ground-breaking feminist article "On Being White: Thinking Toward a Feminist Understanding of Race and Race Supremacy (1983)," and her more recent article, "White Woman Feminist (1992)," since as a "white lesbian feminist" she is theorizing out of her work to address the racisms of feminisms, especially in feminist theories. Because she struggles to theorize gender and race relationally, from the point of view of "white lesbian feminist," I understand her project as related to mine. We are both theorizing the relationality of identity positionings and the power of whiteness. She is motivated to investigate whiteness because her work across differences is failing, and she begins thinking about the causes of that failure. She theorizes that, "If being white is not finally a matter of skin color, which is beyond our power to change, but of politics and power, then perhaps "white" individuals in a white supremacist society are not doomed to dominance by logic or nature" (Fryer, 1983, p. 118). She is struggling with her power and privilege as a "white," thinking that there must be ways to be "white" that aren't constantly employing racism and white privilege. However, her struggling leads her to state that "I can set myself against Whiteness: I can give myself the injunction to stop being White" (p. 127). For Frye, "Whiteness" is the racist enacting of white privilege and power. She believes she can stop acting racist as she stops being "white."

She re-theorizes more complexly her previous understandings of whiteness in "White Woman Feminist." Fryer (1992) is articulating her understanding of the social construction of whiteness by using the example of masculinity:

> I will introduce 'whitely' and 'whiteliness' as terms whose grammar is analogous to that of 'masculine' and 'masculinity.' Being white-skinned (like being male) is a matter of physical traits presumed to be physically determined; being whitely (like being masculine) I conceive as a deeply ingrained way of being in the world. Following the analogy with masculinity, I assume that the connection between whiteliness and light-colored skin is a contingent connection: this character could be manifested by persons who are not "white"; it can be absent in persons who are. (p.151-5)

So, for Frye, "whitely" might be a learned aspect of identity that could be unlearned and is not a biological trait but a conditional connection to skin color.

Frye (1992) describes aspects of whiteliness from her own and other "white" points of view and from the points of view of "people of color." She believes that it is possible to unlearn whiteliness just as men can unlearn masculinity. For Frye, "white women" can disengage from the project of the social creation and maintenance of the "white" race, "by stopping constantly making oneself whitely." It is this position that "holds some promise of our rescuing ourselves from the degraded condition of women in white men's world"(p.166). So Frye's project is to outline aspects of whiteliness in a way that calls attention to its construction, in hopes that "white women" will understand how whiteliness constrains their womanhood, just as masculinity constrains men. Her notion of whiteliness is closely linked to my understanding of learned performance of identity positionings, because this is a constructed identity positioning, not some biological given. Rather, whiteliness is created and recreated through interactions with others. We diverge when Frye suggests one can possibly unlearn whiteliness because I think whiteness is not something that can be undone or unlearned. Rather, I think that the meanings of the performances of whiteness can change and be disrupted by making it visible. In my view, one will always *be* "white," but never monolithically or singularly. However, if being "white" is socially contingent, as she states in the quote above, then meanings of whiteness are never fixed or given but constantly contested and struggled over. For Frye, "being white" may be a way of being that can be contested instead of accepted, may be acted against and worked against instead of accepted as the normal and natural way of being human. Frye's discussion is about contextualizing the constructs of whiteliness so that whitely ways can be struggled against. Frye's work creates a space for me to theorize and consider the performativity of race, since she has illuminated "whitely" as a deeply ingrained way of being in the world, but one that isn't biological.

While Frye's work creates space for conceptualizing whiteness as performative, Ware (1992) begins to ground understandings of whiteness as one of many interconnected temporary identity positionings. Her book, *Beyond the Pale: White Women, Racism and History* (1992), is also driven by her politics and her struggles in working with women across racial differences. She analyzes the connection of "white" women's, especially feminists', self-understandings and how those understandings are shaped historically.

> This book is predicated on a recognition that to be white and female is to occupy a social category that is inescapably racialized as well as gendered. It is not about being a white woman, it is about being thought of as a white woman. In other words I have concentrated on the development of ideas and ideologies of whiteness rather than analyzing what it actually means to grow up white in a white supremacist society. I understand 'race' to be a socially constructed category with absolutely no basis in biology; the term 'racism' encompasses all the various relations of power that have arisen from the domination of one racial group over another. (p.xii)

So "white" womanness is a social positioning that is both raced and gendered. Ware analyzes ideas about what it means to be thought of as a "white woman," while understanding race to be socially constructed. She is concentrating on historical events which shape social categories that, in turn, constrain "white women's" lives. Ware is pointing at history and how historical events shape notions of "white" womanhood. Her book is about searching "for significant moments in the past which would explain how this category was produced" (Ware, 1992, p.xii). As a feminist, and driven by feminist politics, Ware's theoretical approach complicates the formation of white womanhood by discussing how feminism has "developed as a political movement in a racist society" (p.xiii).

Unlike Frye, who analyzes "whiteliness" in the present cultural moment, Ware discusses feminism and whiteness historically, trying to analyze how the constraints of race and racism have always been a part of feminist movements in the West. She complicates notions of social change and political unity by discussing "'strategic identities' which allow opposition to one form of domination without being complicit in another" (Ware, 1992, p. 254). Ware's book doesn't take up what exactly a "strategic identity" might look like or how it might be articulated. Yet I see "strategic identities" as closely related to my conception of identity positionings as multiple and shifting. "Strategic" implies context-based, dependent on the strategy needed in a context, and since contexts change, so must these "strategic identities." Her book tries to illustrate how historical understandings of the dynamics of gender, race, and class undercut people's constant, fixed-identity positionings, making political responses and coalitions more viable. Her work creates a space where I can conceptualize identity positionings as relational, contextual, and historically specific, which I can use to conceptualize identity positionings as multiple and shifting and, building on Frye, also performative. Therefore, Frye and Ware's work has laid important groundwork for understanding "white women" in context and the importance of working for change within a context, and recognition of whiteness, especially how historical events shape our understandings and the performativity of race.

Representations also shape our understandings and performativity of race. The construction of race consciousness, and of whiteness specifically, may be formed by continual visual representations of difference. This possibility motivates Richard Dyer (1988), in his article "White," to discuss the representations of whiteness in movies. Whiteness is described as a culturally constructed category that is represented in Hollywood films as the norm—the natural, inevitable, ordinary way of being human. For Dyer, the strength of normative representations of whiteness is the apparent absence altogether of the typical: "If we are to see the historical, cultural and political limitations (to put it mildly) of white world domination, it is important to see similarities, typicalities, within the seemingly infinite variety of white representation" (p.47). So, in order to question and critique whiteness, it is crucial to identify the homogeneity and commonalities of what appears to be the infinite variety of whiteness. For Dyer, representations of whiteness that can be recognized "as white" are not possible without the presence of an "other," namely "black" people. He analyzes three films that associate whiteness with order, rationality, and rigidity and blackness with disorder, irrationality, and looseness: *Jezebel* (1938), *Simba* (1955), and *Night of the Living Dead* (1969). Dyer (1988) sees the films as portraying:

> ...actual dependency of white on black in a context of continued white power and privilege that throws the legitimacy of white domination into question. What is called for is a demonstration of the virtues of whiteness that would justify continued domination, but this is a problem if whiteness is also invisible, everything and nothing. (p.48-9)

Representations of whiteness are conveyed through differentiation from an Other and expressed in these films in which white domination is contested. Are there no meanings to whiteness and being "white" without a visible present difference from an Other? Perhaps it is this necessary visible representation for Dyer that emphasizes the precariousness of the legitimacy of white domination. The contestation of whiteness, by the "characters of color" and the story line, and the representation of "people of color" with authority over "whites" destabilizes the belief that whiteness is everything and nothing. The visible representation of "white" destabilizes whiteness as erased. In these movies, whiteness actually gets represented. These three movies are used to discuss how whiteness can be 'seen' as represented in particular contexts. Dyer argues that the movies and their representations of whiteness and blackness point at the contextual notions of race. Plus, whiteness is not erased in his particular movie contexts; in fact, whiteness is momentarily made visible by its destabilization. The argument that race is contextually constructed in film seems closely tied to ways that race gets experienced in everyday life: contextually. How I understand and act out whiteness (or don't even think about it) is very different in my apartment compared to in a university classroom. Dyer, in his naming of whiteness as everything and nothing in films, lays the groundwork for my theorizing of whiteness, creating a way to conceptualize the erased nature of whiteness. Moreover, Dyer is analyzing representations of whiteness in specific film contexts, emphasizing the contextual nature of "white" identity positionings through each different film reading. As well as the importance of contextual readings, the points I take from Dyer are that the normalcy of whiteness can be recognized, undercut, and therefore unerased, and that meanings of whiteness can be contested representationally.

While Dyer analyzes how whiteness is conceptualized on film, Ruth Frankenberg in her book, *The Social Construction of Whiteness: White Women, Race Matters* (1993), discusses how thirty "white women" she interviewed conceptualize race in their lives. I turn to Frankenberg here because I want to emphasize that although whiteness has been conceptualized as just the normal way of being human by most "whites," these thirty "white women" highlight that whiteness is not always an erased identity positioning in "white" consciousness. The women's responses are organized into four different discursive repertoires, which Frankenberg uses to explain the complex ways "white women" think about race.

> The key discursive repertoires in question here were, first, modes of naming culture and difference associated with west European colonial expansion; second, elements of "essentialist" racism again linked to European colonialism but also critical as rationale for Anglo settler colonialism and segregationism in what is now the USA; third, "assimilationist" or later "color- and power-evasive" strategies for thinking through race first articulated in the early decades of this century; and, fourth, what I have called "racecognizant" repertoires that emerged in U.S. liberation movements and to broader global struggles for decolonization. (p.239)

I understand these repertoires to be: first, constructing difference in the interests of imperialism and colonialism; second, understanding race as a natural and permanent axis of differentiation and of racial inequality; third, a mode of thinking about race organized around an effort not to "see" or, at any rate, not to acknowledge race differences, the "polite" language of race (Frankenberg, 1993, p.142); and last, the importance of recognizing difference, "but with difference understood in historical, political, social or cultural terms rather than essentialist ones" (p.157).

Frankenberg argues that the "white women" she interviewed lived, negotiated, appropriated, and rejected, sometimes more consciously than other times, the entire array of these four repertoires. Because her project is to analyze how "white women" understand whiteness and its construction, the constructions of her four repertoires work to illuminate how "white women" think about themselves as "white women," and whiteness in general. She argues, "We need to displace the colonial construction of whiteness as an "empty" cultural space, in part by refiguring it as constructed and dominant rather than as norm" (Frankenberg, 1993, p.243). Her discourse moves discussions of race away from "white" as vacant (because it is not) towards a more useful understanding of whiteness as constructed, moreover constructed as dominant. Frankenberg's project is similar to mine, in that she wanted to illuminate how women who identify as "white" conceptualize whiteness to make it visible and enable reconceputalization of whiteness. I lay out her repertoires because these four ways that she understands "white women's" conceptualization of whiteness put into words and make visible the erased race, whiteness. She also makes available for critique and contestation formations of whiteness which I hope to put in relation to gender, sexuality, and other identity positionings.

These four theorists each provide pieces to a complex puzzle of conceptualizing whiteness as something learned, not related to biology. They help us possibly to understand whiteness as a strategic identity that is contextual and changing, to represent whiteness in a way that undoes whiteness as the normal, natural way of being human for most "whites," and to outline exactly how whiteness is conceptualized by "white women" to enable contestation of whiteness as the erased race.

As I build on these four theories about whiteness, I want to take seriously my own positionality as "WASP" and the ways that I have learned not to think about whiteness. I am driven by a desire to work across differences and a desire to understand my racial performativity and to unerase the way whiteness is constantly structuring how I perform my identity positionings, especially within the context of my work in academia. An understanding of how whiteness constantly structures how I move in the world might take away some of the erased, invisible powers of *being* "white," interrupting how "white" is the unspoken, taken for granted, right and normal way to be for "whites." Further, I want to add to these theorists' assumptions about whiteness more emotional aspects of whiteness by investigating my identity positionings, and notions of whiteness from the point of view of blackness.

The construction of "my" identity positionings as "white" person might possibly hinge on absence. I am a descendant of pioneers from Indiana and Kansas and have had ancestors, from England and Germany, in this country since before the Revolutionary War. That lack of connection to any traditions of European ethnicity beyond my knowledge of its existence may constitute an absence of what has been understood as "white" ethnicity (European ethnicity, that is). It seems as though everyone in this "melting pot" country should have some ethnic identity positioning from which to form meanings about their lives and traditions. Yet I experience my history as not having that, my ethnic identity positioning as constructed through U.S. notions of European ethnicity is absent. Perhaps my identity positionings are about that absence or longing to understand what identity positionings might mean for me.

Alicia Ortiz (1991), an Argentine author, writes about her identity positionings in her piece "Buenos Aires." She discusses how the particular history of Buenos Aires, Argentina, wreaks havoc with her identity positionings:

> Why do we have such an absurd need for a solid, deep-rooted, robust, and pink-cheeked identity, a peasant identity anchored for centuries to the same land? Why not embrace an empty self? What is so awful about emptiness once you get used to it? (p.126)

Ortiz is speaking about her identity as *Porteño*, a mix of all the immigrants who have come to Argentina. There is something about not being "anchored for centuries to the same land" that feels familiar to me. Unlike recent "white" ethnic European immigrants, I have been "anchored" to this land, the Plains, almost as long as it is possible for "white" people to be, but not anchored to Europe and those historical traditions. There has been so much time lapsed between immigration and the present that all family traces of the "old country" are gone except some erased understanding of being "white." On the one hand this frees me from the rooted connections to Europe and on the other it leaves me with a lack of historical traditions. In a context where there is the appearance that everyone is supposed to have some understood ethnic or European link, some connection to their identity positionings, something beyond WASP or Daughters of the American Revolution, the lack of that connection, the "empty self" feels like a longing to me. But longing is something; it is not blank, nothing, or normal. Further, it is a longing/absence that is embedded in power relations and historical positionings. Is WASP an ethnicity? Could my conception of my "white" identity positioning as an absence of any ethnic link be useful for thinking about race and power dynamics in this country? How does my understanding of identity positionings learned as absence feed notions of whiteness as invisible, erased by the melting pot? Or does it?

Experiencing whiteness as absence is directly in contrast with how bell hooks (1992) describes "Representations of Whiteness in the Black Imagination." She focuses on "black" people's representations of whiteness in their consciousnesses that are not formed in reaction to "white" or "black" stereotypes, but rather emerge as a response to the traumatic pain and anguish of being "black" that remains a consequence of white racist domination, a psychic state that informs and shapes the way "black" people "see" whiteness (p.169). This is in direct contrast to notions of whiteness as normative. She is actually dealing with the material effects of racist domi-

nation and white supremacy on bodies, "black" bodies. "In white supremacist society, white people can 'safely' imagine that they are invisible to
black people since the power they have historically asserted, and even now
collectively assert over black people, accorded them the right to control the
black gaze" (p.168). It is obvious that many "white" people do not see
whiteness in a similar way. If white domination is a traumatic pain for
"black" people, what is its effect on "white" people? Is race identity about
recognizing societal constraints on all people although with very different
consequences? For hooks, "white" people's "absence of recognition [of
their own race] is a strategy that facilitates making a group the Other"
(p.167). So some "whites'" not recognizing whiteness and taking it to be
the norm is about Othering, constructing ourselves/themselves as regular
in contrast to the unknown, the strange, the peripheral.

So what does all of this mean? I am not sure I can answer that question, but these theories each provide a vital piece to my conceptualization
of whiteness. Each part of how I am choosing to pay attention to and to
question whiteness comes out of some permutation of the above theories.
Whiteness is a socially constructed and learned identity positioning. "White"
identity positionings are historically specific and contextual, different in
New York City than in an "all-white" town in Nebraska. Often the power of
whiteness is in the ways that it is understood as everything and nothing for
"whites," normative but invisible. Understanding the ways that whiteness
is actually conceptualized can open a door to critique and hopefully to different conceptualizations of whiteness. Perhaps, when noticed by "whites,"
whiteness might be a longing, not actually empty or nothing. Moreover, as
hooks (1992) reminds us, the ways that whiteness often is not seen by
"whites" does not mean that there is no impact on "people of color" and no
need to reconceptualize whiteness. These theoretical pieces construct and
ground my conceptualizations of whiteness, providing a framework into
which notions of performativity will be transposed. I use these theories
and the space they create to conceptualize whiteness, and race more generally, as performative. I see this as different from these previous constructions of whiteness because theories of performativity emphasize how knowledge, understandings, and enactments of identities are created over time in
contexts which inhibit and enforce conformity to the normalizing way of
being human. This transposition of performativity, and specifically the
notion of drag, disrupts conceptions of race because of how it highlights
the learned and enforced notions of race and calls into question the biological and physical aspects. So I wonder, is there a way to understand white-

ness and the performativity of race that can explain how whiteness structures the performances of my identity positionings and my understandings of my "WASP" self?

Theoretical Outlines of the Construction and Deconstruction of Sex/Gender/Sexuality

I am not interested in trying to understand whiteness as some fixed, constant notion of biology, or as a social construction. I want to understand how whiteness shapes the performativity of my identity positionings, in hopes of unerasing some of the invisible powers of *being* "white," interrupting how "white" is the unspoken, taken for granted, right and normal way to be for "whites." Building on the theorists above, I turn to queer theory and how notions of gender and sex as socially constructed might lead to a way of thinking about race as socially constructed—not to free race from all meaning but to link it to its historical and social constructedness and to understand racial performances. So, after laying out theoretical constructions of performance from queer theory I will transpose this construction of performance into theoretical constructions of race to create a disruption. I believe that this will both show the similarities between constructions of race and sexuality and theories about them and also highlight the differences, both changing the notion of performance through the transposition and disrupting the context transposed to—constructions of race. Part of this work is to construct and to emphasize the relationality between identity positionings and between theoretical constructions of critical race theory and queer theory.

In order to illuminate the connections between constructions of sexuality and constructions of race, I will outline theoretical constructions of sexuality. Current queer theory is working to construct fluid notions of sexuality because fixed notions of sexuality structure and constrict all lives. This unfixing is based on the unlinking of sex and biology. It goes something like this: sex is constructed and not really based on some "truth" like biology. Therefore, gender, as it has been conceptualized as socially constructed sex, is socially constructed but with no original sex to point to. Sex and gender are just empty signifiers pointing at nothing essential. Because biology is socially constructed and not "true," then biological sex is not "real" but socially constructed. Therefore, gender as the social construction of sex is not based on "real" identity positionings either. There is nothing "real" about biology, sex, or gender. For Judith Butler (1990) in *Gender Trouble*:

> The category of sex and the naturalized institution of heterosexuality are con-
> structs, socially instituted and socially regulated fantasies or "fetishes," not natu-
> ral categories, but political ones (categories that prove that recourse to the "natu-
> ral" in such contexts is always political). (p.126)

Gender and sexuality are not biological "truths" but are constructed political categories. The meanings that get made about gender are under-stood as true because biological sex differences seem irrefutable, not to mention visible. However, biological understandings are not "natural" truths about the universe. They are constructions which explain and enforce cur-rent institutions. Biology has been a way to naturalize and institutionalize the body into two binaries, male/female, man/woman. Butler goes on to discuss the constraints of this context. "The body which is torn apart, the wars waged among women, are *textual* violences, the deconstruction of constructs that are always already a kind of violence against the body's possibilities" (p.126). The body's possibilities are cramped; the ways that people can understand themselves are constricted.

These dualisms—male/female, man/woman—and their naturalization work to constrain peoples' bodies and minds. How we even think about ourselves is contained. Bodies are constrained with respect to gender, sexu-ality, race and so on. Butler discusses constraints with respect to sexuality. In her book, *Bodies that Matter* (1993), she argues,

> . . . constructivism needs to take account of the domain of constraints without
> which a certain living and desiring being cannot make its way. And every such
> being is constrained by not only what is difficult to imagine, but what remains
> radically unthinkable... (p.94)

Not only are bodies constrained by current 'truths,' but so are minds. I would like to say that the radically unthinkable with respect to race for a "WASP" like me might be whiteness. For many "whites" it is unthinkable to actually conceptualize whiteness; most "whites" don't think about be-ing "white" at all. The unthinkable is constraining.

Nevertheless, contestations are always happening. Even within the constraints of biology and the social construction of identity positionings, radically unthinkable things can still happen. Much of this understanding of contestations comes out of Butler's notion that all identities are performative and contextual and that the division of sex and gender is con-tested even at the level of the body (for example, transgender identities).

But bodies are constantly performing sex/gender and sex acts/sexuality. According to Butler, our bodies are always already constrained and the meanings that get made about us, our bodies, are constantly contested. Yet, within those constraints people exist, live, and perform their many constructed and contested identity positionings. Because of the "violence against the body's possibilities," the constraints on our daily lives, performativity of identity positionings is not solely about choice. There are actual material constraints on life. Yet, within those constraints there is still room for personal actions, for agency. Butler explains that agency is not about opposing the constraints, like heterosexisms, but is more a practice of reenactment within the constraints. For example, one performs identity positionings while both being constrained by and contesting heterosexisms. There is still some room to move, to enact myself, to perform identity positionings in context. This results in a paradox, as Butler (1993) discusses:

> The agency denoted by the performativity of "sex" will be directly counter to any notion of a voluntarist subject who exists quite apart from the regulatory norms which she/he opposes. The paradox of subjectivation is precisely that the subject who would resist such norms is itself enabled, if not produced, by such norms. Although this constitutive constraint does not foreclose the possibility of agency, it does locate agency as a reiterative or rearticulatory practice, immanent to power, and not a relation of external opposition to power. (p. 15)

For Butler, agency is not about trying to work outside of racism or sexism. The paradox is that within those oppressions, one is enabled and resists them. So agency comes from being within social categories and using them for the performativity of identity positionings.

This understanding of performativity is also articulated by Peggy Phelan in her book *Unmarked: The Politics of Performance* (1993). For Phelan, performance is a place where the body can destabilize the understandings of a unified subject. She discusses the destabilization with respect to gender: how performance can undercut the unified gendered body by enacting it in ways that undercut and interrupt understandings of male and female, men and women (p.151). This destabilization is within the constraints of oppressions and resists those constraints. This is an example of form and content: the structuring forms of gender can be performed in such a way as to destabilize the content, the unified gendered body.

To clarify further, I am, for instance, constrained by notions of heterosexuality. However it is within those constraints on my person and, in part, because of how notions of heterosexuality require notions and possibilities of homosexuality, that I am also enabled (and have the language of articulation) to articulate myself as "dyke" in a particular contextual situation. What "dyke," and my performance of "dykeness," might mean at Apple Island (a local woman-only space) or in a classroom are very different. The constraints of heterosexuality and context become the material and resources by which I perform dykeness.

Forms of performance that undercut original notions of sex/gender/ sexuality can work in a parodic way. Drag is an example of this. Butler (1990) explains that drag "effectively mocks both the expressive model of gender and of a true gender identity... The performance of drag plays upon the distinction between the anatomy of the performer and the gender that is being performed" (p. 137). Drag is a performance that dislodges notions of gender as "real" and "natural." For example, I can drag femininity, which might reify and at the same time undercut gender roles while also working to undo understandings of myself as a particular sort of "lesbian." However, all of my understandings are made from the fictions of gender, race, class and sexuality. Is there a way to drag race? Is there a way to drag whiteness specifically? Would it dislodge notions of race as "real" and "natural"?

Theorizing the Constructions and Deconstructions of Race

Using these constructions of performance and the paradox of oppressions both constraining and informing the performativity of identity positionings, I will look again at social constructions of race. I think gender, race, class, and sexuality are constantly working together to constrain and enable performativity of identity positionings. My struggle here is the desire to clearly trace ways that whiteness gets erased and reified, but not to do so at the expense of understandings of gender, sexuality, and class. However, I would like to focus on whiteness and ways that constructions of race are disrupted by the transposition of notions of performance. Butler does not ignore how race might intersect with her constructions of the constraints of identity positionings. She explains:

> Given that normative heterosexuality is clearly not the only regulatory regime operative in the production of bodily contours or setting the limits to bodily intelligibility, it makes sense to ask what other regimes of regulatory production contour the materiality of bodies. Here it seems that the social regulation of race emerges not simply as another, fully separable, domain of power from sexual

difference or sexuality, but that its "addition" subverts the monolithic working of
the heterosexual imperative... (Butler, 1990, pp. 17-18)

She wants to complicate the workings of heterosexuality with race, not
as some separate constraint but as a part of the imperatives under, among
and around which we live. Like Butler, I am trying to explicate the complex workings of these constraints together and in relation.

These constraints of race are always related and integral to those of
sexuality and gender, for example. However, perhaps for "whites" one of
the constraints of whiteness is its invisibility and normalcy. Because many
"whites" are so constrained by the racist society in which we/they live, we/
they are unable even to think about constructions of whiteness; it becomes
the radically unthinkable. However, to think about whiteness and to try to
and conceptualize what it might mean to *be* "white" resists the constraint
and works against conceptions of "white" as everything and nothing, and
as the normal, natural way of being human.

While constraints of gender, race, and sexuality are intertwined, histories of gender/sex understandings are very different from histories of race
intelligibility. The labor that it has taken to make raced bodies in history
and the present is very different from that taken to make gendered bodies.
Further, is the theoretical separation that has taken place in this paper between race and gender, privileging one identity positioning before another—
prioritizing sex over race or race over gender? What are the effects of this
theoretical separation since actual bodies cannot be split between race and
gender? Any theory that explicates constraints chooses what will count as
constraints. It is a constant struggle for me—as a "white, middle-class,
able-bodied, thin, Christian-raised, academic, lesbian, Midwestern theorist"—to work against continually assigning priority or importance to certain identity positionings and constraints over others.

History might be the turn that is necessary to a theory that tries to
destabilize race, and explain what makes destabilizing race different from
destabilizing gender and sex. The history of the category of race, and the
social and cultural labor that it took to produce that category makes understanding the construction of race different from that of sex/gender/sexual-
ity. For example, take the analysis of whiteness from David Roediger's
recent book *The Wages of Whiteness: Race and the Making of the American Working Class* (1991). In his discussion of the historical construction
of "white working class" identity positionings, he examines the pleasures
of the constructions of whiteness. He outlines W.E.B. DuBois's arguments
about race and class constructions of the working class in the U.S. around

the turn of the century. DuBois was very clear about the various racial constructions. Roediger (1991) constructs DuBois's argument as follows:

> As important as the specifics are here, still more important is the idea that the pleasures of whiteness could function as a 'wage' for white workers. That is, status and privileges conferred by race could be used to make up for alienating and exploitative class relationships... White workers could, and did, define and accept their class positions by fashioning identities as 'not slaves' and as 'not Blacks'. (p.13)

Therefore, whiteness became some sort of status that was normalized and, in this case, blackness became the "Other." Because of the way that whiteness came to serve as a wage for "white" workers and the history of who counts for "white" in this country, the history of whiteness is different from the history of the biological sex/gender binary and its relation to heterosexuality. Historically, "the status and privileges conferred by race" have been different from those conferred by sex/gender/sexuality, although related. The difference lies in the ways that gender and sexuality are intimately linked. Historically there have been conceptions of gender identity positionings that explain how men have certain traits and women have "opposite" traits. Moreover, sexuality then emerged out of and in relation to those gender relations. For example Rubin (1984), in her article "Thinking Sex: Notes for a Radical Theory of the Politics of Sexuality," discusses just this historical connection, "The development of this [current] sexual system has taken place in the context of gender relations. Part of the modern ideology of sex is that lust is the province of men, purity that of women" (p. 307). Thus, the organization of conceptions of sexuality is based historically on gender relations. Furthermore, Sedgwick (1990) explains that definitionally gender is part of the determination of sexuality in a way that neither gender nor sexuality is definitionally intertwined with race (p. 31). However, she instantly complicates this separation by stating, "to assume the distinctiveness of the *intimacy* between sexuality and gender might well risk assuming too much about the definitional *separability* of either of them from determinations of, say, class or race" (p. 31). In other words, because race, class, gender, sexuality, and other identity positionings are so intertwined to believe that two of them, namely gender and sexuality are more closely linked than the others may well be problematic because of the ways these identity positionings all mutually constitute each other.

Moreover, the intimate links between race, gender, and sexuality take place at the level of the body and in a social context of oppressions and privileges. Butler (1993) notes:

92

> Rather than accept a model which understands racism as discrimination on the basis of a pregiven race, I follow those recent theories which have made the argument that the "race" is partially produced as an effect of the history of racism, that its boundaries and meanings are constructed over time not only in the service of racism, but also in the service of the contestation of racism. (p. 18)

This is indicative of the paradox of agency discussed above. Our understandings of race and our racial performances have been constructed by and experienced in our daily lives, within the constraints of racism. Since the constraints of racism are not traumatic in the same ways for most "whites"—"WASPs" like myself for example—as for "people of color," is it possible that many "white" people experience whiteness as normal, nothing? Can a "WASP" understanding of the constraints of whiteness in her life destabilize this assumed nothingness and invisibility of whiteness? Further, because whiteness is not consciously experienced—is experienced as nothing for many "WASPs"—the way the constraints of whiteness work for most "WASPs" is that we/they understand our/themselves to be the normal and natural way of being human. The common-sense conception is "race is about people of color." So, the radically unthinkable for many "whites" might be to somehow conceptualize whiteness and its constraints as a race. Performing our/their whiteness—me performing my WASPness—has always been about the specificity of being human, not about constructions of whiteness. Thus, the theoretical turn that positions whiteness and understandings of race as constraints within which we make meanings about ourselves may enable some "whites" to recognize the erasedness of whiteness (that we/they may not have before) and the pleasures and privileges behind the work of that erasure.

Hence, the transposition of how queer theory destabilizes sex/gender takes on notions of race might go something like this: skin color is constructed and not really based on some "truth" like biology. That is to say, what is seen and understood as skin color—more melanin in the skin for example—and the meanings made from those understandings are all constructed. Therefore, race, as it has been conceptualized as the social constructedness of skin color, is socially constructed but with no original "real" biological truth behind it. Skin color and race are just empty signifiers pointing at nothing essential. All identity positionings are performative and contextual, and the division of skin color and race is contested even at the level of the body (for example passing as a race one knows one is not). Bodies are constantly performing raced selves and raced acts, but those performances are often within the constraints of the understandings of whiteness as blank, normative, and the radically unthinkable for "whites." Within these understandings, these constraints, people are living their lives and refiguring themselves contextually. Paradoxically, performance lies both within the service and the contestation of racism.

Disruptions created by the transposition of these notions of performativity into constructions of race are twofold. First, the thought that skin color is not a "real" genetic fact disrupts how race is often taken to be a "natural" category, as opposed to sexuality, which is understood as a "choice." Also disrupting race as natural is to conceptualize what "race" means in the context of racist society—that it is both through the constraint of racism and in contestation of it that meanings are made about racial identity positionings. Also the transposition links constructions of sexuality more strongly to constructions of race, emphasizing their relationality. Performativity also emphasizes this relationality because no one is constructed of just one identity positioning: I could never just "be white" and I am never "white" outside of a society that is constantly constructing meanings about whiteness. The performativity of my whiteness is within the constraints of racism and also contesting those constraints.

What might this performance of identity positionings actually look like? I believe that Patricia Williams, in her book *The Alchemy of Race and Rights* (1991), might perform an example of multiple understandings of her identity positionings and what it means to "be her." Each moment that she comes in contact with constraining social categories, the categories change and shift and so does Williams. That is not to imply, however, that race has no bodily effects and is dispensable. Williams notes, "While being black has been the most powerful social attribution in my life, it is only one of a number of governing narratives or presiding fictions by which I am constantly reconfiguring myself in the world" (p.256). Thus, for Williams, her race forms a constraint upon her life but it is also the asset she uses to confront and work against the constraints of racism. This is the paradox in which identity positionings are made and unmade in contexts (Butler, 1990, p.247, note15). Thus, the constraints of whiteness (or gender, or heterosexuality) also provide me with the means and understandings to reshape myself.

How might media representations of contesting taken-for-granted understandings of race look? Perhaps Anna Deavere Smith's one-woman presentation of the 1991 riots in Brooklyn, *Fires in the Mirror*, might be an example. She, in her "raced" and "gendered" body, embodies nineteen different portraits of people from the "Jewish" and "black" communities based verbatim on interviews she conducted. The riots started after a "black" child was run over by a "Jewish" man, and in response a "Jewish" student was stabbed by a few "black" youths. Smith appears to portray the people as "true" to her understandings of them. I don't believe Smith is parodying these people, but rather her performance undercuts the rigid meanings of race. She in her "black female" body "is" the person she has interviewed in the context of the interview, if only for a moment. She takes on their mannerisms, their intonations, and their looks as much as she can. She is her "black woman's" body as "white" official, as "Jewish woman," as "black youth." It is her "as" someone that points to the construction of identity positionings and undercuts the "realness" of race and gender. At the same time it enacts the realness of the actual, painful events of the riots and the aftermath. She drags race and gender in her performance.

Thus one can not only drag sex and gender, but also drag race as well. Moreover, through thinking about dragging race, the concept of drag becomes racialized, so drag cannot be totally free from conceptions of race as it might have been in the past. Thus, race, like sex/gender/sexuality, can be conceptualized as performative, as learned over time and through contexts of experience. The performativity of whiteness might be the ways that it becomes understood as the normal, natural way of being human for "whites." Also, just thinking about, talking about, and performing whiteness are ways to undercut its invisibility and normalcy. Are there actual performances of whiteness that undercut it as the "point from which we tend to identify difference" (Carby, 1992, p. 193)

Northern Exposure and Constructions of Whiteness

The actors on the television show *Northern Exposure* are often able to perform within the constraints of race in such a way that can be understood as dragging race. *Northern Exposure* started in the summer of 1990. It was conceptualized as series about a "white Jewish" doctor from New York City paying back his loans by living and working in a small Alaska town. Cicely, is a small town populated by "whites" and "Native people." Within the context of historical racial tension, Alaska did not move "Native people" to reservations. Thus the doctor is the outsider, the Other, as are most viewers from mainland United States. Looking at an episode of the show illustrates the performativity of whiteness. I want to specifically look at the episode about "white healing myths" as an example of what performances of whiteness and its constraints might look like. Also the performances of whiteness in this episode work to unerase, or expose, it, as opposed to performing it as the natural way of being human.

The white healing-myth episode of *Northern Exposure*, aired fall 1993, works to undercut notions of whiteness in parodic and unfixing ways. Leonard, a local "Native" healer, is researching "white culture" because some of his clients are assimilating and crossing over to "the white community." He wants to understand "white culture" better so he can meet the needs of his partly assimilated clients. He starts by collecting "white" healing stories, telling Hollings, the "white" local tavern owner, "Traditionally healers, such as myself, have found that storytelling has great curative powers. People are fortified by parables, legends, you might call them. In our culture the theme is some act of faith, or perseverance." He then discusses Paul Bunyan with Hollings. He asks him, "How does this character's story impact on your daily life? Are you aware of his influence?" Hollings responds that he hasn't thought of him in years. This response is similar to those that Leonard gets from all the "white" people that recount their understanding of "white" popular cultural myths and their understandings of "white culture" to him.

Leonard's quest can be understood as unerasing whiteness and highlighting its performance. He is asking specifically for what Butler calls the "unthinkable" from the "white people." Moreover, because he is "Native American," he has the ability to ask about "white culture"; for him, whiteness is thinkable. Because of the history of oppression of "native" peoples by "whites," Leonard is in a position to be able to *see* "white culture" just as bell hooks argues that "black people" can.

Just as in the interchange between Leonard and Hollings, each "white" person has a confused response about what meanings might be important from their stories. This can be interpreted as pointing out the constructedness of whiteness and the conflicts that arise when "whites" are called to perform the unthinkable, to think about whiteness and meanings about whiteness. The "white" people willingly recount numerous stories, like the one about the girl with the beehive who finds maggots in it, or was it black widow spiders? The "whites" perform what appears to be pleasure in telling these stories, and they are clearly confused in response to Leonard's questions about the stories' meanings. The repetitious performance of "white" confusion implies parody; the parody and humor comes from the excess, of confusion. The excess also questions some search for deeper meaning in the stories. Because there is this excessive, rather comic confusion, can there really be deeper meanings about "white culture"? More-over, is there such a thing as "white culture"? Can "white culture" exist without deeper meanings? Does the excess and confusion point to the absence of deep meaning about "white culture" and represent the erasure of whiteness?

The excess and the confusion around whiteness point to how deeply erased whiteness is for the "white" people. Leonard finally gets so frustrated that he gives up his project and begins talking about his problems with Chris, the "white" philosopher/radio DJ in town.

L: I have failed, Chris...I can't locate the white collective unconscious.

C: I wouldn't feel too bad about that, you know, Western culture hasn't really carried the baton on folklore and mythology. The rise of Christianity put the kibosh on that, and then gospel hits the #1 best seller list and everything else gets remaindered.

L: The stories are interesting in some anthropological context, I guess, but mostly they seem to apply to high school students. There's often some mishap involving a rodent or something from the arachnid family and the victim of this misadventure invariably reacts negatively, goes ballistic, freaks out, has a hairy fit, culminating in either insanity or litigation.

C: Yeah, not much you can use there.

L: I simply can't find any healing properties in these fables. White people don't seem concerned at all with using mythology to heal themselves. In fact, they seem intent on making each other feel worse. So, I am abandoning the project.

C: Hey, Leonard, I don't think you gotta do that. There's gotta be something to be learned from this maybe, maybe its just indicative of how threatened we feel in the wake of the industrial revolution.

L: How's that?

C: Well you know it's not just the clock maker and the clock anymore. Everything is rolled off the assembly line, you know. We feel rattled by the anonymity of our possessions. Hey, where'd that come from? Who's this guy? Who can I trust? I mean mass production gave rise to capitalism, but undermined the individual, which in turn killed god. We as a society have filled that vacuum with fear and paranoia.

L: How does the rise of capitalism explain the one about the young woman in the Volkswagen?

C: Oh yeah, right. The drive-in movie, Spanish fly, gear shift deal. I don't know, brother, you're on your own there.

Leonard and Chris discuss the possible meanings or lack thereof in these myths, but then undercut their own understandings. They seem to wrestle with the constraints of whiteness and historical meanings shaping it, like capitalism. Their struggling seems to imply the difficulty of connecting culture and whiteness. The excessive exposure of the difficulties and confusion calls attention to it. Likewise, Chris cannot really focus on whiteness and shifts the discussion to capitalism, class, and religion as identity positioning markers, for "whites," in the place of race. Yet, the meanings about whiteness that get discussed in their conversation are not fixed or closed down. In fact, Chris and Leonard's conversation and the meanings about whiteness that they make call attention to the lack of talk about whiteness instead of erasing it. Further, their conversation undercuts the notion of the universal, biological, spiritual truth, because it doesn't explain the one about the young woman in the Volkswagen (all the information we as viewers are given about the story is the vague reference Chris makes). Also humor works to destabilize the seriousness of their struggle. It appears as if they are both struggling to understand meanings about whiteness, but it is not so serious that there is no humor or pleasure.

Telling and making stories are performances that are raced. In the context of this show it seems as though the "whites'" performances of the stories from "white" popular culture represent whiteness. Since these stories are performances, it is not surprising that Leonard's search for stories ends at a site of performance, a movie theater. He is watching an Orson Welles movie with Ed, a young "Native" healer in training and filmmaker wannabe. Leonard refers to movies possibly being the answer he was searching for, the "white" medicine, because Ed says he feels better watching them. "They say it's magic," Leonard says. Interpreting movies as "white" healing stories points to the escapist pleasure of movies. Ed experiences movies as magic in their perfection. Orson Welles made *Citizen Kane* "perfectly" says Ed, "without even trying." Because they appear perfect, movies erase the work of their own construction. That natural appearance of the perfect movie world can let one escape one's life and feel better, as Ed does. Movies, therefore, might be the perfect healing for people whose race is the radically unthinkable. The natural erasure of the film's construction reinforces the natural erasure of the construction of whiteness as a race.

Yet, "white" healing myths as movies and the idea of naturalness of movies and race get undercut when Leonard asks Ed about Rosebud and by the discussion of the search for Rosebud in *Citizen Kane*. The movie is driven by the search to find the meaning of "Rosebud," Kane's final word on his deathbed. No one in the movie ever knows who Rosebud is, but the final scene shows a burning sled with Rosebud written on it. For the viewer this points at the possible futility and emptiness of the search for the mean- ing of Rosebud. Even though Rosebud is just a sled, the search for the meaning of Rosebud drives the entire plot. Leonard asks Ed if anyone in the movie ever figures out the meaning of Rosebud. By trying to under- stand whiteness through one artifact—myths—Leonard is engaged in an equally futile search. However, his search calls attention to the complexity and power of whiteness. The search for the truth of "white" healing stories might be undercut by acknowledging the futility of the search for Rosebud, an empty sign. Thus the healing stories might also be empty, unfixed, with no true meaning. Even though the search for "real" meaning in the stories is shown to be meaningless it might not undercut the performances of white- ness. The performances of whiteness and the confusion around whiteness still call attention to and unerase "white."

I think this episode points at ways in which "whites" are constrained, yet it also parodies whiteness and its constraints. Leonard's search under- cuts the notion that "white culture" is blank. The other actors perform their whiteness in parodic ways, telling their supposed cultural myths. The cul- tural myths are humorous and that humor works to undercut notions of "real" cultural truths. Even Chris in his theories about capitalism can be read as portraying and undercutting whiteness, especially since often white- ness is read through other identity positionings, particularly class, for ex- ample "white trash." Their parody, their humorous performances of white- ness, their drag of whiteness highlight how there may be no *real* "white" identity positionings, just these constant parodic imitations. The final end to the search—"white" healing stories as movies—points at how represen- tations may shape thinking, yet they have no original, and thusthere is no *real* "white culture" and the search might be futile. In this way, the imita- tive nature of whiteness itself is highlighted.

What Might All This Mean?

I will try and pull together some of the threads of this paper, not to tie them up into a nice bow, but to make sure nothing is stranded. Whiteness has been theorized by some "whites" trying to contextualize and historicize it. These theorists—Frye, Ware, Dyer, and Frankenberg—have laid the groundwork upon which I have understood my whiteness and theorized about the performativity of whiteness. From Frye, I take the possibility of thinking about "whiteliness," a construction of identity positioning that a "white" person can work against, an oppressive way of being than can be unlearned. Ware has helped me to understand the history of feminist constructions of whiteness and the importance of historicizing whiteness. I am conscious of representations of whiteness and ways that they can be made more visible from Dyer's discussion of three films. Frankenberg's understandings of how thirty "white women" think about whiteness has grounded my thinking about my whiteness and how I, as "white," can begin to theorize about it. These "white" theorists have each lent their different impressions of whiteness to my own. Also, in my classroom practices, I try to keep in mind hooks's discussion of the harm of whiteness upon "blacks" and the invisibility of that harm to most "whites," so that I don't unconsciously continue that harm through my pedagogy.

These ways of thinking about being "white" are the context in which I have discussed the performativity of whiteness. I have explored here how thinking about whiteness as both a performance that constrains how I think about myself and as an understanding of myself that allows me to change and shift understandings of my identity positionings. Although whiteness might be radically unthinkable for some "white" people, it still constrains our/their lives. There are performances of race that can unerase whiteness, making it thinkable and hence transformable. The ways that Anna Deavere Smith performs both her identity positionings and those of the people she interviewed simultaneously point at the constructedness and performativity of race and gender. Chris and Leonard's discussion of "white" popular cultural myths points at whiteness in ways that unerases it and undercuts understandings of universal normative truths. I have tried to theorize some aspects of being "white" to call attention to whiteness and its constructions. Attention to whiteness makes it no longer radically unthinkable, unerasing its invisible constraining power, possibly allowing for some ability to change the constraints of whiteness. Moreover, conceptualizing race as performative highlights drag as a tool to interrupt whiteness as the normal and natural way of being human for "whites." This use of drag transforms conceptions of drag as well as conceptions of whiteness and, in turn, emphasizes the performativity of whiteness and the racial component of drag. As whiteness becomes visible and its normalcy is undercut through reiterative performances, perhaps whiteness can become more thinkable for "whites," and less the point from which difference is judged. Maybe "whites" dragging whiteness can create small cracks in the seamless normalcy of whiteness, making it impossible to continue to conceptualize whiteness in the same old way, which in turn makes it impossible to construct difference in the same old way.

Through discussions of the constructions of sex/gender/sexuality and their similarities and differences to constructions of race, I have highlighted the relationality of these identity positionings. Moreover, since I transposed notions of performance from queer theory on to notions of race disrupting and transforming conceptions of race as natural, which I take as a project from the field of critical race theory, I have constructed a relationship between queer theory and critical race theory.

This is just a start, a trial at talking about whiteness in hopes of creating a space in which to take seriously the erased nature of whiteness for most "whites." We can begin to move toward unerasing whiteness and contextualizing its positionality, toward keeping whiteness situated. Yet, is discussing race as performative and as a constraining aspect of everyone's life a way to disassociate from the actual pain that gets inflicted on real people's lives in this country? As a "white woman," am I again centering on myself and my own struggle with identity positionings? By concentrating on writers constructed by and writing about whiteness, am I missing some complexities that writings by "people of color" could add? Further, is this another way for me as a "white" to try and escape the guilt of white privilege by deconstructing and recontextualizing notions of race? Moreover, is there a way to talk about understandings of identity positionings that doesn't fragment gender, race, and sexuality, let alone class, ability and other identity positionings?

References

Anzaldua, G. (1987). *Borderlands: La frontera, the new mestiza.* San Francisco: Spinsters Aunt Lute.

Bad Object-Choices. (Eds.). (1991). *How do I look? Queer film and video.* Seattle, WA: Bay Press.

Butler, J. (1990). *Gender trouble: Feminism and the subversion of identity.* New York: Routledge.

Butler, J. (1993). *Bodies that matter: On the discursive limits of "sex".* New York: Routledge.

Carby, H. (1992). The multicultural wars. In G. Dent (Ed.) *Black popular culture.* (pp.187-199).

Crimp, D. (Ed.). (1987). *AIDS: Cultural analysis, cultural activism.* Cambridge, MA: The MIT Press.

Dyer, R. (1988). White. *Screen, 29* (4), pp.44-64.

Frankenberg, R. (1983). *The social construction of whiteness: White women, race matters.* Minneapolis: University of Minnesota Press, 1993.

Frye, M. (1983). On being white: Thinking toward a feminist understanding of race and race supremacy. In M. Fryer (Ed.) *The Politics of Reality: Essays in Feminist Theory.* Trumansburg, NY: The Crossing Press.

Fryer, M. (1992). White woman feminist:1983-1992. In M., Fryer (Ed.) *Willful virgin: Essays in feminism.* Freedom, CA: The Crossing Press.

hooks, b. (1992). Representations of whiteness in the black imagination. In b. hooks *Black Looks: Race and Representation.* Boston: South End Press.

Northern Exposure. (1993). White healing myth episode.

Ortiz, A. (1991). "Buenos Aires. In P. Mariani (Ed.). *Critical fictions: The politics of imaginative writing.* Seattle: Bay Press. 115-130.

Phelan, P. (1993). *Unmarked: The politics of performance.* New York & London: Routledge.

Roediger, D. (1991). *The wages of whiteness: Race and the making of the american working class.* London: Verso.

Rubin, G. (1984). Thinking sex: Notes for a radical theory of politics of sexuality. In C.Vance (Ed.) *Pleasure and danger: Exploring female sexuality.* Boston: Routledge &Kegan Paul (pp. 267-319).

Sedgewick, E. (1990). *Epistemology of the closet.* Berkeley:University of California Press.

Smith, A. D. (1991). *Fires in the mirror.* PBS production.

Ware, V. (1992). *Beyond the pale: Women, racism and history.* London: Verso.

Williams, P. (1991). *The alchemy of race and rights.* Cambridge: Harvard University Press.

CHAPTER SIX

The Blues: Breaking The Psychological
Chains of Controlling Images
Robin Good

. . . to evert the critical gaze from the racial object to the racial subject; from the described to the describers and imaginers; from the serving to the served.
—Toni Morrison

Racism in America is certainly a highly charged topic in the contemporary United States, considering the L.A. uprising following the Rodney King trial and the distinctly polar emotional responses of whites and blacks elicited by the acquittal of O.J. Simpson. Also, there has arisen in recent times a distinct anger openly expressed by white people towards people of color. This anger is an expression of how some white people see themselves in our society today— as vulnerable and as victims.

The U.S. has undergone three recessions within the past fifteen years; simultaneously, the nation's industrial base has witnessed massive restructuring and downsizing due to a shift away from heavy manufacturing industries towards service industries. This has led to massive lay offs and falling wages and benefits for those who remain unscathed by the layoffs. The working class has been the hardest hit by these events, leaving it with an acute sense of vulnerability to fates seemingly beyond its control. A falling standard of living and the resultant sense of loss and deprivation has led to white working class resentment directed at minority groups who are perceived to be getting preferential treatment via affirmative action. These minority groups, many whites believe, are getting "white jobs" at the expense of white, working class people (Rubin 1994).

This anger has been expressed in three specific ways. First, there has been an increase in support for conservative politicians who advocate repealing many of the victories of the civil rights movement— restricting or abolishing affirmative action, for example. Second, there has been an increase in the formation and support of white supremacy groups. Pennsylvania, for example, has seen a dramatic increase in the number of these hate groups. In 1994, there were 18 such groups. In 1995, these were 39. This makes Pennsylvania second in the nation (behind Florida) in terms of the number of hate groups within a state (Cheng 1995; Kim 1995). An interesting aspect of the growth of white supremacy groups in Pennsylvania involves their formation in areas of Pennsylvania that are almost exclusively white. The anger directed toward minority groups is being expressed even though there is little or no *direct* competition between whites and nonwhites for jobs in these white areas. As Lillian Rubin points out in her book, *Families on the Fault Line,* "as the economic vise tighten[s], despair turn[s] to anger...[and] this anger isn't directed so much at those above as at those below. And when whites at or near the bottom of the ladder look down in this nation, they generally see blacks and other minorities" (Rubin, 1994, pp. 240-241). Third, this anger has been expressed through an increase in racial incidents. Again, taking Pennsylvania as an example, in 1988, 181 racial incidents were documented. In 1992, 417 of these incidents were documented over twice the number of occurrences within a four-year time span (Cheng 1995, p.1A).

Racial tension, racial unrest, and racial inequality have been a part of American culture, politics, and law since the beginning of Anglo colonization of North America. The interracial dynamics of white privilege and nonwhite oppression still exists. The legacy of antimiscegenation laws, even though outlawed since 1967, continue to shape people's current notions of "proper" relationships and marriages. Likewise, belief systems (still largely shaped by pre-1900 notions of race differences) influence present concepts of racial identity, masculinity and femininity, sexuality, who is permitted to marry into a family, who is allowed to live in one's neighborhood, who is authorized to attain positions of power, privilege, and prestige (Frankenberg, 1993).

If America is to address racism, to begin to move away from unequal and unjust relationships and towards relationships which are more humane, dignified, respectful, egalitarian, and life-affirming, then it is best to begin by looking closely at these relationships-close enough so as to reveal current structures of power which serve to privilege some and exclude and oppress others. At this vantage point, whiteness can be viewed as a normative state of existence in America-a yardstick by which to measure and evaluate *everyone*. Whiteness carries with it privileges, advantages, acceptance, and power; other colors do not. Often in subtle and unconscious ways, these privileges are played out. To make this differential in power and privilege clearly visible and conscious is the first step in the critique and transformation of relational inequalities (Collins 1991; Frankenberg 1993; Giroux 1994)

Making Whiteness Visible in the Classroom

The classroom can serve as a site in which to uncover and make visible these positions of privilege and oppression. Furthermore, the classroom can serve not only to critique these positions but to offer a project of possibility— an imagining and carrying out of new ways of relating which are life-enhancing to people of all colors, sexes, ethnicities, classes, and sexual orientations (Giroux 1994). This chapter describes a curriculum and pedagogy whose purpose is to make explicit whiteness as an ethnic category, a particular vantage point in American society. This curriculum and pedagogy looks specifically at white perceptions of black women and how these perceptions have been historically shaped and codified into "controlling images" that objectify the black woman, dehumanizing her and limiting her possibilities for self-definition. Four images will be explored: the mammy, the matriarch, the welfare mother, and the Jezebel. These images have served to keep black women in their place— that is, they have been created and used by white society to justify the continued oppression of black women.

The Cartesian dualism that underpins Western ways of seeing helps us to understand these white perspectives. This either/or way of viewing the world is responsible for the "white gaze"— the objectification and subjugation of the Other, the Other in this case being black women. At this point, the chapter examines the notion of black women's resistance to these controlling images. The forum for resistance is black women's blues. The song lyrics of such blues singers as Bessie Smith, Ma Rainey, Billie Holiday, Nina Simone, and Aretha Franklin can often be seen not only as an expression of a black woman's experiences with oppression and injustice, but as a literal and figurative means of "finding a voice": that is, a means by which to articulate an identity which is *self*-determined rather than externally determined.

Central to creating this self-determined identity is the need for new types of social relationships— ones grounded in a both/and perspective. Rather than viewing the world in a dualistic, exclusionary, and hierarchical manner which orients relationships in terms of domination and subjugation, this perspective sees the world as a continuum. In this context, social relationships become interconnected and inclusionary leading to equal, complementary, and overlapping subjectivities. Rather than a win/lose orientation, it is a win/win orientation predicated on respect, dignity, and the inherent worth of all living things. It is a striving for self-Other liberation. Thus, current notions of gender and race, and especially the notions of superior male/inferior female and superior whiteness/inferior blackness, are criticized and transformed.

Also central in creating new types of social relationships is the need to look at racism not simply as a black problem but also as a white problem. Thus, we begin to become conscious of how white people are complicitous in perpetuating racism individually and collectively. Ruth Frankenberg in *The Social Construction of Whiteness: White Women, Race Matters*, speaks of the need for race-cognizance- the awareness that race makes a difference in both nonwhite AND white peoples' lives and that racism is a significant factor in shaping contemporary U.S. society (Frankenberg, 1993).

The goals of this curriculum are as follows:

-to understand how the dualistic way of looking at the world fosters unequal relationships.

-to understand how history has shaped current racist discourse.

-to "make visible" white privilege and how its correlate, whiteness as the norm, have served to create denigrating images of black women that are used as justification for continued black oppression by white people.

-to look at racism as a white and a nonwhite problem.

-to examine-via black women's blues music- black women's resistance to these controlling images and how these songs offer a *self-determined* identity which serves to humanize and dignify black women.

-to use the information on controlling images and the resistance to these images through blues music as the basis for a class discussion that uncovers students' positionalities-that is, now the student's race, gender, class, and ethnicity serves to privilege or oppress him or her.

-to use the class discussion to critique unequal relationships.

-to examine a new type of social relationship- one grounded in a both/and perspective- which offers the possibility for inclusivity, for a balancing of power and privilege, and for fostering a more humane society.

History as Shaper of Present Reality

In order to understand racism and other unequal social relationships, it is important to understand how history has shaped our current worldview and discourse, which then serves to foster and perpetuate unequal relationships. Four hundred years ago, Rene Descartes articulated a way of looking at and understanding the world which continues to the present day- the dualistic, either/or conceptual framework. It has become the key component of Western thinking.

This type of thinking shapes people's perceptions and values and thus shapes their decisions, actions, and interactions on an individual level, a community level, and an institutional level. Dualistic thinking categorizes people, things, ideas, and the natural world— for example, black or white, male or female, reason or emotion, culture or nature, fact or opinion, mind or body. These categories gain meaning only in relation to their counterparts. That is, the characteristics of a category, for example black, are different from the characteristics of its counterpart, white. Characteristics for one category are excluded from or are viewed as opposite of the characteristics of its counterpart. Categories, therefore, are not seen as overlapping or complementary but as fundamentally different and distinct. Thus, either/or thinking is an exclusionary and reductionist way of looking and thinking about the world (Collins, 1991).

Furthermore, these categories are rarely considered different AND equal but are usually seen as different and unequal. Hence, one category becomes superior to the other: white is superior to black; male is superior to female; reason is superior to emotion; culture is superior to nature; fact is superior to opinion; and mind is superior to body. In this hierarchical system of thinking, the category that is considered inferior becomes objectified as the Other, viewed as an object to be controlled, dominated, and manipulated by the superior category. This in turn leads to oppression and subordination of the inferior category. Patricia Hill Collins (1991) argues that the overall social relationship in Western societies where either/or thinking is employed is one of domination and subjugation. Collins further asserts that as long as one category is viewed as the inferior Other, there is ideological justification for race, class, and gender oppression.

This dualistic perspective underpins scientific or essentialist racism—a theory first articulated in the 1800s that still influences current concepts of race. Scientific racism is a theory of racial hierarchy which is based on biology and evolution— that is, there is a biological difference between races and, consequently, some races are more highly evolved than others. According to this theory, the white race has evolved more than any other race due to a superior genetic makeup (Frankenberg, 1993).

Once race was made into a difference, difference became a rationale for racial inequality and, consequently, the basis for judgments and rankings, domination and oppression. In the colonization of North America, for example, the notion of Manifest Destiny— God's sanction of white people as the rightful possessors of the continent was premised on this cosmological view. The biological superiority of the white race was seen as justification for the insistence (via treaties and force) that the Native Americans "get off" of white man's land. Similarly, the view of white genetic superiority was the justification for slavery that white people could own an "inferior" black person. It is the notion that "we're better than them," and it still serves to justify current racist and sexist beliefs.

Some of the most blatant racist and sexist beliefs present in our current society center around the constructions of masculinities and femininities along racially differentiated lines. Foremost is the notion of the sexuality of men and women of color as animalistic, excessive, or exotic. In sharp contrast to this view of a "primitive" sexuality of people of color, is the view of white people's sexuality as "civilized" and "restrained." This clearly delineated conceptual construct of racial sexuality arose from scientific racism whites as more highly evolved and therefore more "civilized," and people of color as less evolved and therefore more "primitive," more like animals.

Arising from such notions of sexuality linked to race are various myths and stereotypes. For example, the stereotypic figures of Jezebel and Mammy arose from this view of nonwhite sexuality. Likewise, the myth of the African American male as a sexual aggressor or rapist arose from the notion of men of color as animalistic, supersexual beings. This myth had its origins immediately following slavery as white men sought rationalizations for continued repression of black men: that is, the need to "protect" white women and their "civilized" sexuality from black men and their "primitive," overly aggressive sexuality. Scientific racism also provided the rationale for antimiscegenation laws (laws prohibiting interracial marriages or sexual relationships). The argument was to keep white and nonwhite people separate so as to keep the white race "pure" and genetically superior. The rationale continues to influence present notions of racial boundaries— that is, what constitutes the norm today for marriages and neighborhoods is monoraciality (same-race marriages and same-race neighborhoods). Transgressors of these boundaries were and still are viewed negatively. White women, for example, who marry or date across racial lines are seen as sexually "loose," as sexually radical, as sexually unsuccessful (that is, they could not attract a white male so they have to settle for a man of color). Furthermore, children born to interracial couples are viewed today in negative terms— in fact, more negatively than the black couple because blood has been mixed, the superiority of the white genes has been diluted. Thus, these children are viewed by many in today's society as doomed. Unable to gain the acceptance of either the white culture or the nonwhite culture, they are sometimes forced to live as outcasts (Frankenberg, 1993).

Maintaining Otherness: Controlling Images of Black Women

Dualistic thinking and scientific racism, as stated earlier, are based on the notion of difference, of otherness. White culture viewing itself as superior, as the norm— has, throughout U.S. history, needed the Other in order to define its normalcy, its boundaries. To define boundaries, someone has to stand at the edges, at the margins, signalling a clear line as to who is "in," and considered normal and safe, and who is "out," and considered abnormal and threatening (Collins, 1991; Frankenberg, 1993). The Other in American society is anyone who is not a white male, for even within whiteness, "otherness" exists, as white women are not considered equal to white men and, hence, are denied some of the privileges of white men.

Let us examine more closely how one particular group of people, black women, have been regarded as the Other by the white dominant culture, and how creating and maintaining images of black women as the Other provides ideological justification for race, gender, and class oppression. According to Collins:

Portraying African-American women as stereotypical mammies, matriarchs, welfare recipients, and hot mommas has been essential to the political economy of
domination fostering Black women's oppression....As part of a generalized ideology of domination, these controlling images of Black womanhood take on special
meaning because the authority to define these symbols is a major instrument of
power. In order to exercise power, elite white men and their representatives must
be in a position to manipulate appropriate symbols concerning Black women.
They may do so by exploiting already existing symbols, or they may create new
ones relevant to their needs....[Furthermore,] the objective of stereotypes is not to
reflect or represent a reality but to function as a disguise, or mystification, of
objective social relationships (Collins, 1991, p.67-68).

In short, these controlling images are designed to make racism, sexism, and poverty appear to be natural, normal, and an inevitable part of
everyday life.

The dominant ideology of the slave era fostered the creation of four
interrelated, socially constructed, controlling images of black womanhood,
each reflecting the white dominant group's interest in maintaining and jus-
tifying black women's subordination. The prevailing ideology functioned
to mask contradictions in social relations affecting all women. "True"
women possessed four cardinal virtues: piety, purity, submissiveness, and
domesticity. Elite white women and those of the emerging middle class
were encouraged to aspire to these virtues. African-American women en-
countered a different set of controlling images.

The Mammy

The first controlling image applied to African American women is that
of the mammy— the faithful, obedient domestic servant. Created by the
white dominant group to justify the economic exploitation of house slaves
and sustained to explain black women's long-standing restriction to domestic service, the mammy image represents the normative yardstick used
to evaluate all black women's behavior. By loving, nurturing, and caring
for her white children and "family" better than her own, the mammy symbolizes the dominant group's perceptions of the ideal black female relationship to elite white male power. Even though she may be well loved and
may wield considerable authority in her white "family," the mammy still
knows her "place" as obedient servant. She is the black woman who has
internalized the mammy image. She has come to see herself as a mammy.
In doing so, she has accepted her subordinate position. In acting out the

mammy image, she serves to replicate superior white/inferior black relationships, exactly the intention behind the creation of the mammy image.

The mammy image is important because its aim is to shape black
women's behavior not only as women but also as mothers— that is, black
women are encouraged to transmit to their own children the deference behavior they exhibit as they live out the mammy role. By teaching black
children their assigned "place" in white power structures, black women
who internalize the mammy image potentially become effective conduits
for perpetuating racial oppression. Therefore, the mammy image is an extremely important psychological means by which the white dominant culture can keep present AND future black women subservient, docile, and
accepting of their racial and gender oppression.

The mammy image also serves a symbolic function in maintaining gender oppression. Images of black womanhood serve as a reservoir for the
fears of Western culture: the fears of the physical female. Juxtaposed
against the image of white women promulgated through the cult of true
womanhood, the mammy image as the Other symbolizes the oppositional
difference of mind/body and culture/nature thought to distinguish black
women from everyone else. Mammy, harmless in her position as slave,
unable because of her all-giving nature to do harm, is needed as an image,
a surrogate to contain all the fears of a physical female. The mammy image
buttresses the ideology of the cult of true womanhood, one in which sexuality and fertility are severed. "Good" white mothers are expected to deny
their female sexuality and devote their attention to the moral development
of their offspring. In contrast, the mammy image is one of an asexual woman,
a surrogate mother in blackface devoted to the development of the white
family (Collins, 1991).

The Matriarch

The fact that the mammy image cannot always control black women's
behavior as mothers is tied to the creation of the second controlling image
of black womanhood. Though a more recent phenomenon, the image of
the black matriarch, again created by the white dominant group, fulfills
similar functions in explaining black women's placement in interlocking
systems of race, gender, and class oppression. Prior to the 1960s, female-
headed households were certainly more common in African American communities, but an ideology racializing female-headedness as a causal fea-

ture of black poverty had not emerged. Since then, the mammy continues to typify the black mother figure in white homes, the matriarch came to symbolize the mother figure in black homes. Just as the mammy represents the "good" black mother, the matriarch symbolizes the "bad" black mother. The modern matriarchy thesis contends that African American women fail to fulfill their traditional "womanly" duties. Spending too much time away from home, these working mothers cannot properly supervise their children and are a major contributing factor to their children's school failure. Furthermore, as overly aggressive, "unfeminine" women, black matriarchs allegedly emasculate their lovers and husbands. These men, understandably, either desert their partners or refuse to marry the mother of their children.

Portraying African American women as matriarchs allows white people to blame black women for the success or failure of black children. Assuming that black poverty is passed on intergenerationally via value transmission in families, an elite white male standpoint suggests that black children lack the attention and care allegedly lavished on middle-class/upper-class white children and that this deficiency retards black children's achievement. Such a view diverts attention from the political and economic inequality affecting black mothers and children and suggests that anyone can rise from poverty if he or she only receives good values at home. Those African Americans who remain poor are blamed for their own victimization. Using black women's performance as mothers to explain black economic subordination links gender ideology to explanations of class subordination.

The image of matriarch also supports racial oppression. Black family structures are seen as deviant because they challenge the patriarchal assumptions underpinning the construct of the ideal "family" father, mother, children. The absence of black patriarchy is used as evidence for black cultural inferiority. Black women's failure to conform to the cult of true womanhood can then be identified as one fundamental source of black cultural deficiency (Collins, 1991).

The Welfare Mother

A third, externally defined, controlling image of black womanhood that of the welfare mother appears tied to black women's increasing dependence on the post-World War II welfare state. Essentially an updated version of the breeder woman image created during slavery, this image provides an ideological justification for efforts to harness black women's fertility to the needs of a changing political economy. The post-World War II political economy has offered African Americans rights not available in former historical periods. African Americans have successfully acquired basic political and economic protections from a greatly expanded welfare state, particularly Social Security, Aid to Families with Dependent Children, unemployment compensation, affirmative action, voting rights, antidiscrimination legislation, and the minimum wage. In spite of sustained opposition by Republican administrations in the 1980s, these programs allow many African Americans to reject the subsistence-level, exploitative jobs held by their parents and grandparents. Job export, deskilling, and increased use of illegal immigrants have been used to replace the loss of cheap, docile black labor. The large numbers of undereducated, unemployed African Americans, most of whom are women and children who inhabit inner cities, cannot be forced to work in exploitative conditions. From the standpoint of the dominant group, they no longer represent cheap labor but instead signify a costly threat to political and economic stability (Collins, 1991).

Controlling black women's fertility in such a political economy becomes important. The image of the welfare mother fulfills this function by labelling as unnecessary and even dangerous to the values of the country the fertility of women who are not white and middle class. A closer look at this controlling image reveals that it shares some important features with its mammy and matriarch counterparts. Like the matriarch, the welfare mother is labeled by white dominant culture as a bad mother. But unlike the matriarch, she is not too aggressive. On the contrary, she is not aggressive enough. She is portrayed as being content to sit around and collect welfare, shunning work and passing on her bad values to her offspring. Typically portrayed as an unwed mother, she violates one cardinal tenet of Eurocentric masculinist thought: she is a woman alone. As a result, her treatment reinforces the dominant gender ideology positing that a woman's true worth and financial security should occur through heterosexual marriage.

In the post-World War II political economy, one of every three families is officially classified as poor. With such high levels of poverty, welfare state policies supporting poor mothers and their children have become increasingly expensive. Although in reality there are larger numbers of white rural single mothers who are poor, hence debunking the notion that the welfare mother is equated with blackness, nevertheless the image portrayed by the media remains that welfare equals black single mothers with lots of children. Thus creating the controlling image of the black welfare mother and stigmatizing her for own poverty and that of African American communities shifts the angle of vision away from structural sources of poverty and blames the victims themselves. The image of the welfare mother thus provides justification for the dominant group's interest in limiting the fertility of black mothers who are seen as producing too many economically unproductive and state-dependent children (Collins 1991).

The Jezebel

The fourth controlling image— the Jezebel, whore, or sexually aggressive woman— is central in this nexus of elite white male images of black womanhood because efforts to control black women's sexuality lie at the heart of black women's oppression. The image of Jezebel originated under slavery when black women were portrayed as being sexually aggressive wet nurses. Jezebel's function was to relegate all black women to the category of sexually aggressive women, thus providing a powerful rationale for the widespread sexual assaults by white men typically reported by black slave women. Yet Jezebel served another function. If black slave women could be portrayed as having excessive sexual appetites, then increased fertility should be the expected outcome (and during the era of slavery, more black children meant more slaves, an economic advantage to the slaveholder).

This fourth image of the sexually denigrated black woman is the foundation underpinning elite white male conceptualizations of the mammy, matriarch, and welfare mother. Connecting all three is the common theme of black women's sexuality. Each image transmits clear messages about the proper links between female sexuality, fertility, and black women's roles in the political economy. For example, the mammy, the only somewhat positive figure, is a desexed individual. The mammy is typically portrayed as overweight, dark, and with characteristically African features— in brief, as an unsuitable sexual partner for white men. She is asexual and therefore is free to become a surrogate mother to the children she "acquired" not through her own sexuality. The mammy represents the clearest example of the split between sexuality and motherhood present in Eurocentric masculinist thought.

In contrast, both the matriarch and the welfare mother are sexual beings. But their sexuality is linked to their fertility, and this link forms one
fundamental reason why they are negative images. The matriarch represents the sexually aggressive woman, one who emasculates black men and
will not permit them to assume roles as black patriarchs. She refuses to be
passive and thus is stigmatized. Similarly, the welfare mother represents a
woman of low morals and uncontrolled sexuality, factors identified as the
cause of her impoverished state. In both cases black female control over
sexuality and fertility is conceptualized as antiethical to elite white male
interests (Collins 1991).

Taken together, these four prevailing interpretations of black womanhood form a nexus of elite white male interpretations of black female sexuality and fertility. These interpretations are translated into images that serve
as psychological chains for white AND black people. That is, if these images become accepted and internalized by white people, they provide justification for the continued oppression and subordination of black women.
If they are accepted and internalized by black women (as the white culture
hopes they will be), they make continued oppression and subordination
easy to maintain because there is no resistance by black women to the status quo. In both cases, controlling images lock those people who internalize them into a view of black women which is limiting, objectifying, and
ultimately dehumanizing. In this manner, controlling images replicate and
perpetuate the "white gaze" and unequal relationships.

Music as a Form of Resistance and Self-Defintion

People cannot live outside of the dominant ideology and its attendant
controlling images (Frankenberg, 1993). On the contrary, everyone is embedded in it. However, there is always an interaction occurring between the
self and the dominant ideology. As people try to understand their experiences and lived world in relation to the dominant ideology, multiple reac-
tions are possible: they can accept and internalize the dominant ideology
and serve to replicate and perpetuate it; they can reject all of the dominant
ideology and create their own definitions of selfhood, womanhood, blackness, and so on; or they can reject *parts* of the dominant ideology yet remain complicitous with other parts of it (Frankenberg 1993). People's re-
actions, understandings, and actions are complex because people simultaneously inhabit multiple spheres of oppression. A black woman, for ex-

ample, occupies at least two spheres: that of a woman and that of a black person. If she is also part of the working class, then she also inhabits a third sphere— that of lower class. If she should also be a lesbian, she would occupy a fourth sphere— that of sexual orientation (Collins 1991).

Music, especially the blues, is one location in which black women have literally found a voice. It is a forum through which they are able to resist and reject controlling images and instead define themselves. In other words, the blues have become a way in which black women can articulate their own personal experiences of subjugation while simultaneously expressing the possibility of changing and overcoming it (Collins, 1991). Outright criticism or rebellion by black women against the externally defined and imposed representations of black womanhood (the mammy, matriarch, welfare mother, and Jezebel) was and is difficult— even dangerous— as those who occupy the dominant position in society have the power to ignore, trivialize, and even silence critics and rebels of the status quo. Conventional channels through which people express their views and criticisms— books, newspapers, magazines, television, radio, the political realm, the business realm, the world of academia— have been, for the most part, closed to people of color. Those in control of those channels have been and still are predominately white males. The most commonly heard views and criticisms expressed through these channels, therefore, are those of white males. All other voices— often deemed by white males as inferior, less important, not the "real" truth— are often suppressed.

Therefore, black women's resistance to the psychological slavery of controlling images was and is often accomplished in more subtle and covert ways or in "safe" contexts. One of these "safe" contexts was and is through music. Music has always been central to African American culture. Thus, it became a natural channel through which black women could express their lived reality— the experiences of being a black woman in a white racist and sexist society. The essence of blues poetry is life itself: its aches, pains, grievances, pleasures, and brief moments of glory. It also provides a wellspring of solace and hope. Thus, the blues are paradoxical in that they contain the expression of the agony and pain of life as experienced by black women in America, yet the very act of articulation demonstrates resilience, toughness of spirit, and the desire to shape existence while living in the midst of oppressive contradictions. For black women, the blues provide them with a voice— not only heard by other black people but by white people as well. During the 1920s and 1930s, recordings and performances made by famous blues singers— such as Ma Rainey, Bessie

Smith, Alberta Hunter, and Sippie Wallace— became very popular with white people. Cabarets and show palaces were packed. Today, the blues are still popular. What many white people may not have realized then or now, however, was that behind the beautiful melodies and the sometimes soulful, sometimes toe-tapping rhythms, were lyrics often expressing black women's dislike and discontent (even anger) with the status quo. Thus, even though the *channel* was available through which to express their views and criticisms, the message that black women were trying to convey to their white audience— that they did not want to be dominated and controlled in thought or behavior by white culture— went largely unheard, or at least not taken seriously.

The classroom, then, can be a place where the message of the blues can be studied and discussed, where white people can become aware, and hopefully begin to take seriously, the "heart" of the blues: the injustice and dehumanization of oppression felt by black women due to the unequal racial and gender relationships in America which privilege white males over all others. Awareness of this unequal power structure must be combined with the study of *how* white males maintain this unequal structure. Creating controlling images which serve as thought and behavior control is one way to replicate and perpetuate white male dominance. Therefore, examining these controlling images and how they function to shape not only black women's images of themselves but also shape *white people's* images of black women is critical to the understanding of how oppression operates in American society. The blues, carrying the voice of black women, can then be used to discover how black women view themselves and how they would like others to view them and to treat them.

The lesson of the blues would involve a three-step critical analysis:

  -uncovering the dualistic structure that underpins gender, racial, and class relationships and which creates and perpetuates privilege and oppression.
  -examining controlling images and how they serve to replicate privilege and oppression.
  -listening to the blues, to how black women perceive themselves and would like others to perceive them as well. If put into action, these new views would lead to a new type of social relationship: one based on equality and justice.

Class discussion could include such questions as:
   -What is this song about?
   -What problem(s) is the singer grappling with?
   -How does this particular singer view the problem?
   -What solution(s) does this singer offer for the problem?
   -Does this solution serve to break the dominant ideology/controlling
    images in some manner or serve to replicate it?
   -If the song offers alternative definitions of people, relationships, or
    situations, how do they differ from the dominant ideology?
   -Have you (the student) ever experienced a similar situation/
    problem?
   -What solution(s) did you devise for this situation/problem?
The class discussion should include these questions as well:
   -How does whiteness shape the view of the self?
   -How does whiteness shape the view that white people have of other
    white people?
   -How does whiteness shape the view of the nonwhite person?
   -How do these views serve to maintain the current power differential
    by objectifying and dehumanizing the nonwhite person?
   -What are our own multiple positionalities (race, gender, class,
    ethnicity, sexual orientation)?
   -What privileges do these positions hold?
   -In what ways do these positions oppress?
   -How can we imagine, articulate, and act in ways which promote
    more egalitarian, more humane, more dignified relationships?

"Mississippi, Goddam"

Let us apply the above set of questions to a specific blues song, "Mississippi, Goddam." This song addresses the issue of inequality between white and black people in America.

   Alabama's got me so upset
   Tennessee made me lose my rest
   Everybody knows about Mississippi, Goddam.

> Hound dogs on my trail
> School children sittin' in jail
> Picket lines, school boycotts
> They said it was a Communist plot.

The lyrics are pointing out the social reality of the 1950s. The lyrics give a general idea of what happened but more specific information would be very important and pertinent at this point. What DID happen in Alabama? In Tennessee? What DOES everyone know about Mississippi? It would be relevant to students to read about and to watch footage of events that happened between blacks and whites during this time period: Martin Luther King, Jr.; George Wallace; school boycotts, bus boycotts, restaurant sit-ins; passive resistance; rallies for equality and civil rights; police using dogs, billyclubs, and fire hoses on black people; Jim Crow laws; segregated restaurants, theaters, schools; lynchings; Ku Klux Klan activities....

It was a period of time when black people began to openly express their desire for equality. As the song, "Mississippi, Goddam" states:

> Don't tell me, I'll tell you
> Me and my people just about due
> You don't have to live next to me
> I just want equality for my sister, my people, and me.

Knowing about the blatant inequalities between black and white people in the 1950s makes it quite apparent why the song states "Me and my people just about due." The song even asks:

> Why don't you see it?
> Why don't you feel it?
> I don't know. I don't know.

Meaning, why can't the white dominant group *see* this blatant inequality and injustice? Why can't they *feel* it? Black people see it and feel it. It is quite clear to black people that they are not receiving the privileges and power that accompany the dominant position in society. "Mississippi, Goddam" expresses the frustration, consternation, even anger at this obliviousness by whites— their inability to see and do anything about the gross inequalities.

In addition to making a statement about the blatant inequalities alluded to in references to Alabama, Tennessee, and Mississippi, this blues song also deals with the less obvious— controlling images.

> Yes, you lied to me all these years
> You told me to wash and clean my ears
> And talk real fine just like a lady
> And you'd stop calling me Sister Sadie.

The reference to Sister Sadie can be associated with the Jezebel controlling image. Both terms refer to sexually aggressive black women. The "you" in this stanza refers to white people and how they think of and explicitly call black women Sister Sadie. This stanza points out how black women have been "told" (it is implicit that they are being told by whites) that if they act like a lady they would not be called Sister Sadie anymore. Acting like a lady is defined, however, not by black women but by white culture: having clean ears and talking "real fine," that is, not in the black vernacular. What frustrates and angers this singer is not necessarily that she must adopt the white group's definition of lady in order to be considered and treated an equal to white people, but that she *has* adopted this standard, this definition and STILL is not being treated with equality. As she says, "Yes, you lied to me all these years."

"Mississippi, Goddam" goes on to talk about more "lies" told to black people by white people.

> Oh, this whole country's full of lies
> Y'all gonna die and die like flies
> I don't trust you anymore
> When you keep sayin', "Go slow."
>
> But that's the trouble— too slow
> Desegregation, mass participation, unification— too slow
> Do things gradually and bring more tragedy.

White people have been telling black people that desegregation, mass participation, unification— all actions which would help equalize privileges and power between black and white people— must go slow. And that is the trouble, says the song. TOO SLOW. "Do things gradually and bring more tragedy." The lyrics can be interpreted as saying that white people are telling black people that change must occur slowly. The song is implying that black people *have been waiting* for equality to come. But to no avail. Inequality continues to exist, and it does not appear that it will end if black people simply wait a little longer.

This stanza is expressing not only the frustration of waiting for equality which is not materializing, but also the realization that doing "things gradually...[will only] bring more tragedy"— that is, more injustice and inequality. This particular stanza is asserting that the white dominant group has purposely lied to blacks. By making black people *think* that equality was slowly coming, white people could, in actuality, maintain the status quo without any protest from black people. In other words, the "we must go slowly" talk is exactly that— talk. It is a ploy used by white people to keep black people quiet and in their subordinate position. It is a controlling mechanism for maintaining white privilege and power.

> The singer, when saying
> I don't trust you anymore
> When you keep sayin', "Go slow."
> But that's just the trouble— too slow...
> Do things gradually and bring more tragedy

. . . is declaring that she *knows* the ploy being used and is refusing to continue believing the "lies" being told to her by white society. She is aware, in other words, of the controlling mechanisms (Sister Sadie and acting like a "real" lady and the "go slow" tactic) being used by the white group to maintain their privileged position. And now aware, she is breaking the psychological chains of the controlling images. This blues song does not explicitly offer new self-definitions. However, it does make clear that equality between black and white people is desired.

The goal, in this type of analysis of the blues, is to create an awareness among white students of the privileges that come with their whiteness, and that these privileges come about because they occupy a dominant position in relation to others who are not white. Furthermore, to maintain the dominant/subordinate relationship structure, mechanisms are needed that will replicate and perpetuate this structure. One of these mechanisms is the creation of controlling images by the dominant group. These controlling images are effective in perpetuating this unequal structure as long as a majority of both white and black people believe that these are right and natural. As soon as enough whites or blacks begin to question the "rightness" or "naturalness" of these images, their power to control people's thoughts and actions is broken. Therefore, studying the blues can make white students aware of controlling images— what they are and the power they exert over themselves and black women. In short, the blues can expose these images for what they are: psychological chains for both white and black people. By exposing and resisting them, the blues open up the possibility for the white culture to view black women in a new way— a way which is dignified and humanizing. And this, ultimately, opens up the possibility for new types of relationships— ones not grounded in dualism but rather in a both/and framework. Classrooms, then, can be transformative sites, aiding in the creation of more humane, more just, and more egalitarian human relationships.

Suggested Blues For The Classroom

What follows are some specific songs performed by the legendary blues artists of the 1920s and 1930s which can be studied. The lyrics can be found in the references as indicated. Many more songs and their lyrics are discussed in the books by Harrison, 1988; Lieb, 1981; Cone, 1922 and in the article by Russell, 1982.

1) "Get It, Bring It, Put It Right Here" Bessie Smith (Russell, 1982, p.132)

   -Breaks the controlling image of matriarch. The song describes the desire to construct a relationship of equality between black men and black women in the home.

2) "Prove It On Me Blues" Ma Rainey (Lieb, 1981, p.124)

   -A powerful statement of lesbian self-worth.

   -Breaks the mammy controlling image. Black women's sexuality is depicted as natural and normal. Furthermore, lesbianism is depicted as natural and normal.

   -Breaks the Jezebel controlling image. Song depicts sexuality and lesbianism in a positive manner.

3) "Tricks Ain't Walkin' No More" Bessie Jackson (Russell, 1982, p.134)

   -Breaks the welfare mother image. Depicts a black woman as *wanting* to work and be financially independent.

   -Breaks the Jezebel image. Tells black women to refuse to prostitute themselves no matter how bad the economic situation is for them.

4) "Sports Model Mamma" Rosalie Hill (Harrison, 1988, p.107)

   -The song brags about a black woman's sexiness— double entendres used.

   -Breaks the mammy and Jezebel images. Depicts a black woman as proud, sure of herself, and unashamed of her sexuality.

5) "Up The Country Blues" Sippie Wallace (Harrison, 1988, p.88)

   -Breaks the mammy, matriarch, welfare mother, and Jezebel images. The song is an assertion of power and respect for self and black womanhood in general.

6) "Mean Tight Mamma" Sara Martin (Collins, 1991, p.101)

   -Breaks the mammy image. Tells black women to reject the confining images of beauty as defined by white culture and to express pride in African American features.

   A few songs by Aretha Franklin, a current blues singer:

7) "Respect" (Collins, 1991, p.108,110)
    -Breaks the mammy, matriarch, welfare mother, and Jezebel images.
    Extols the belief that being black and female is valuable and wor-
    thy of respect from others, especially from black men.
    -Breaks the welfare mother image as the singer is demanding re-
    spect on the basis of her economic self-reliance.
8) "Do Right Woman—Do Right Man" (Collins,1991, p.185)
    -Breaks the matriarch image. The blues tradition provides the most
    consistent and long-standing text of black women who demand that
    black men reject stereotypic sex roles. This song encourages black
    men to define new types of relationships, ones that are based on
    mutual respect, faithfulness, financial reliability, and sexual expres-
    siveness.
    -Breaks the mammy, matriarch, welfare mother, and Jezebel images.
    Makes the claim that men and women are equally human, that
    women are not playthings.
9) "Change Is Gonna Come" (Collins, 1991, p.112)
    -Expresses the need for persistence and endurance in the journey
    towards self-definition.
    -Asserts that actions of self-definition change the world from one
    in which black women merely exist to one in which they have some
    control. This is an empowering process for black women.

Other forums for the expression of black women's resistance to and
rejection of the dominant ideology and for the expressions of self-definition can be found in literature and in films. Studying all of these forums
could comprise a unit of study or an entire college course. Studying several forums would provide a richer learning experience for students, as
they would be exposed to several learning avenues— sight (films), sound
(music), and imagination (literature). Popular culture, such as current films,
TV shows, pop/rock music, and MTV, is also a rich avenue by which to
explore notions of dominant ideology, standards of masculinity/femininity,
controlling images and negative stereotypes, complicity with or rejection
of the dominant ideology, and alternative forms of self-definition.

Some recommended books by black women writers:
    -*I Know Why the Caged Bird Sings,* Maya Angelou
    -*Sweet Summer*, Bebe Moore Campbell
    -*Lemon Swamp and Other Places,* Mamie Garvin Field and Karen Field

-"The Johnson Girls," a short story by Toni Cade Bambara
-*Sula, The Bluest Eye, Beloved,* Toni Morrison
-*The Color Purple*, Alice Walker
-*Zami*, Audre Lorde
Some recommended films by black women filmmakers:
    -Illusions and Diary of an African Nun, Julie Dash
    -Gotta Make that Journey: Sweet Honey in the Rock, Michelle
     Parkerson
    -Hair Piece, Ayoka Chenzira
    -Losing Ground, Kathleen Collins

For more information on black women filmmakers, see Campbell, 1983. More general information on black women in film can be found in Mapp, 1973.

References

Bessie Smith: American blues singer [video]. (1988). Warner Amex Satellite Entertainment Co. Princeton, N.J.: Films for the Humanities.

Campbell, L. (1983). Reinventing our image: Eleven black women filmmakers. *Heresies 4*(4): 58-62.

Cheng, V. Ex-Aryan warns of growing hate trend. (1995, Nov. 9). *Centre Daily Times,* p.1A.

Collins, P. H. (1991). *Black feminist thought: Knowledge, consciousness, and the politics of empowerment.* New York: Routledge.

Cone, J. H. (1972). *The spirituals and the blues: An interpretation.* New York: The Seabury Press.

Giroux, H. A. (1994). Insurgent multiculturalism and the promise of pedagogy. In D. Theo Goldberg (Ed.), *Multiculturalism: A critical Reader.* (pp. 325-343). Cambridge, Mass.: Blackwell Publishers.

Harrison, D. D. (1988). *Black pearls: Blues queens of the 1920s.* New Brunswick, N.J.: Rutgers University Press.

Kim, S. Going past the hate. (Nov. 6, 1995). *Centre Daily Times*, p.1A.

Lieb, S. R. (1981). *Mother of the blues: A study of Ma Rainey.* Boston: The University of Mass. Press.

Mapp, E. (1973). Black women in films. *Black Scholar 4*(6-7): 42-46.

Morrison, T. (1993). *Playing in the dark: Whiteness and the literary imagination.* New York: Vintage Books.

Rubin, L. B. (1994). *Families on the fault Line: America's working class speaks out about the family, the economy, race, and ethnicity.* New York: HarperCollins Publishers.

Russell, M. (1982). Slave codes and liner notes. In G. T. Hull, P. B. Scott & B. Smith *But Some of Us Are Brave.* (pp.129-140). Old Westbury, N.Y.: Feminist Press.

CHAPTER SEVEN

White Women Teaching in the North:
Problematic Identity on the Shores of Hudson Bay
Helen Harper

I should mention to you that for quite a while when I got here, I looked at myself a lot. I kept physically looking at myself. Because I kept thinking, What do I look like? It was very strange. What do I look like to them? I kept trying, because I'd never seen myself as the oppressor. I could never see myself as— even though I'm white, because I always felt I was on the periphery, I never felt really Wonder Bread white. And I *was* all of a sudden. And I would look all the time. I remember asking myself questions like, How white am I? I did that a lot. It was very weird.

—Robin

In her first year of teaching, Robin[1] was employed in a small northern First Nations community. Previously she had been a student in the faculty of education in which I teach and was one of the few in her class to secure a teaching job. Robin struggled (and continues to struggle) most intensely and self-consciously with an identity formulated in, against, and beyond notions of femininity, whiteness, and teacher, as organized through the history, practices, and identities available both inside and outside the reserve where she taught.

This chapter is part of a study that investigates how white women teaching in isolated northern Aboriginal communities create and negotiate a sense of themselves and their work. The study is part of a larger project on white women teachers in Canada and their role in, and preparation for multicultural and antiracist education. The intention of this work is to make visible the cultural texts through which white women teachers forge an identity, and the processes of identification by which they assume or do not assume particular images or constructs of the teacher. It is hoped that this project will produce a larger, clearer, and more dynamic picture of the history and process by which gendered and racialized teacher identities are assumed and negotiated. Such a picture may indicate how to intervene more effectively in the preparation of teachers from a dominant culture for work in antiracist education with both minority and majority students.

This initial study, conducted in the Spring of 1996, involved ten women who were teaching in fly-in Cree communities located on the shores of Hudson Bay. Of the ten women, seven were first-year teachers, eight were white, one South Asian, and one Aboriginal teacher who was from outside the band community. This chapter focuses in part on Robin, for she was most articulate about her experience and appeared ideally suited for, and desperately wished to work in, an alternative school setting. However she was not able to create or re-create herself to her satisfaction in the school or in the First Nations community in which she resided. Even problematically, she was never "at home" with herself in the profession or the community. The sense she makes of her experience in this context renders visible notions of whiteness, Nativeness, femininity, masculinity, and a radical teacher identity that have organized educational discourse in Canada. Her experience speaks in important ways to teacher education programs and focuses attention on a history that organizes professional identities along race, class and gender lines.

This chapter and the larger study of which it is a part draw on scholarship from three related areas: antiracist education, post-structuralism, and postcoloniality, and in particular the history of white women in the context of British and Canadian imperialism. The impetus for this work comes initially from the politics and pedagogy of anti-racist education. The first section of this paper examines the antiracist education and white identity and then briefly traces two subject positions of the white Lady teacher: "Lady Bountiful" and "Janey Canuck." The last section of the paper returns to Robin and her struggle with and against these positionings. The paper concludes with the implications of her struggle for teacher education.

Cream in the Coffee: AntiRacist Education and White Identity

Antiracist education focuses on how schools name, define, and negotiate cultural and racial differences. Moreover it confronts educational policies and practices that reproduce race together with gender, sex, and class and other inequalities. This "inclusive antiracist education" offers a powerful alternative to the responses that have historically characterized the production and treatment of human difference in Canadian schooling (Dei, 1994, 1995). Such responses have included the suppression of difference through assimilation, an insistence on a "natural" difference requiring segregation, the denial of difference with a focus on equal treatment for all, and celebration of difference by way of multicultural education (Harper, in press). Antiracist education interrogates how human difference is named and enacted. In terms of identity, antiracist education examines issues of power and powerlessness in relation to how racialized identities are produced and normalized in school contexts. In part this means a focus on the practices by which identities are produced and translated into the everyday; into "common sense" or what seems natural or normal. What is deemed normal and natural becomes hegemonic and largely invisible. This is particularly true with the practices and identities of dominant culture. As Russell Ferguson explains:

> In our society dominant discourse tries never to speak its own name. Its authority is based on absence. The absence is not just that of the various groups classified as "other," although members of these groups are routinely denied power. It is also the lack of any overt acknowledgment of the specificity of the dominant culture, which is simply assumed to be the all-encompassing norm. This is the basis of its power." (1990, p. 11)

Whiteness, functioning as an invisible norm, "colonizes the definitions of other norms, class, gender, heterosexuality, nationality and so on—it also masks whiteness as itself a category" (Dryer, 1988, p. 45).

While whiteness is frequently the invisible norm, at times it is rendered visible. For example, the term *poor* frequently assumes blackness in many places in the United States (personal communication with Professor Wright, University of Tennessee, 1995). If indeed, blackness becomes the invisible norm associated with poverty in certain historical and geographical locations, then it is not surprising to discover that whiteness often must be explicitly stated when referring to people living in poverty. Hence the expression and identity "poor white trash," one of the few instances in which whiteness is explicitly named. It is important then to note when and for what reason specification does or does not occur. In many versions of multicultural education it is apparent that neither dominant culture nor whiteness is named. Rather information about other races and cultures is simply added to the curriculum and highlighted at particular moments. As noted by Richard Dryer, this kind of curricular reform serves to keep invisible the authority and power of dominant groups and turn nondominant groups into the exotic:

> Looking with such passion and single-mindedness at non-dominant groups has had the effect of reproducing the sense of the oddness, differentness, exceptionality of these groups, the feeling that they are departures from the norm. Meanwhile the norm has carried on as if it is the natural, inevitable, ordinary way of being human. (1988, p. 44)

The importance for antiracist education, of highlighting white identity, in this instance, the representation and performance of the "white woman teacher" lies in making visible taken-for-granted assumptions and practices in order to understand and challenge structures of white power and authority.

This is not easy work. Exposing the workings of identity formation is socially and psychologically disturbing. Intervention means reworking identities and identifications that have, for better or worse, have secured people to the world. There can be comfort in what is familiar and seemingly stable. However the stability is largely illusionary. From the perspective of poststructural theory, identity is an ongoing process rather than a fixed state. Individuals actively negotiate an identity with and against the positionings available to them at any one historical moment.

Central to this study and its larger project are questions of how white identities get organized and negotiated. That is, what is the history of white subject positionings that have dominated social life, and what is the nature of their power, socially and psychologically? In particular, when and how does whiteness become an invisible norm? What are the contradictions and alternatives that must be actively ignored and excluded or in some way negotiated in the formation and performance of white identity? White femininity is particularly interesting in the context of historical and contemporary colonialism since it is often a shifting and contradictory position, both the visible and invisible, both at the center and at margins of colonial education. Since white women may well continue to have a presence in the teaching profession, and considering the diversity of the students with whom they will be or are now working, it would seem important to examine how white femininity is organized and negotiated. This is particularly important in the context of minority education; in this case in the context of Aboriginal education.

Lady Bountiful and Janey Canuck: White Women and the Empire

There has been increasing interest in the role of white women and their complicity and resistance to imperialism (cf. Blunt & Rose, 1994; Chaudhuri & Strobel, 1992; Trollope, 1983). The study of white women offers a disruption in the narratives of the British colonialism in that it "helps to destabilize the binary oppositions between both male/female and colonizer/colonized" because "the intersection of colonial and gender discourses involves a shifting, contradictory subject positioning, whereby Western women can simultaneously constitute 'centre' and 'periphery,' 'identity and alterity'" (Blunt & Rose, 1994).

For white women teaching Aboriginal students in the Canadian North, students and teachers directly confront a history of Canadian, British, and French colonialism that exposes their previous and current understandings of self and other. They confront positionings from in and outside First Nations communities that offer dramatic identificatory moments. Two positionings documented in history of British imperialism are that of the mother-teacher in service to the empire and that of English lady traveler and her adventures in the colonies.

The English mother of empire is referred to by Ford-Smith (1992) as: "Lady Bountiful." "Lady Bountiful" is a representation of the white lady missionary or teacher that emerges during the time of British imperialism. It is an image in which, "notions of imperial destiny and class and racial superiority were grafted onto the traditional views of refined English motherhood to produce a concept of the English woman as an invincible global civilizing agent" (Ware, 1992). The image of "Lady Bountiful" is particular salient in terms of the teacher or colonial governess who was seen as having a unique duty to bring civilization to the 'uncivilized." Initially, in the early 1800s, her role was to educate British working-class women in religion, morality, and hygiene. However, her sphere expanded with imperialism to anywhere the British flag was flying. In India direct appeals were made to "well-trained, accomplished English ladies, capable of doing good to their Indian sisters both by instruction and by personal example" (Ware, 1992). The ideal of femininity propounded by the British to the colonies became the white woman, the embodiment of chastity and purity who acted as a "civilizing" force.

The specific image of the white lady teacher is of a spinster headmistress, intelligent but thwarted in her academic pursuits by her gender and possibly her social class, whose maternal instincts and academic interests have been directed towards her "Native" charges. Embodied, she was the sponge or mediating agent between the subaltern and the colonial state. The intersection of white lady teacher and motherhood and colonialism is particularly powerful because "Lady Bountiful" epitomized purity, chastity, and goodness, understood increasingly as selflessness. Her selflessness was bound inextricability to administering to the needs of others, not to her own. She is and was the consummate caregiver. According to Ford-Smith (1992), this image and role carries with it the imperative "to know and the incredible arrogance of that imperative to know." Lady Bountiful must know and feel what is wrong and be able to fix it. For "Lady Bountiful" to be bountiful she needs to know, to feel, and to be in control. She needs to be at the centre but at the same time her needs—her own "self" remains absent. Her ability to act as the civilizing force, to be the white mother-teacher in the service of the empire, is dependent upon her need to be at the centre, knowing and helping her charges. As a missionary-teacher, if she doesn't know, if she can't be in control, can't feel, or can't act, there is guilt as well as the fear that is unmotherly or unladylike or unChristian.

The white Lady Traveler off on her adventures in the colonies is also in service to the empire, and she also needs to be at the centre, knowing and understanding the foreigners she meets. She is the consummate researcher and teacher, reporting her experiences back to in England, teaching about "the other." She is represented in women like Mary Kingsley (*Travels in West Africa*, 1887); Mary Hall (*A Woman's Trek from Cape to Cairo*, 1907); and Lady Isabella Bird (*A Lady's Life in the Rocky Mountains*, 1879). Often these women travelers were single, mature, and wealthy. Many traveled after the death of parents or husbands left them with money and without responsibilities. Unless missionaries, they traveled privately for travel's own sake, since few institutions, with the exception of the church, included women in their overseas recruitment (Blake, 1992). Her gender is significant in that it allowed her "a woman's perspective" to see and record areas of life that male colonial administrators and explorers were unaware of or unable to experience. Her whiteness is played out in that she is both insider and outsider. As a traveler as opposed to a colonist, she is not part of the community, so is allowed greater eccentricity, which often meant more freedom than white women settlers or native women. At the same time, as a traveler, the white women has no long term commitment to the community she is visiting. But if she is seen as too much the outsider, too white, it would be too difficult her to investigate and experience "the other." For both Lady Bountiful and the white Lady Traveler, whiteness as an ever-present norm must be largely ignored or suppressed, since their "selfless-ness" is necessary in order to know and experience the colonized. The focus needs to be on the "other," not her "self."

Lady Bountiful and the white Lady Traveler are evident in historical documents and literature often as part of the positioning of the white lady teacher. To some degree, one can see Lady Bountiful in Anne Langton, a spinster from England who devoted her life chiefly to housekeeping for her brothers in Canada during the early 1800s. According to her diaries, Anne Langton was not particular enamoured of her "untutored children of the forest" but nonetheless believed it was her duty to spread British culture to the inhabitants of the Canadian backwoods (Prentice, 1991). There is evidence that current multicultural educational policy and practices in Canada employ the same image of Lady Bountiful, demanding the the teacher know and save "hapless" minority students, while her own whiteness and white privilege remain unacknowledged (Harper & Cavenaugh, 1994). *Janey Canuck Abroad* (1901) and *Janey Canuck in the West* (1905) written by Emily Murphy, *Canadian Crusoes* (1850) by Catharine Parr Traill, and *Roughing it in the Bush* (1852) by Susanna Moodie offer images of the white lady adventuress in Canada. These women were often settlers, rather than travelers, who wrote to encourage support immigration to Canada. The image of Janey Canuck is overtly Canadian. She was the "female counterpart of "Jack Canuck, the popular cartoon figure of the 1890s who had become the symbol of the naive, youthful, self-confident and brash Canadianism of the day" (Basset, 1975, p. xi). Through the persona of Janey Canuck, Emily Murphy depicted Canada as a place of adventure and rejuvenation for Europeans: "The hardy Northern environment of Canada is a fertile breeding ground where the tired, ailing Anglo-Saxon race, exhausted and numbed by the unhealthy conditions and decadence of the late nineteenth century city life, could be revitalized" (Basset, 1975, xix). Both the white Lady Traveler and Lady Bountiful, among other discursive positions, are evident in the history of Aboriginal education.

Aboriginal Education in Canada and the Role of White Women

Women currently 65 percent of the teaching positions in the Northwest Territories and in the Yukon (Canadian Teachers Federation, 1993). Many of these teachers are white and originally from southern Canada. White women do not have a long history in northern Canada. Initially the Hudson Bay Company, which was given a monopoly in the late 1600s for fur trading in what was referred to at the time as Rupert's Land, did not permit its male employees to bring their wives and/or female relatives. Hudson Bay employees were not settlers but traders who would return to England once their service was finished. As a result, many of the fur traders took Native women as wives in the practice "á la façon du pays" (Van Kirk, 1980). These "country wives," as they were called, were instrumental in the fur trade, establishing contacts with Indian tribes and bands, serving as translators, and educating husbands and generally ensuring their survival in a harsh, alien environment. Later, mixed-race women produced from these liaisons became the preferred wives. However, as white presence in the North grew, the prohibition against white women was lifted and white women, the "tender exotics," became fashionable as wives for white men, even though the very qualities that made them desirable, refinement and fragility, were a handicap in the North. As in other countries, the presence of white women resulted in increasingly overt racism. Fur traders often abandoned their country wives and children to marry white women. English school teachers were considered particularly desirable (Healy, 1923). White women, "the delicate flowers of civilization," became the sign of civilization and refinement. As teachers and nuns, they were there to bring salvation and progress to Aboriginal women and children and men. Although some white women did stay in the North, more often they were temporarily stationed there, and would then leave with their husbands for other positions in the South or back in Britain.

In terms of education, historically the role of white teachers and their relation to Aboriginal students, though highly problematic, was abundantly clear. Until 1969 the education of Aboriginal children was under the auspicious of the Federal Department of Indian and Northern Affairs. Until then the objective of education had been to suppress Aboriginal culture and languages in efforts to "improve" Aboriginal children with the goal of assimilation, or, failing that, of "fitting the Indian for 'civilized' life in his [sic] own environment, a goal it [also] failed to achieve" (Ashworth, 1995, p. 26, emphasis). The psychological scars of cognitive imperialism and colonization experienced in various Aboriginal residential, industrial, and day schools, are apparent in the communities and in the schools to this day. It is not surprising that there exists very negative views about white teachers, as Battiste & Barman (1995) indicate: "Aboriginal peoples began to see educators, like their missionary predecessors, as nothing more than racists, patriarchs and oppressors who hid behind fine-sounding words or ideology. Their objectives were viewed as tainted and hypocritical" (p. viii.).

The notion of the ideal teacher has changed dramatically in Aboriginal schools. In the late 1960s the Federal government sought to transfer its responsibility for Aboriginal education to the provinces. However there was considerable opposition to this proposal from the National Indian Brotherhood. In a policy paper entitled "Indian Control of Indian Education," the Brotherhood argued for the right of Aboriginal peoples to administer educational programs for their own children, rather than either the federal or provincial governments. Although the initial concern was with administration, this demand has come to include greater control over the curriculum. The result has been a redefinition of the purpose of Indian education with a key commitment to salvaging Aboriginal language, and culture and transmitting those cultures and their unique world views (Battiste, 1995). In 1973 the Federal government accepted that commitment in principle and began establishing Indian education training centres at various universities for the training of Aboriginal teachers. The desire was that Aboriginal teachers who know and understand their own culture should become the norm in First Nations Communities. In 1975-76, 53 communities had assumed control over their schools; by 1991-92, the number had increased to 329 (Kirkness, 1992).

The position of the white Lady teacher organized by Lady Bountiful or Janey Canuck has become extremely problematic for both Native communities and the white women teachers who continue to be employed in these areas. Some of the struggles experienced by Robin in her first year of teaching speak directly to these subject positions.

Robin: Contending with Lady Bountiful:

"I Have Always Existed on the Periphery." —Robin

Robin, the first-year teacher whose words began this paper, worked in a band-operated school in a small fly-in community on the shores of Hudson Bay. Although the senior administrators were Aboriginal and male, the vast majority of the teachers were, like Robin, young, white, female, and from the south. There continues to be a shortage of qualified Aboriginal teachers, and so white teachers continue to be recruited. Like the other teachers participating in the study, Robin and I had a series of formal and informal interviews and casual telephone calls after her arrival on the reserve. In addition to the interviews, I visited the reserve where she taught. During my short visit I observed her class, and participated in all the school and social events that she did. For Robin, her connection both with the white teachers and with the aboriginal community was not easy to negotiate in terms of her notion of teacher identity.

In the course of our interviews, Robin described herself as an individual who has not lived what she considers a traditional white middle class life. She was not raised in a traditional middle class nuclear family and grew up in a series of working class neighborhoods. For a time she lived in downtown Detroit and described how she was the only white student in her kindergarten class. She was in French immersion school but felt marginalized there because of her family's socioeconomic status. In terms of her education, Robin often described herself, both as a student and as a student teacher, as someone who resisted schooling. She explained, "I was terrible at school. I was suspended a lot in elementary school; I detested high school." But she enjoyed reading and writing. In her own words, Robin "devoured books" and "loved to write," and this drew her to university and to an honors degree in English. Robin was not particularly enamoured by her experience in the faculty of education. As evident in the transcripts, she experienced difficulty identifying with her fellow student teachers, associate teachers, and professors. She remarked, "I hated my first practicum experience ... I felt I was in disguise. I was supposed to be like them [the other teachers] and I just couldn't be." Robin was appalled by the fact there were so few men in the elementary program and so few people of color in the program generally. She saw herself as far more politically radical than other students in the faculty, and in that regard definitely in the minority. Several times Robin defined herself as marginalized— as having "always existed on the periphery."

From her account, what appears to have kept her in the program and in the profession in part is her reading of radical pedagogy, in particular the works of Henry Giroux. Her reading gave her "some hope I can do this [teaching]." Not only did she identify with radical pedagogy but she spoke of students who are marginalized in classrooms. "During my practicum I would ask myself which student am I not paying attention to, or which student have I or my associate [teacher] missed. So often I could see myself in that classroom as that student."

The construct of the white radical teacher is one formulated largely on the notion of living on, to use Robin's words "the periphery," or more commonly living on the borders or in borderlands (Giroux, 1992; Haig-Brown, 1995). It is an identity which becomes intelligible to itself when whiteness becomes other to itself. That is, it is a white identity understood and articulated against dominant white culture. This is the position of the radical pedagogue, but also to a degree the subject positioning of Lady Bountiful and the white Lady Traveler, who themselves push convention by traveling and working in the geographical and social margins of the empire. The white Lady Traveller, in particular flaunts, Victorian notions of femininity by travelling privately, often alone, in foreign lands. However, neither the white Lady Traveler or Lady Bountiful is out to deliberately challenge British imperialism, and in fact the work of white women in the colonies generally served to reinscribe the values and beliefs that underlie British colonialism (Chaudhuri & Strobel, 1993).

Considering how Robin defines herself, it is not surprising that she decided to pursue a teaching position in an minority community. She remembered her decision: "I would try to teach, but I would never ever teach in southwestern Ontario. If I had to teach in the suburbs, I would go insane." Robin initially applied for a teaching position in other countries and in northern Ontario and eventually one. Despite her desire to teach outside of white, middle class, suburban southern Ontario, her decision to go north was still a struggle. Robin deliberated at length both before her job interview and afterwards. She describes her concerns: "I had reservations about whether I could teach Native children because I'm not Native, because I was just such an outsider. How I could do that or if I had the right. I didn't know if I had the right to invite myself into someone else's community." When asked what she had thought she offered the reserve, Robin replied: "I don't know if I thought I had anything to offer. I felt that I wasn't going to do any more damage. I think that's more it. I felt like I respected that they were their own community and I was an outsider. I felt I could be sensitive. I at least thought there was a question. I may not know the answer but I knew there was a question."

Defining herself against a history of white teachers who have damaged Aboriginal culture, and at least knowing "the question(s)," Robin could imagine a place for herself within the reserve. Evidently so too could the Aboriginal officials who hired her, but the experience proved difficult. The place and identity of teacher she imagined as home was not easy to create.

At the time of the visit Robin was planning to leave the community and she declared herself unsuccessful. When asked what advice she would have for other white women considering a teaching job on a Northern reserve, she stated: "I think they should really think about why they want to be there. Think of their motives for coming. But really there's no way to prepare for this. No way. If they're coming for the money they will probably be more successful than I am, but I don't want them here." Robin did not directly name what for her would constitute success. She did name and describe incidents in which her fears of damaging Aboriginal culture, of becoming or being positioned as racist, came into the fore. What haunts many of these incidents is the historical legacy of Lady Bountiful and white Lady Traveler.

The White Mother-Teacher and the Transient Teacher

As cited at the outset of this paper, Robin found a personal identity as white and in particular white and oppressor disconcerting. Having defined herself against a construct of white dominant society, to be viewed within this construct left her questioning her own identity within this construct — "how white am I?" She questioned her own complicity within practices that have supported white imperialism and racism. Comparing herself with other whites in the community she did believe she offered something different and was hurt and dismayed by her inability to be differentiated from this construct of whiteness. Over the course of the interviews she described numerous incidents where this lack of differentiation was particularly painful. She pointed to official discourses in the community: "We're actually not considered a part of the community—the white people. In all official LEA [Local Education Authority] documents we're defined as transients: the hospital staff, the teaching staff, some of the workers at the Northern Store." Robin did not see nor want to be seen as transient. While she was told by her male white colleagues that white women rarely stay and realized that for all intents and purposes the white population is transient, she expected some space to be viewed outside of this identity.

Another incident involved a meeting organized by school authorities to deal with school violence. During this meeting non-Natives teachers were asked to leave. This caused agitation among everyone, and eventually the teachers were invited back in. Robin found this very distressing. She described the event:

They have been trying to get this behaviour code for years but no one from the community will ever show up to meetings. The teachers feel like they're working on a battleground. We need that document. And the first thing to come out of superintendent's mouth is that teachers should not have any part at all—sorry, white teachers should not have any part at all helping in drawing up this document. It was a slap in the face. And he prefaced that by saying these teachers are transients. He reiterated that. 'Teachers are not part of the community. They will not stay; they will be gone, and we will be left.' Which I can sort of understand and I agree that it has to come from the community, but we're going to be the ones to enforce the rules, plus a lot of parents don't know what's going on in the school ... We care about students and we're working with them. We know what's going in the day-to-day operation of the school.

At this point she saw no space to define herself in the community, outside of a transient identity, no acknowledgment of the relationship of the teacher to students. Although white teachers were permitted back into the meeting, the incident remained for Robin a "slap in the face." The nature of the insult is more apparent when Robin speaks about another incident involving a primary school teacher:

There was a primary teacher here last year who at one point referred to her students as my kids, 'oh my kids doing this.' I do that. J— does that. We all do that. And a parent overheard it and freaked out and it was a very big thing. And that teacher was sat down and there was meetings. The community was really upset when they found out because they are not your kids and don't you ever think they are your kids ... I have a really hard time not being emotionally involved with my students—not caring about them but I know that's not welcomed.

The desire to be the mother-teacher neglects the history and racial construction of the "white" mother-teacher and her contemporary and historical relationship with Aboriginal students and their communities. This local incident plays out a power struggle between the white mother-teacher and the Aboriginal mother over her children that is occurring on a larger scale as First Nation peoples seek greater control over the education of their children. In the history of Aboriginal education it has been the white transient female and male teachers who, as agents of the Federal government, have been central in the educational decisions for and about Aboriginal children. It is a difficult position to relinquish. Lady Bountiful and the white Lady Traveler are seductive images. It is difficult to resist the desire to be central in someone's life, and to be given the illusion of transcending one's social and historical location and one's own privilege to "know" and "help" others. And it is predictable that there is guilt, as Robin comments:

I know it's going to be really, really hard to leave this place. There's a lot of guilt associated with leaving here. I can never promise my students that I'm going to be here for them. I could never promise that I'll be here next year. Some ask for

this. Some want to but are too afraid because they don't get it. A lot of the hatred
they feel for us is because we do go.

For Robin and the other white teachers and, most importantly, for Aboriginal children and their communities, there needs to be another white
teacher identity in the North. As long as white women continue to teach in
aboriginal communities, a new relationship between white women teachers
and their students needs to be forged. This begins with making visible the
history and discursive constructions that have affected and continue to affect the social and political terrain.

Conclusion: Teacher Education

I have learned to take risks. As a non-Native person focusing on First Nations
education, I have come to accept myself and the work I do as part of what has
become my culture—a culture of the border...I have found justification for my
work in terms of efforts to work by the side of the oppressed to combat racism...This
border world has become my home. (Celia Haig-Brown, 1995, pp. 238-239)

What is the education that white women teachers need in order to do do
border work successfully— to find a home in the border world, as Celia
Haig-Brown describes. It may be that at this time white teachers will not
find a home, albeit a problematic one, in the North. That is, they will not be
able to negotiate an identity with themselves or with others in these contexts. Their work and their lives will need to be located elsewhere. But
North is everywhere, that is, the situation of white teachers teaching in
minority contexts can be found in many urban and rural centres in southern
as well as in northern Canada, so that the need to provide a rearticulated
white teacher identity is pressing. A faculty of education in its preservice
program might be a site where an intense rearticulation of teacher identity
can occur. In the case of white women, this rearticulation may be possible
if programs include opportunities for engagement with: 1) postmodern
notions and processes of identity, displacement, and home; 2) the history
and discursive construction of white women teachers; 3) the histories and
strategies of negotiating identity, collectively and individually; and 4) the
rewriting of Lady Bountiful and the white Lady Traveler in the texts of the
lives of professors, teachers, and students. All of this should be done in
consultation with minority communities. What is also required is ongoing
education and support of those teachers who are seeking ways to redefine
the nature of teacher identity in order create better a better education expe-

riences for their students and their communities.

While respecting the efforts of First Nations communities to hire their own teachers and accepting the possibility that Robin may well have been replaced by an aboriginal teacher with more intimate knowledge of the community and its culture, I believe that in the meantime she could have offered much to her students, if she had been given support. On the part of the Faculty of Education, I think a more overtly political teacher education program, more intensely engaged with issues of equity and social justice, and the rewriting and renegotiation of teacher identity both individually and collectively, would have helped her immensely.

As the racial, cultural, and linguistic diversity in all our school populations increases, the need for such a program becomes all the more critical. Without it, white women teachers may continue to become Lady Bountifuls and white Lady Travelers, at best conflicted, at worst blindly reinscribing colonial purposes and aims in Canadian classrooms.

Notes

1. Robin is pseudonym.

References

Ashworth, M. (1993). *Children of the Canadian mosaic: A brief history to 1950.* Toronto: OISE Press.

Bassett, I. (1975). Introduction. In E. Murphy's *Janey Canuck in the West* (1975 ed). Toronto: McClelland and Steward Ltd.

Battiste, M. & Barman, J. (1995). *First Nations education in Canada: The circle unfolds.* Vancouver: UBC Press.

Bird, I. (1879). *A lady's life in the Rocky Mountains.* London: John Murray.

Blunt, A. & Rose, G. (1994).*Writing women and space: Colonial and postcolonial geographies.* New York: Guilford Press.

Canadian Teachers Federation (1993). *Progress revisited: The quality of (work) life of women teachers.* Toronto: Canadian Teachers Federation.

Chaudhuri, N. & Strobel, M. (1992). *Western women and imperialism: Complicity and resistance.* Bloomington: Indiana University Press.

Dei, G. (1994). Anti-racist education: Working across difference. *Orbit, 25,* (2), 1-3.

Dei, G. (1995). Integrative anti-racism: Intersection of race, class, and gender. *Race, Gender and Class, 2,* (3), 11-30.

Dryer, R. (1988). White. *Screen, 29,* (4), 44-64.

Ferguson, R. (1990). Introduction: Invisible centre. In R. Ferguson et al. (Eds.) *Out There: Marginalization and Contemporary Culture,* (pp. 9-14). Cambridge: MIT.

Ford-Smith, H. (1992). *ReMaking white ladies: The construction of gendered whiteness in the Caribbean.* Paper presented at the O.I.S.E. 1993.

Giroux, H. (1992). *Border crossings: Cultural workers and the politics of education.* London: Routledge.

Haig-Brown, C. (1995).

Hall, M. (1907). *A woman's trek from Cape to Cairo.*

Harper, H. (in press). Difference and diversity in Ontario schools. *Canadian Journal of Education.*

Harper, H. & Cavenaugh, S. (1994). Lady bountiful: The white woman teacher in multicultural education. *Women's Education 11,* (2), 27-33.

Healy, W.J. (1923). *Women of Red River.* Winnipeg: Peguis Publishers.

Kirkness, V. *First Nations and schools: Triumphs and struggles.* Toronto: Canadian Education Association.

Kingsley, M. (1887). *Travels in West Africa.* London: MacMillan and Co.

Murphy, E. (1901). *Janey Canuck abroad.* Toronto: McClelland and Steward Ltd.

Murphy, E. (1905). *Janey Canuck in the West.* Toronto: J.M. Dent & Sons.

Prentice, A. (1991). From household to school house: The emergence of the teacher as servant of the state. In R. Heap & A. Prentice (Eds.) *Gender and education in Ontario: An historical reader,* (pp.25-48). Toronto: Scholars' Press.

Traill, C. Parr (1923). *Canadian crusoes: A tale of the Rice Lake plains.* Toronto: McClellan and Steward.

Trollope, J. (1983). *Britannia's daughters: Women of the British empire.* London: Pimlico.

Van Kirk, S. (1980). *Many tender ties: Women in fur-trade society in Western Canada, 1670-1870.* Winnipeg: Watson & Dwyer.

Ware, V. (1992). *Beyond the pale: White women, racism and history.* London: Verso.

CHAPTER EIGHT

The Study of the Construction of White Masculinity in Advertising in Multicultural Education
by Ernest M. Mayes

Advertising is a very powerful visual medium through which many ideas are articulated to the public sphere. Every day, the average American sees a multitude of television commercials and print ads containing images of constructed versions of reality. Moreover, many theorists argue that advertising defines gender roles for men and women (e.g. Barthel, 1988; Williamson, 1978). In the critical analysis of advertising, the stereotypical depiction of women, particularly white women, has been a hot topic for researchers (Yanni, 1990). However, some researchers have started to pay attention to advertising practices involved in the depiction of white males and masculinity.

Jackson Katz (1995) discusses the construction of white masculinity in advertising in the article "Advertising and the Construction of Violent White Masculinity." The author notes that much of the research that has been conducted on racial representation in the media has focused on African Americans, Hispanics, or Asians, but not "Anglo Whites." Katz notes that violence is typically gendered as a male behavioral trait by society. He points out that violent themes are often closely linked to the depiction of white masculinity in advertising. Part of the reason for this is that advertising often stresses differences such as gender, with its imagery:

> Advertising, in a commodity-driven consumer culture, is an omnipresent and rich source of gender ideology. Contemporary ads are filled with images of "danger-

ous"-looking men. Men's magazines and mainstream newsweeklies are rife with ads featuring violent male icons, such as uniformed football players big fisted boxers and leather clad bikers (Katz, 1995, p. 135).

Thus, masculinity is often associated with violence and femininity with passivity. His aim in writing the article was to show how "hegemonic constructions of masculinity in mainstream magazine advertisements normalize male violence" (Katz, 1995, p. 134). He mentions the concept of masculinities which are defined by socioeconomic class, sexual orientation, and racial and ethnic differences. Thus, the author seems to suggest that there is a hierarchy of masculinities with white middle- class males as the hegemonic norm. Moreover, white male masculinity could possibly be viewed as the model for other masculinities to emulate. Overall, he says that more attention should be paid to the construction of violent masculinity in advertising and violent acts committed by boys and men across the country.

It is during childhood and adolescence that conceptions of gender differences are formed psychologically. In the article "Gender Schemata: Individual Differences and Context Effects," Signorella and Lisbeny (1987) discuss the notion of gender schemata in developmental psychology and its role in the development of identity. Gender schemata are described as the "cognitive structures representing information related to gender" (Signorella and Lisben, 1987, p. 1). The authors note it is important to understand that the formation of gender identity occurs in relation to knowledge of gender-typed traits, activities, occupations, and attitudes. This fact is strongly noted by advertising executives who promote goods aimed at the youth culture in America (Goulart, 1969). Thus, the examination of sex role stereotyping in advertising is very important, because advertisers develop their marketing campaigns using strategies that reinforce gender segmentation to sell products (Carlsson-Paige, 1990).

It is very important that students become aware of the nature of advertising as a constructed system of intended meaning. The relationship between the viewer and the advertisement is very complex. Shields (1990) states that visual texts can replicate dominant cultural discourses concerning race, ethnicity, sexual orientation, class, age, and gender. Moreover, she points out that the average person participates in the process of interpretation when looking at visual texts, such as advertisements:

> Meaning is not found intricately woven into the fabric of the text to be unearthed
> by a trained scholar, nor is the meaning of a text to be defined solely in individual
> psyches. The ability of a visual text to communicate meaning involves an intri-
> cate interplay between the codes and messages encoded into the text at the time of
> its production and the cultural experience and subjectivity the spectator brings to
> the viewing of that image (Shields, 1990, p. 25).

Correlations can be made between the positioning of a given product
in an advertisement and the social values of our society (Wernick, 1991). It
has been theorized by researchers that advertisers use the nuances of ideology in relation to culture in order to influence consumers to purchase their
products.   Ideology has been termed as a level of reality, subjective and
objective, at which humans orient meaningfully to their world, collectively
and individually.   It can encompass the symbols, values, cosmologies, norms,
and ideals that are culturally arranged systematically by society (Wernick,
1991, p.23).

Frith (1990) discusses how semiotic analysis can be used as an ad-
equate tool for examining cultural values in advertising.   She argues that
ads are not merely sales tools, but cultural artifacts that shape human consciousness and reflect the values and mores of society.   She notes that a
method developed by Gillian Dyer is very useful in decoding advertisements.   Dyer (1982) developed the method for the textual analysis of advertisements from techniques used in art criticism by Erwin Panofsky.
Panofsky used iconographic analysis to study the imagery and symbols in
paintings. Most importantly, Panofsky discusses the idea of three levels of
meaning that can be ascertained from paintings as a form of visual communication: denotative, connotative, and ideological. Dyer states that one
can also look at advertisements at these three levels. At the primary level,
one would notice the subject matter of an advertisement. This level would
include the colors displayed, the amount of body copy used, and the figures
and/or models used within the ad. At the next level one would examine the
subject matter in relation to culture, taking into account allegorical imagery, cultural themes, and motifs. The last level involves uncovering cultural ideologies that are present within the advertisement.

A critical analysis of ads in magazines will help students discover themes
associated with white masculinity that are repeated time and time again.
The following are themes that students may discover along with ads that
are explicative of them The ads are briefly analyzed using semiotics.

Theme 1. The equation of athletics with technological progress

The first ad is for the Power IDE from Future Domain computer software company. It appeared in the December 1995 issue of *Windows Sources*. Most ads for technological products have only white male models. Very often in ads, technological advancement is associated only with whiteness. This one features two white male models, one a body builder and the other an average-looking guy. The body builder is shown wearing bright red gym shorts and matching shirt. However, the other meeker model is shown in flannel boxer shorts and a plain white T-shirt. The average-looking guy is here used symbolically to represent outdated computer software. The software he stands for is noted in the copy as being "feeble" and "slow." The viewer may interpret that the average looking model also has those characteristics, because he looks like a stereotypical nerd. On the other hand, the software that the bodybuilder stands for is noted as having "real muscle." Thus, the Power IDE is better because it is "stronger."

The second ad appeared in the May 1995 issue of *Details*, and it is for the Tacoma truck from Toyota. The ad depicts two Toyota trucks juxtaposed in a beach setting with wind surfboarders sailing on a nearby lake. The headline reads: "The Arrival of the Fittest." In an inset, the engine inside the truck is shown with the following copy: "New powerful 190-hp 3.4 V6 engine outmuscles the competitor's best and biggest V6's." Moreover, the body copy reads: "Stronger. Faster. Better. That's the GOAL of every competitor. To OUTPERFORM the field. To be the BEST there is." Thus, it appears as if technological progress is being equated with athletic competion.

Theme 2. Masculinity indicated by the sexual conquest of women

This next ad which appeared in the Spring 1995 issue of Esquire Gentleman, is for Bernini cologne. It features a female model lying on a bed, whose face is shown in profile. The model is apparently naked, because she is barely wrapped in bedsheets. The copy of the ad reads: "Sometimes she recalled his scent so vividly, she would lie there, aroused by her own imaginings." The imagery in this ad alludes to the notion that sexual prowess is necessary for a man to be considered truly masculine. The ad also attempts to tie the usage of this product to sexual virility, because the model has been overwhelmed by the sexual prowess of her lover (i.e. the smell of his cologne).

Theme 3. The depiction of the white male as violent predator/hunter

The next ad, for Tippman paintball guns, appeared in the January 1996 issue of *Action Pursuit Games*. Several images of different models paint ball guns are shown, with brief discriptions of their capabilities. For example, one gun featured has an "optional sniper barrel." Paintball activities are similar to military war games in which opposing teams hunt each other with guns and fire paint pellets at one another to mark a target strike. Very often, the color red is used to simulate blood. Ads for real guns would never be able to point out that they could be used to shoot people, but an ad for a paintball gun can. The copy reads: "While other kids in Indiana were playing basketball, the Tippmanns were making the woods a terrible place to be." The prey in this ad are men who participate in these paintball activities. In the ad, a close-up of the face of a startled paintball gunman is shown in front of blurred tree limbs. With this weaponry, enemies from the opposing units can be neutralized easily, as the copy suggests: "So it's not surprising that when the dust settles, you can bet the last person standing is holding a Tippmann."

In conclusion, the study of the construction of white masculinity in advertising in multicultural education would be helpful to all students. As stated earlier, the majority of the critical analysis of ads has focused only on women or minorities. Unfortunately, the concerns of minority groups may be studied, but not practiced in the classroom. Many times minorities at predominantly white universities are singled out to discuss racial issues by their professors. Moreover, minorities often have to "sever identification with their minority group" in order to attain success at these institutions (Kincheloe, 1995, p. 152). In a classroom setting, the examination of the depiction of white males in advertising can help students explore whiteness in relation to many issues, including whiteness as a social norm, cryptoracism, white privilege, the invisibility of whiteness, white anger, and racism.

References

Barthel, D. (1988). *Putting on appearances: Gender and advertising.* Philadelphia: Temple University Press.

Carlsson-Paige, N., & Levin, D. (1990). *Who's calling the shot?: How to respond effectively to children's fascination with play and war toys.* Philadelphia: New Society.

Dyer, G. (1982). *Advertising as communication.* New York: Methuen, Inc.

Frith, K., T. (1990). "Undressing advertisements: A technique for analyzing social and cultural messages," presented at the 1990 Association of Education in Journalism and Mass Communication Conference.

Goulart, R. (1969). *The assault on childhood.* Los Angeles: Sherbourne Press, Inc.

Katz, J. (1995). Advertising and the construction of violent white masculinity. In G. Dines & J.M. Humez (Eds.), *Gender, race and class in media.* London: Sage Publications.

Kincheloe, J. L. (1995). *Toil and trouble: Good work, smart workers, and the integration of academic and vocational education.* New York: Peter Lang.

Shields, V. (1990). Advertising visual images: Gendered ways of seeing and looking. *The Journal of Communication Inquiry ,14,* 25-39.

Signorella, M. L., & Lisben, L. (1987). *Children's gender schemata.* San Francisco: Jossey-Bass.

Wernick, A. (1991). *Promotional culture: Advertising, ideology and symbolic expression.* Newbury Park, CA: Sage Publications.

Williamson, J. (1978). *Decoding advertisements: ideology and mean-*

CHAPTER NINE

Developing a Pedagogy of Whiteness in the Context of a Postcolonial Hybridity: White Identities in Global Context
Peter McLaren

In a pedagogy of whiteness, critical multiculturalists attempt to un-settle both conservative assaults on multiculturalism and liberal paradigms of multiculturalism; the latter in my view simply repackage conservative and neo-liberal ideologies under a discursive mantle of diversity. In un-dertaking such a project, I have tried in a modest way to advance a critical pedagogy of whiteness that will serve a form of postcolonial hybridity.

It is true that the concept of hybridity has been used in a powerful way to counter essentialized attempts at creating monolithic and "authentic" forms of identity (McLaren, 1995; Hicks, 1991). However, Fusco rightly reminds us:

> Too often...the postcolonial celebration of hybridity has been interpreted as the sign that no further concern about the politics of representation and cultural exchange is needed. With ease, we lapse back into the integrationist rhetoric of the 1960s, and conflate hybridity with parity. (1995, p. 76)

Since not all hybridities are equal, we must attach to the term an ideo-logical tacit nominal qualifier. In making this assertion, Ragagopalan Radhakrishnan (1996)provides us with an important qualification. He main-tains that we should distinguish between a metropolitan version of hybrid-ity and postcolonial hybridity. Whereas the former is a ludic form of ca-pricious self-styling, the latter is a critical identitarian mode. Metropoli-tan hybridity, notes Radhakrishnan, is "characterized by an intransitive and immanent sense of jouissance" while postcolonial hybridity is marked by a "frustrating search for constituency and a legitimate political identity" (1996, p. 159). Metropolitan hybridity is not "subjectless" or neutral but is a structure of identitarian thinking informed by the cultural logic of the dominant West. Postcolonial hybridity, on the other hand, seeks authenticity in "a third space that is complicitous neither with the deracinating imperatives of Westernization nor with theories of a static, natural, and single-minded autochthony" (p. 162). It is within such a perspective that educators are called to create una pedagogía fronteriza.

Critical multiculturalism (Kincheloe and Steinberg, 1997) as a point of intersection with a critical pedagogy of whiteness supports the struggle for a postcolonial hybridity. Gómez-Peña captures the concept of postcolonial hybridity when he conceptually maps what he calls the "New World Border":

> ...a great trans- and intercontinental border zone, a place in which no centers remain. It's all margins, meaning there are no "others," or better said, the only true "others" are those who resist fusion, mestizaje, and cross-cultural dialogue. In this utopian cartography, hybridity is the dominant culture; Spanish, Franglé, and Gringoñol are linguas francas; and monoculture is a culture of resistance practiced by a stubborn or scared minority. (1996, p.7)

A revolutionary multiculturalism must engage what Enrique Dussel (1993) calls "the Reason of the Other." The debates over modernity and postmodernity have a different set of valences in Latinoamerica for los olvidados, for the peripheralized, for the marginalized, and for the wretched of the earth. Dussel writes about this distinction, from his own Latin American context:

> Unlike the postmodernists, we do not propose a critique of reason as such; but we do accept their critique of a violent, coercive, genocidal reason. We do not deny the rational kernel of the universalist rationalism of the Enlightenment, only its irrational moment as sacrificial myth. We do not negate reason, in other words, but the irrationality of the violence generated by the myth of modernity. Against postmodernist irrationalism, we affirm the "reason of the Other." (p. 75)

Whites need to do more than remember the history of colonialism as it affected the oppressed; they need to critically re-member such history. As Homi Bhabha (1986, p. xxiii) reminds us: "Remembering is never a quiet act of introspection or retrospection. It is a painful re-membering, a putting together of the dismembered past to make sense of the trauma of the present." This means piercing the vapors of mystification surrounding the objectification of human relations within bourgeois consciousness in order to construct new forms of subjectivity and agency that operate within a socialist political imaginary.

What I am advocating is a revolutionary multiculturalism, a critical pedagogy of whiteness, that moves beyond the ludic, metrocentric focus on identities as hybrid and hyphenated assemblages of subjectivity that exist alongside or outside of the larger social totality. Revolutionary multiculturalism, as I am articulating the term, takes as its condition of possibility the capitalist world system; it moves beyond a monoculturalist multiculturalism that fails to address identity formation in a global context, and focuses instead on the idea that identities are shifting, changing, over-lapping, and historically diverse (Shohat, 1995). Revolutionary multiculturalism is a politics of difference that is globally interdependent and raises questions about intercommunal alliances and coalitions. According to Ella Shohat, intercommunal coalitions are based on historically shaped affinities, and the multicultural theory that underwrites such a coalitionary politics needs "to avoid either falling into essentialist traps or being politically paralyzed by deconstructionist formulations" (1995, p. 177). Shohat articulates the challenge as follows:

> Rather than ask who can speak, then, we should ask how we can speak together, and more important, how we can move the dialog forward. How can diverse communities speak in concert? How might we interweave our voices, whether in chorus, in antiphony, in call and response, or in polyphony? What are the modes of collective speech? In this sense, it might be worthwhile to focus less on identity as something one 'has,' than on identification as something one 'does.' (1995, p. 177)

Revolutionary multiculturalism recognizes that the objective structures in which we live, the material relations tied to production in which we are situated, and the determinate conditions that produce us, are all reflected in our everyday lived experiences. In other words, lived experiences constitute more than subjective values, beliefs, and understandings; they are always mediated through ideological configurations of discourses, political economies of power and privilege, and the social division of labor. Revolutionary multiculturalism is a socialist-feminist multiculturalism that challenges the historically sedimented processes through which race, class, and gender identities are produced within capitalist society. Therefore, revolutionary multiculturalism is not limited to transforming attitudinal discrimination, but is dedicated to reconstituting the deep structures of political economy, culture, and power in contemporary social arrangements. It is not about reforming capitalist democracy but rather transforming it by cutting it at its joints and then rebuilding the social order from the vantage point of the oppressed.

Revolutionary multiculturalism must not only accommodate the idea of capitalism, it must also advocate a critique of capitalism and a struggle against it. The struggle for liberation on the basis of race and gender must not remain detached from anticapitalist struggle. Often the call for diversity and pluralism by the apostles of postmodernism is a surrender to the ideological mystifications of capitalism. The fashionable apostasy of preaching difference from the citadels of postmodernist thought has dissolved resistance into the totalizing power of capitalist exploitation. In this regard, Ellen Meiksins Wood rightly warns:

> We should not confuse respect for the plurality of human experience and social struggles with a complete dissolution of historical causality, where there is nothing but diversity, difference and contingency, no unifying structures, no logic of process, no capitalism and therefore no negation of it, no universal project of human emancipation. (1995, p. 263)

The challenge is to create at the level of everyday life a commitment to solidarity with the oppressed and an identification with past and present struggles against imperialism, against racism, against sexism, against homophobia, against all those practices of unfreedom associated with living in a white supremacist capitalist society. As participants in such a challenge, we become agents of history by living the moral commitment to freedom and justice, by maintaining a loyalty to the revolutionary domain of possibility, and by creating a collective voice out of the farthest reaching "we"—one that unites all those who suffer under capitalism, patriarchy, racism, and colonialism throughout the globe.

Subaltern ethnicities can become a focal point for a critique of Enlightenment rationality and its stress on universalizing Western notions of sameness and difference. They can also become a pivot position from which to challenge the structuring of intersubjective relations by global white supremacist patriarchal capitalism. In this case, the illusion of symmetrical intersubjectivity is countered from the standpoint epistemology of the oppressed. As Linda Martin Alcoff (1996) notes, identity in this case does not constitute an opposition to sameness but rather an opposition of substance to absence—of having an identity to not having an identity. Identity can give a person substantive visibility in a world that tries to make her invisible. Yet there is another way of situating agency that is not compatible with ethnic identification but which becomes important in developing a coalitional politics of anticapitalist struggle. I believe that this concept of agency—agency as singularity—is also important in developing forms of critical agency as a counterpraxis of resistance to the globalization of capital and consumer ethics.

While identity politics can provide points around which a counter hegemonic politics can coalesce, there exists the frequent problem of essentialized identities and the difficulty of developing necessary coalitions among new social movements that do not rely on the modernist logic of difference and a humanist conception of the subject. Because identity politics largely relies on a modernist logic of difference, we strongly need to consider a rethinking of agency that does not rely on identity politics to mount a challenge to the dominate social order. This suggests approaching the concept of subjectivity as a position from which one experiences the world and thus as a "contextually produced epistemological value" (Grossberg, 1996 p. 98) that is "always inscribed or distributed within cultural codes of differences that organize subjects by defining social identities" (p. 99). Such an understanding of subjectivity can lead to a theory of Otherness based on positivity and effectivity rather than negatively defined difference. In this sense, agency has more to do with identifications or affiliations than with ethnicity. Whereas subjectivity operates in terms of the types of experience that are available, agency has to do with "a distribution of acts" (Grossberg, 1996, p. 102). The questions surrounding agency that need to be asked by a critical pedagogy of whiteness include: What are the forms of agency that school can make available to individuals and groups? How can subject positions and identities be articulated into specific fields of activity and along particular vectors?

I agree with Larry Grossberg (1996) that agency may be more a matter of "singular belonging" than structures of ethnic or political membership, and more the case of an "elective community" that exists within the "structured mobilities" of everyday life. In my view, agency cannot easily be conflated with questions of cultural identity in the sense that it marks not a modernist subject agent of liberal humanism but rather a place where one acts practically and tactfully and with revolutionary purpose. Agency has to do with the spatial relations of places and how people are distributed within them.

Grossberg notes that oftentimes a politics of ethnic identity is grounded in a modernist logic of difference in which the "other" is defined by its negativity and which gives rise to a politics of resentment. What is necessary, therefore, is to develop a theory of agency in which culture is not grounded in the idea of difference and the logic of individuality but rather is viewed as productive. Secondly, this calls for educators to move beyond the modernist concept of the subject-agent underwritten by a liberal humanism. The alternative, according to Grossberg (1996), "is to begin to construct a theory of otherness which is not essentialist, a theory of positivity based on notions of effectivity, belonging and, as Paul Gilroy (1993) describes it, 'the changing same' (Grossberg, 1996, p. 97). Grossberg argues that agency is not so much a question of cultural identity built around a modernist logic of difference and individuality but rather a matter of spatial relations built upon a logic of temporality and overlapping mobilities. Grossberg notes:

> The question of agency is, then, how an access and investment or participation (as a structure of belonging) are distributed within particular structured terrains. At the very least, this suggests that agency as a political problem cannot be conflated with issues of cultural identity or of epistemological possibilities. In other words, agency is not so much the 'mark of a subject, but the constituting mark of an abode? (1996, p.100).

My notion of a pedagogy of whiteness is not to decry identity politics. Identity politics is undeniably important in assisting ethnic groups to resist oppressive relations within a white supremacist capitalist patriarchy. My fundamental concern is organizing revolutionary praxis and social transformation productively around the revolutionary pivot points of anticapitalist struggle in which agency is neither limited to nor does it exclude-agential spaces of ethnic struggle. In my view, collective agency needs to be produced within spaces of mobility and belonging articulated within the spacial and temporal axes of resistive and transformative power. Here it is important to emphasize that social agency must be rethought within a criticalist project of revolutionary transformation in such a way that does not discursively privilege an economic determinism that universalizes the historical inevitability of labor and the economy and that relegates individual identity to a bourgeois swindle of fulfillment. Further, social agency (race, class, gender, sexuality, nationality) needs to be understood not as a form of economic overdetermination but rather as the product of social relations that are constitutive of the agency of class. That is, social agency needs to be analyzed within the contextual specificity of its historical effects. I am maintaining that cultural, political, and economic processes are mutually constitutive of social agency, as agency can be more productively read as an historically specific confluence of discursive and material processes. In this context a pedagogy of whiteness cannot be separated from issues of globalization, economic imperialism, and the complex politics of human agency.

Critical agency formulated both as a singularity linked to place and as a form of critical ethnicity are necessary for the development of a counterpraxis capable of challenging both local and globalized forms of white patriarchal capitalism and hegemonic articulations of white identity. At times we must allow our faith in revolutionary praxis to overwhelm the cynical reason of our age, a reason that lies halfway between wakefulness and a fitful sleep, a reason that contributes to ensuring the asymmetry of power between the rich and the poor. We must advance toward an unconditional assent to struggle, to victory, to life.

Notes

* Sections of this text appear in *Multiculturalism* (in press) *Educational Foundations* (in press) and Peter McLaren. *Revolutionary Multiculturalism*. Boulder, Colorado: Westview Press, 1997.

References

Alcoff, L., M. (1996). Philosophy and racial identity. *Radical Philosophy*, (75), Jan/Feb, 5-14.

Bhabha, H. (1986). Remembering Fanon. In F., Fanon, *Black Skin, White Masks*. (foreword). London: Pluto Press.

Dussel, E. (1993). Eurocentrism and m. *Boundary 2, 20* (3), 65-77.

Fusco, C. (1995). *English is broken here: Notes on cultural fusion in the americas*. New York: The New Press.

Grossberg, L. (1996). Identity and cultural studies: Is that all there is? In S. Hall & P. DuGay (Eds.), *Questions of cultural identity*. London: Thousand Oaks Sage, 87-107.

Gómez-Peña, G. (1996). *The new world border*. San Francisco, CA: City Lights Bookstore.

Hicks, Emily. (1991). *Border writing*. Minneapolis, MN: University of Minnesota Press.

Kincheloe, J. & Steinberg, S. (1997). *Changing multiculturalism: New times, new curriculum*. London: Open University Press.

McLaren, P. (1995). *Critical pedagogy and predatory culture*. London & New York: Routledge.

McLaren, P. (1997). *Revolutionary multiculturalism: Pedagogies of dissent for the new millennium*. Boulder, CO: Westview Press.

Radhakrishnan, R. (1996). *Diasporic mediations*. Minneapolis, MN & London: University of Minnesota Press.

Shohat, E. (1995). The struggle over representation: Casting, coalitions, and the politics of identification. In R. de la Campa, E. Kaplan & M. Sprinker, (Eds.), *Late Imperial Culture*, 166-178. London & New York: Verso.

Wood, E. M. (1995). *Democracy against capitalism: Renewing historical materialism*. Cambridge, United Kingdom: Cambridge University Press.

CHAPTER TEN

The Making and Unmaking of Whiteness, Gender, and Class in College Classrooms [1]
Frances Maher and Mary Kay Thompson Tetreault

> All of us felt so wholesome after we cleaned ourselves on her. We were so beautiful when we stood astride her ugliness. Her simplicity decorated us, her guilt sanctified us, her pain made us glow with health ... Her inarticulateness made us believe we were eloquent. Her poverty kept us generous. Even her waking dreams we used, to silence our own nightmares. [2]
>
> —Toni Morrison

This quote from Toni Morrison's novel, *The Bluest Eye*, shows how people construct themselves through demonizing and exorcising the figure of the "other," in this case a powerless black girl called Pecola Breedlove. Throughout the novel Morrison offers illustrations of the ways in which dichotomizing white as the norm and black as different shape notions of gender and class in the African American world, and by extension in the white world as well. When Morrison made "our" beauty contingent on Pecola's ugliness, or our generosity contingent on her poverty, she was emphasizing the ideological and cultural freight of associating white standards of beauty with virtue and truth, the "normal" against which the "other" is demonized, or disappears. Her work has illuminated the ways in which white norms of beauty, sexuality, and motherhood operate in discourses of gender, as well as the ways in which assumptions of whiteness operate in discourses of class and other forms of domination.

Remembering these insights prompted us to examine the racialization of femininity and sexual attractiveness in classes in our recently published book, *The Feminist Classroom*.³ In this chapter, we return to the classrooms we studied to see the dynamics of the cultural production of whiteness in shaping the discussions of gender and class. Agreeing with scholars who have observed that whiteness is both assumed and continually in need of assertion, always being constituted as it was simultaneously being challenged and resisted, we decided to focus on what happens in classrooms where the majority of students are white. We found that even when issues of gender and class identity were the ostensible topics of discussion, they played out against the backdrop of the assumption that *everyone* was white. What role does this assumption play in white students' construction of their own places within gender and class as well as racial hierarchies?

In our subsequent reanalysis of the data we gathered for *The Feminist Classroom*, we found that exploring the theme of positionality became the most salient theme in understanding our own whiteness as well as that of the students. Positionality is the concept advanced by postmodern and other feminist thinkers that validates knowledge only when it includes attention to the knower's position in any specific context.⁴ While position is always defined by gender, race, class, and other significant dimensions of societal domination and oppression, it is also always evolving, context dependent, and relational, in the sense that constructs of "female" create and depend on constructs of "male"; "black" and the term "of color" are articulated against ideas of "white." Thus people's locations within these networks are susceptible to critique and change when they are explored rather than ignored, individualized, or universalized.

In this spirit of critique, we began our explorations of the role of whiteness in shaping the construction of knowledge in the college classroom shortly after the book was published. In this essay, as well as others, we have taken up different aspects of this issue.⁵ Our thinking has been shaped throughout by writers and scholars such as Toni Morrison, David Roediger, Elizabeth Ellsworth, Andrew Hacker, and Karen Sacks who have variously explored the cultural constructions of the categories "white" and "black," or "white" and "of color." Although from different disciplines, these writers all challenge the assumption that racial differences are "natural states" deducible from physical characteristics. They assert that these categories of race depend on each other for their elaboration as meaningful entities, as well as for the multiple and evolving significance attached to them.⁶ Whiteness, like maleness, becomes the norm for "human"; it is the often silent and invisible basis against which other racial and cultural identities are named as "other," measured, and marginalized.

Roediger, Sacks, and Hacker show how notions of whiteness change over time, interacting with constructions of nationality and class and how class hierarchies are reproduced through racial positionings. Roediger explores ways in which nineteenth-century white workers learned to depend for their self-definition on their sense of themselves as white by defining themselves against black slaves and freedmen.[7] The concept of who was white also changed to include successive groups of European immigrants, just as immigrants themselves changed to fit into some concept of whiteness. Indeed to become white has often been constructed as synonymous with becoming truly American. America's larger systems of racial formation often confounded religion and race as well. For example, Hacker observes that Irish-Catholic immigrants took longer to shed an alien identity because Catholics were not regarded as altogether white, and Jews were kept at the margin of white America because they were not Christians.[8] Further, Sacks shows how this concept of whiteness evolved as Jews "became white folks" following World War II. Roediger asserts that "the central implication of the insight that race is socially constructed is the specific need to attack whiteness as a destructive ideology rather than to attack the concept of race abstractly."[9] In other words, the concept of whiteness itself operates as an unseen but powerful system of dominance that must be uncovered in order to get at the operations of racism in our society.

As we turn now to use theories of whiteness and positionality as lenses to reexamine some of our classroom portraits, we will be able to see more clearly how whiteness was constructed, and how that construction shaped the discourse of gender and class. Our examples will reflect class discussions in which whiteness is assumed as a normal condition of life rather than a privileged position within networks of power. It appears to be a safe, well-marked path, powerful because it is an invisible one to whites, which allows discussions of race to slide effortlessly forward as notations of features of "the other."

Constructing Social Class as White and Male

We turn first to the ways white males constructed their masculinity and class positions, using the assumption of whiteness as part of their guiding ideological framework. The first course we look at is a senior seminar in Literary Theory, at a small liberal arts college. Nine students were enrolled, five males and four females, all white, several of whom were in their late twenties to mid-thirties.[10] This discussion from which the following excerpt is drawn concerned the ideas of a prominent French feminist, Julia Kristeva, as analyzed in Toril Moi's book, *Sexual/Textual Politics*.[11] The initial focus on Kristeva was "derailed" when the professor, who is white, used "class" to show how the same term can have different meanings.

Her comment led to an extended argument about whether women could be seen as a class; two males fought vigorously against the idea, and one female defended it. Ralph, who referred to himself as a "former SDSer," began this debate by saying, "I'm rejecting sexes as defined as classes; I think classes are defined by economics."[12] Jane, who was in her late twenties, replied: "Right, and economics are defined by gender." Ralph's next remarks- that "gender is defined by economics," that "it has less to do with you know, sexual oppression in itself as it does [with] power, or acquisition, or ownership," made Jane bristle. She responded, "That seems so irrelevant to this-you argue that it's power and acquisition, but the fact of the matter is a high majority of women are making less money [than men]." Ned came to Ralph's defense, asserting at one point that "if you look at gender, you will see all women as being oppressed," implying that all women are not oppressed in economic terms.

These students did not mention race at all as part of their discussion of class analysis, but we can examine how unconscious assumptions about race and gender drove the discussion. Ralph, for example, drew class divisions along both gender and racial lines as well, unconsciously constructing class as both white and male while simultaneously claiming class as the primary oppression. In this discussion, sex belonged only to women; men's gender is not named. Therefore Jane's introduction of gender into the analysis is treated by Ralph and Ned as an introduction of women. When Ralph said, "it has less to do with sexual oppression than power or ownership," he is resisting the introduction of women's oppression into the equation because it muddied the water and because class oppression has no gender (i.e. it is assumed to be male against male.) Jane's earlier comments about working class women's lower wages (when compared to working-class men's wages) led only to a stalemate about whether gender or class is the primary oppression. That stalemate continually reinforces and normalizes the idea that the working class (and the ruling class, too, presumably) is male.

But are the students constructing the working class as white, as well as male? After a while the teacher introduced the concept of positionality to break the stalemate. She said:

> What we need is a description that is not based on categories but on positionality, on relations. No group is in and of itself oppressed or marginal. It's only in relation to something else. So that, women we can say are marginal compared to men. But Black women are marginal compared to white, middle-class women.

> What is perceived as marginal at any given time depends on the position one occupies. You have to see centrality and marginality, oppression, oppressor and oppressed as relational concepts. That is, they are marked by difference, not by any positive kind of thing. (So) you have to keep the whole thing moving.

> Feminism posits itself as a counter to patriarchy. It argues that patriarchy is central and women are marginal. The working class has been fairly ignored in the feminist movement ... Black women's struggles have been marginal to the feminist movement. The feminist movement in this country, by and large, has been white and middle class. So, already they have reinscribed that same center-margin dichotomy within itself.

Ralph then asked his teacher, "What determines White and middle class? I still have problems with this." The teacher responded, "Well, again you have to see it as relational, not a positive kind of term." Ralph then relied, "Well, that is different, then. It is negative, you know."

In our original analysis of this class, we worried that women's oppression could be ignored in the relativism of such an approach. We observed gender oppression being given a back seat to the males' assertion of economic class as the main oppression, which we thought enabled them to ignore the issue of male privilege. We saw male dominance enacted, not only in their vocal domination of the discussion, but also in the way Ned and Ralph collaborated in opposing Jane. Even though we noted that their own position was not critiqued or made visible by either the professor or the students, we also inadvertently equated gender primarily with women.

What we did not see were the powerful ways in which the students and teacher were constructing maleness and whiteness as the norm, both for economic classes and for people in general. While the teacher's use of positionality challenged the students to break out of the categories they were debating and to see them all in relation to each other, race and gender were still presented as sets of complementary opposites and exclusions (women compared with men, Black women compared with white women.)

While the professor called centrality and marginality into question as shifting and relational concepts, "marked by difference, not by any positive kind of thing," she failed to articulate (nor did we pick up) the power relationships that produce these forms of centrality and marginality in the first place, namely whiteness and maleness.

Ralph's class analysis may have been his way of expressing a covert identity politics, one whose central figure is not working people in general, but the working-class white male. If Ralph were to include the perspectives of women and blacks in his construction of the working class, this might challenge the primacy of class oppression, and make the interrelations of class, gender, and race oppression more complex. In a subsequent interview, Ralph reaffirmed his view of the importance of class while continuing to construct it as white and male. He wondered if it would ever be possible to "quantify human needs," and thought that paying attention to gender detracted from human needs. "Once you consider gender issues, you're immediately led to the sword of economic theory ... and I haven't seen any fundamental change in the level of suffering among women." Again, "gender" is "women." He, like Ned, denied his privilege but also feared its loss. Ned told us he preferred Kristeva's call to deconstruct the hierarchies over "feminism's idea of a feminist self," which he viewed as "a limitation on the human self." Better to erase all differences than risk the reversal of the hierarchies that a feminist self implied. Both wished the whole notion of gender would go away, and presumably race as well, because white males, in his formulation, have no gender (and perhaps no race) themselves.

Despite the professor's assertion that "what we need is a description that is not based on categories," this discussion of race presupposed the categories "black" and " white" as a binary opposition, rather than exploring the ways in which, even in this discussion, these categories (as well as the categories "woman" and "man") actively produce each other. Race only entered the picture with the inclusion of "Black women," whereas, like maleness, whiteness had been central to the identity of the working class in this discussion all along. But whiteness, like maleness, had been central to the identity of the working class in this discussion all along. In short, this whole discussion, in which the students resisted the inclusion of race and gender, was profoundly "racialized" and "genderized."

Constructing Whiteness in Individualized Terms

We found this tendency to construct social class in implicitly white and male terms in other discussions in *The Feminist Classroom* as well. Moreover, in one case where whiteness was actually acknowledged, its treatment as an aspect of individual identity worked to mask its operations on deeper social and ideological levels. Our next example comes from an honors freshman writing class of five male and five female students at a large comprehensive university, which, as a state institution, draws upon a less affluent, predominantly white, student body.[13] This discussion treated issues of social class in much more concrete terms than the previous example, perhaps due to the participants' location nearer the bottom of the social class hierarchy. In our book, we described the discussion as reflecting many white students' typical attitudes towards social class, where middle class status is assumed for all white people, leaving the category "poor" as a marker for blacks and avoiding exploration of the wide class differences among white people themselves.

As an introduction to *The Women of Brewster Place*, Gloria Naylor's novel about working class Black women in an urban setting, the professor, a white middle class female, wanted the students to look at the structural elements of class, race and gender oppression, and see how they are interrelated. In response to her question, "Have any of you read any books that talked about social class," the male students (no females spoke) described class in anecdotal terms, telling stories of financial upward mobility. One student contrasted rich people who "can afford to do what they want" with those who have only a "moderate" amount of money, who "cannot just go crazy; they are saving up and investing."

> It's really like a slap in the face, you've got the jobs just because you're Black or Asian, they're not saying you got the job because you're better or more qualified, [but that] we need your minority groups because our supervisor is going to come down on us.

When the teacher later on sought to turn the discussion back to race, we saw one of the rare instances in our data where the construct of race included the idea of whiteness:

The consciousness level in the United States has been raised, where we're much more highly aware of gender issues. Whereas race, white people don't often think of racial identity in terms of their own identity, what it means to be a white person. ... The minority races are much more conscious of who they are. That's not true for whites in America, that the first thing you identify with as "who are you?" is white.

Our original analysis in *The Feminist Classroom* characterized this comment as showing how the teacher "helped her students confront racial issues," and we still associated "race" with African Americans, not whites. Upon further reflection, we see this remark, and indeed this whole discussion, as a vivid example of the extreme individualism in mainstream culture. While the students assert that class position is determined by individual upward mobility, the students also seem to be unconsciously noting structural factors, such as snobbery: "class is what someone else makes it." However, these factors are always experienced in individual terms; "I could not be upper class." This perspective is carried over to their dismissal of Affirmative Action policies as unfair acts of favoritism, a personalized "slap in the face." But again this "slap" is read as coming from "your minority groups;" Blacks are seen not as individuals here but as a group. Yet, because of their construction of Affirmative Action as a threat to their individual mobility rather than a response to a group history of discrimination, they spouted the worst stereotypes about unqualified people getting jobs.

These students tell a familiar narrative of discrimination, one in which they feel simultaneously victimized as individuals by groups from both above and below. However, only the latter group is racialized, and seen as "the other." Whiteness is unconsciously constructed and relied upon here as the social glue normalizing their connection to other, "higher-up" whites, thus stabilizing an inherently unstable situation. The professor could not get her white students to understand the position of Blacks because they didn't understand their own position as whites. Although they understood something of class privilege, through their lack of it, they could not see themselves as privileged within the social relations of race.

We now see that even the teacher's insightful last remark about white racial identity, while ahead of our own thinking at the time, still casts whiteness in individualized rather than structural terms-as an issue of "what it means to be a white person." Indeed, this excerpt illustrates that the acknowledgment of whiteness as an individual attribute does not automatically lead to an expanded understanding of its social structural relations, or of its ideological power; rather, people may acknowledge their whiteness simply as a self-justifying or self-excusing marker of relative personal privilege, and no more. That whiteness is a social construction organizing people into social relations of dominance and oppression, through which some individuals benefit, eluded us at the time as well. Moreover, we now wonder if, among the students who spoke, their exploration of their class and race resentments assumed maleness as another unmarked attribute of their identity, an assumption which would have accounted for the female students' silence in that discussion. Assumptions of whiteness took another form in our next example, however, as students explored issues of femininity and beauty from different, but no less complex, racial/ethnic positions.

Whiteness, Sexuality, and Femininity

One of the most telling examples of the racialization of femininity and sexual attractiveness took place in a course, "Women Writers Since 1800." The class was composed of seventeen women and five men, ranging from freshmen to seniors, and was taught at the same liberal arts college as our first excerpt. The teacher began one class by asking if anyone had written in their journal about Emily Dickinson in response to the discussion of her poetry in the previous class. Nancy, a Japanese American woman who sat at the edge of the room and had not spoken during our previous observations, nodded, and began to read from her journal entry. She based part of her entry on a poem that begins, "I'm Nobody! Who Are You?"[14]

> I couldn't help thinking of the idea of a mute culture within a dominant culture. A "nobody" knowing she's different from the dominant culture keeps silent and is surprised to find out there are others who share this feeling. But they speak only to each other and hide otherwise. This is what it must have been like being a woman and thinking against the grain. But don't tell! At least if you are silent and no one knows, you can continue to live your inner life as you wish, your thoughts at least still belong to you. If "they," the somebody's, find out, they'll advertise and you'll have to become one of them.

Nancy then turned to some comments about Poem 327:[15]

> But looking at this poem it's problematic, there is a price to pay, and it isn't always voluntary. Infinite vision seems to come from suffering through enforced pain. "Before I got my eyes put out I liked as well to see-As other Creatures, that have

Eyes and know no other way." You can run around in ignorant bliss until something breaks through this level of illusion, takes out the "eye" that makes it possible for you to view the world this way and once you see through it, you can't go back, trying to face yourself backwards would "strike you dead." I'm not articulating this well but it's like growing awareness.

A silly example: It's like watching a Walt Disney movie as a child where Hayley Mills and these other girls dance and primp before a party singing "Femininity," how being a woman is all about looking pretty and smiling pretty and acting stupid to attract men. As a child I ate it up, at least it seemed benign, at the most I eagerly studied it. But once your eye gets put out and you realize how this vision has warped you, it would split your heart to try and believe that again, it would strike you dead.

In our interpretation of this class, we concluded that Nancy was rejecting her earlier attempt to model herself on Hayley Mills, a prototypical white American teenager of the 1960s, and embarking on a second rite of passage in which she recognized the harm of modeling herself on such a trite stereotype of American femininity. In the invocations of both Emily Dickinson's poetry and of Hayley Mills, who is young and blond, Nancy's images of femininity and of womanhood are not only images of superficial physical characteristics associated with whiteness, but of female sexuality as well. Neither in the class discussion nor in our original interpretation was this point taken up. By concentrating on her evocation of gender oppression, we allowed Nancy's recognition of the harm of modeling herself on a stereotype of white femininity to pass us by. We also did not see that Hayley Mills' "beauty" depended on Nancy's "otherness" for its intensity. This oversight reveals the extent to which we too had internalized the complex interplay of physical beauty and sexuality that on the one hand primarily constructs femininity as white, and on the other hand fails to understand the extent to which women of color also carry around a white norm of beauty.

Nancy's musings underscore the physical and visual power of race as part of imagining one's appearance to others, and therefore one's effect on others. How does one read and internalize messages of beauty and ugliness, visibility and invisibility, as inscribed on one's body? Feminist theorists have long since taught us the importance of understanding the ways in which women internalize "the male gaze," learning how to see themselves as objects of others' viewpoints rather than subjects of their own construction. We have learned from Nancy the extent to which physical racial identification confers instant ascribed identity, and with it social status. However, since we as white women are often not conscious of our race, we do not experience our bodies as a "raced" as many women of color do.

A subsequent interview with Nancy, who grew up in a Japanese American family in a small Finnish community in the Northwest, "where there were three Japanese families that lived down our little road," leads us to wonder, now, about how much Nancy had in fact internalized white images. As a young Asian American, did she after all identify as "white" most of the time?

> We were the only Japanese family that went to school in a Finnish community. (If) you look at my yearbook, everyone is blond and tall and then there is us. We grew up in this community where we're obviously very different physically, but since we grew up there we didn't really perceive ourselves as very different. Whenever we were among a lot of other Japanese, we would notice that and feel, "Oh, look, everybody's Japanese!"

We are now also struck by the complexity of Nancy's racial identification-"We're obviously very different physically, but we didn't really perceive ourselves as very different." Writers on whiteness like Andrew Hacker, Neil Gotanda, and others have pointed out that one of the most pernicious aspects of American racism has been its rigid construction of anything "nonwhite" as Black. The confusion caused by these dichotomies has left some Asian Americans, for example, identifying as white and others as junior versions of blacks.[16]

The impact of the ideal of "pretty and blond" on Nancy's sense of herself as a woman, and the cost of "living in the roles" of the dominant culture, meant that Nancy had to see herself in terms of Hayley Mills, or not Hayley Mills, before she could construct an alternative vision of who she was. But who "was" she, in terms of "black" and "white"? What are the fault lines and discontinuities that emerge when the category of "whiteness" as description offers up only mixed messages to an Asian-American woman? The vivid, visual nature of the lesson Nancy learned about whiteness is shown in the language she used to name the end of innocence-"how this vision has warped you."

Nancy's use of visual images reminds us that mirrors are also metaphors for showing us how others see us, and therefore for the impositions of ideology and culture into our multilayered consciousness of self. Adrienne Rich wrote about the pain of looking into a mirror and the impossibility of merging the way you see yourself with the ways the outer world experiences you.

> When those who have the power to name and to socially construct reality choose
> not to see you or hear you, whether you are dark-skinned, old, disabled, female, or
> speak with a different accent or dialect than theirs, when someone with the au-
> thority of a teacher, say, describes the world and you are not in it, there is a mo-
> ment of psychic disequilibrium, as if you looked into a mirror and saw nothing.[17]

To reconceptualize the assumptions that construct beauty, as did Nancy, is to claim the possibility and necessity of reconstructing the mirror so that you are in it. As Nancy wrote: "Once you see through it, you can't go back, trying to face yourself backwards would 'strike you dead.'"

Assumptions of Whiteness and Commonalities Among Women

While the previous discussion focused on constructions of "difference" within gender, students in an all female class yearned for ways to identify with all other women, even women who were markedly different in experience and background from themselves. This perspective was heightened, at this historically women's college, by the recent decision to admit men.[18] In the process, however, they first identified race and then suppressed it, engaging in a strategy that legal scholars label as nonrecognition or racial transparency.[19] One student, in a journal entry, approached *Sula* as a narrative of patriarchy, rather than racism. She searched for commonalities between white and black women by exploring one issue of positionality and knowing: how white and African American, lesbian and straight, readers and writers of texts can communicate with each other. The student had written in her journal:

> Barbara Smith [a Black feminist critic] says, Writing about Black women writers
> from a feminist perspective and about Black lesbian writers from any perspective
> at all [is] something dangerous. ... Perhaps it would be less presumptuous and less
> offensive for the white women critics to try to comprehend the feminist or lesbian
> issues within Black women's literature. These ideas and issues may prove to be
> starting points for Black and white women to understand and interpret each other's
> literature more intelligently. ...
>
> One of the issues that Toni Morrison's Sula explores is the value system imposed
> on women by patriarchy and the conflicts between women that arise when women
> defy these value systems. ...While white women can never expect to express a
> total understanding of the Black woman's experience, they can express concern
> and understanding in those areas of Black women's lives and literature that paral-
> lel their own.

In proposing that lesbianism and feminism can help white readers to understand African-American women's literature, the student explicitly positioned the other students with regard to Morrison's two main characters, Sula and Nel, by gender, in effect ignoring Barbara Smith's. At the student's suggestion, the class began discussing lesbianism in the novel. As another student put it, Sula says that no man could ever be the perfect companion, and maybe there is that-that struggle between being heterosexual and lesbian in the relationship between Nel and Sula.

It was not until much later, however, that the issue of race was raised for the first time, as part of the discussion of Sula's character. The class turned to debate whether Sula was acting like a man, and the sole African American student finally broke in to capture a main theme of Morrison's novel: Because each had discovered years before that they were neither white nor male, and that all freedom and triumph was forbidden to them, they had set about creating something else to be. [20] This African American student grappled with Morrison's idea in her comment:

> I think that's a problem because a lot of times we're talking about how they're not men and they're not white, like you know here they are, they're stuck being Black women, you know, this horrible fate, and I think that Sula tried so hard to be a man. ... I don't know, she really has masculine qualities to me, and - it's as if she can't accept herself the way she is. But society's not going to accept her the way she's trying to be.

The student, who had held back during the semester from raising the topic of race, only to do so in this, the last class, was the first person, except for the other student's journal entry, to mention race. The professor took up the African American student's views, acknowledging how tricky, scary, and difficult it is for white middle-class feminists to talk about Black women's writing, especially when they're writing about a community that's not particularly middle class. She then challenged the students to take the position of African-American women for the first time, rather than hiding behind their gender similarities. She elaborated:

> But that's not the whole story. And it's important to keep in mind that racism and sexism are not neat little separate packages, and now we're going to attend to sexism and then later we'll attend to racism maybe makes it twice as large. ... In ways that may not be expectable, a Black woman is going to feel an allegiance to women, and an allegiance to Blacks, that often those two are going to clash, and sometimes she's going to feel an allegiance to both simultaneously. ...

And I've sometimes had the sense in reading some Black women's work ... that
there are certain aspects of these works that in a way seem kind of male identified
(maybe because of) an allegiance to blackness. ... Violence is something that in
some Black women's writing is more acceptable. ... It makes me really uncomfortable - I don't want violence to be acceptable. But how can white women be
sensitive to women of other races if we don't try to at least raise the possibility of
different attitudes toward things that we thought it wasn't possible to have different attitudes toward?

This class revealed the workings of racial nonrecognition. The journal
writer initially positioned herself as a white woman, and by extension everyone else in the room but the African American student. Despite efforts
at racial neutrality, there was an underlying assumption of a white norm
and the black other. Implicit in their discussion of Sula and Nel was the
assumption of commonalities of gender experience among all women that
left uncomplicated, and glossed over, differences among white women and
between white and black women. This suppression of race continued until
the African American student's remark about Nel and Sula stuck being Black
women. After the student made race explicit, the professor challenged the
white students to notice race for the first time rather than suppressing it.

The professor reproduced, however, the dominant culture's practice of
focusing on the race of African-Americans rather than whites. She spoke of
the dominant culture's bifurcation of African American women by con-
trasting their allegiance to women on the one hand and to blacks on the
other. Her analysis of the interaction of racism and sexism with regard to
black women did not include a similar analysis for white women, nor ways
in which white women are male identified. What was left unexplored was
white women's relationship to white men in the service of racial privilege.
The different attitudes of black women rather than those of white women
became the problem. This separation of the woman from the color, to para-
phrase Chinosole, one of our professor informants from San Francisco State,
most likely reinforced the white students' views of gender, race, and sexual
orientation as fixed and separate categories of identity, even though the
teacher emphasized that they interacted and were not additive quantities. In
her response, the professor struggled for a way to mark and appreciate that
her own attitudes, not Morrison's, might be the different ones that ought to
be examined.

This discussion illustrates a phase in white feminist theory where women were most often constructed as white.[21] In part this is because much of feminist theory was grounded in personal experience and obscured the predominance of white women in building the theory.[22] This focus on white women and gender as the major issue subordinated race, class, and sexual orientation, while ignoring white women's skin privilege. The white students in this class had the intellectual tools to understand that feminism challenged claims to the universality of gender but did not yet understand that their detachment about race was a mark of their own racial privilege. This class discussion also illustrates the problematic contexts in which many white feminists work. The racial insulation of their classrooms, as well as the enforced silence of many lesbian students, means that gender is often discussed apart from the racial, class, and sexual dynamics that give it more complex meanings.

Conclusion

In this reanalysis of our book, we can see how constructions of gender and class, as well as race and ethnicity, are "made" and enforced largely in and through the operations of unacknowledged assumption that everyone is white. We have seen whiteness operate both differentially and simultaneously, as "always more than one thing"; it has been physical description, individual identity, and, throughout, a "dynamic of cultural production and interrelation" operating "within a particular time period and place, and within particular relations of power."[23]

During the discussions of social class in the literary theory course and the honors freshman writing course, the students assumed both maleness and whiteness as the norm in their discussions of working-class unity and middle-class mobility. From the unacknowledged perspective of the dominant position, both "race" and "gender" were properties of the "other," leaving both the middle class and the working class as white and male. While in the honors freshman writing class, whiteness was constructed primarily as a matter of individual identity, in the literary theory class the white students fretted about the ways in which "race," and to a lesser extent, "gender," interrupted the theoretical unity of the oppressed that they were seeking within feminist theory. Based on physical description as a marker for social location, both groups of students assigned "race" to minorities, especially to blacks, while staying oblivious to their own position as whites.

The next two examples showed the working of whiteness operating in and through discussions of gender issues. For Nancy, "breaking through illusion" was necessary to confront whiteness both as physical description and feminine ideal. To her, the ideology of appropriate gender roles, all the way from "looking stupid to attract men" to being a good mother, was derived from white stereotypes that were neither named nor deconstructed. In the discussion of *Sula*, assumptions of whiteness as a basic concept of "woman" led the students to focus on the heroines' feminine attachments, their lesbianism, rather than to acknowledge their racial oppression; even when the lone African American student pointed this out, the group identified "race" with African American women only, refusing to acknowledge whiteness as a social position. In both these discussions we can see race as a bipolar construct, with black and white as the two poles, operated to make all "difference" oppositional in nature, so that black lives could not be normal, but only the obverse or the exception to those of whites — whether in *The Bluest Eye*, a Hayley Mills movie, or *Sula*. Also caught in this dualism, the Asian, Filipina, and Hispanic students lacked any appropriate "mirror" for their identities. Finally the pervasive power of whiteness as a feature of the intellectual dominance of the academy, wherein the universalized knower and known are always assumed to be white, can be seen everywhere in these discussions.

However, we also saw the beginnings of the "unmaking" of whiteness in these class discussions, and in other conversations we had as we concluded writing *The Feminist Classroom*. The professor in the honors freshman writing course included whiteness in her construct of race. The teacher who led the discussion of *Sula* has been preoccupied in the ten years since we observed her with the problem of how a white professor and a group of white students can tackle the topic of race in America. In an interview she said:

> I want them to think of other possibilities in life than what they start with ... There are some things I think they kind of get, but they don't live their whiteness; I don't live my whiteness. I'm working hard to see how to do that.[24]

As we work to unmake the pernicious effects of race and gender privilege in college classrooms, it is useful to return to Adrienne Rich's mirrors as a metaphor for seeing this unmaking. White professors and their students need to think about one professor's advice to her African American students at Spelman on how to use a mirror to reclaim their bodies:

> So I tell my students, the way I look at the "beauty myth" is about trying to look into a mirror and trying to see yourself. In a very systematic way thinking about those socio-cultural corporate entities that keep you from seeing and appreciating who you are-your face, your breasts, everything. And then we move on from there to how to wipe the mirror clean. Not with Windex, which involves buying something already packaged, but with vinegar and water, which is something that your mother told you will cut through the dirt in a real special way.[25]

To reclaim all our bodies against all the "sociocultural corporate entities that keep (us) from seeing and appreciating who we are" means different things to different ones of us. Whereas for African Americans it means wiping the mirror clean of the distortions of racism, for whites it means beginning to see in the mirror those relationships of domination that mark whiteness as a position of oppression. For whites, living our whiteness, to quote Elizabeth Ellsworth, involves being "simultaneously ignorant and knowledgeable, resistant and implicated, committed and forgetful, ambivalent, tired, enjoying the pleasures and safety of privilege; effective in one arena and ineffective in another."[26]

Notes

1. The title for this article was inspired by the conference, "The Making and Unmaking of Whiteness," University of California, Berkeley, April 12 13, 1997. Some of this article appeared in slightly different form in a recent essay in the Harvard Education Review, entitled "Learning in the Dark, How Assumptions of Whiteness Shape Classroom Knowledge, Summer, 1997.

2. Quote p.1, The Bluest Eye (New York: Pocket Books, 1972), p. 159.

3. Frances A. Maher and Mary Kay Tetreault, The Feminist Classroom: An Inside Look at How Professors and Students Are Transforming Higher Education for a Diverse Society (New York: Basic Books, 1994). In this article, we include excerpts from four classes at three different institutions. The first one is from a seminar in literary theory at Lewis and Clark College. The second is from an honors freshman writing course at Towson State University. The third is from a course on women writers since 1800, also at Lewis and Clark College. The fourth is from a class on feminist criticism at Wheaton College.

4. Maher and Tetreault, The Feminist Classroom, chapter one.

5. Maher and Tetreault, "Learning in the Dark: How Assumptions of Whiteness Shape Classroom Knowledge," Harvard Educational Review, 67:2, Summer 1997, pp. 321-347; Tetreault and Maher, "'They Got the Paradigm and Painted It White': Maximizing the Learning Environment in Higher Education Classrooms," Duke Journal of Gender Law & Policy, 4:1, Spring 1997, pp.197-212.

6. Tony Morrison, Playing in the Dark: Whiteness and the Literary Imagination (New York: Vintage, 1993); David Roediger, Towards the Abolition of Whiteness: Essays on Race, Politics and Working Class History (New York: Verso, 1994); Elizabeth Ellsworth, "Double Binds of Whiteness," in Off White; Readings on Society, Race and Culture, ed. Michelle Fine, Lois Weis, Linda C. Powell, and Mun Wong (New York: Routledge, 1997), pp. 259-269; and Elizabeth Ellsworth, "Working Difference in Education," Curriculum Inquiry, forthcoming; Andrew Hacker, Two Nations, Black and White, Separate, Hostile, Unequal (New York: Ballantine Books, 1995); Karen Brodkin Sacks, "How Did Jews Become White Folks?" in Gregory and Sanjek, Race, pp. 78-102.

7. Sacks, "How Did Jews Become White Folks?"; Roediger, Towards the Abolition of Whiteness, pp. 13-14.

8. Hacker, Two Nations, p. 8.

9. Roediger, Towards the Abolition of Whiteness, p. 3.
10. One of us was always present in the classroom as an observer, in this case, Mary Kay Tetreault. All discussions were taped and later transcribed and edited.
11. Moi, Toril, Sexual/Textual Politics; Feminist Literary Theory, Methuen, London and New York, 1985. See Maher and Tetreault, op cit., pp. 72-76, for a discussion of this class. The quotes in this essay are not always fully quoted in the book; we returned to the data to reexamine it for other issues.
12. Students for a Democratic Society was a student movement in the 1960s that opposed the war in Vietnam and worked for civil rights.
13. Maher and Tetreault, op cit., 178-185.
14. Thomas H. Johnson, ed. Complete Poems of Emily Dickinson (New York, Macmillan, 1967); Poem 288.

> I'm Nobody! Who are you?
> Are you —Nobody—Too?
> Then there's a pair of us?
> Don't tell! They'd advertise—
> you know!
>
> How dreary—to be—Somebody!
> How public—like a frog—
> To tell one's name—the live-
> long June
> to an admiring Bog!

15. Poem 327 (Johnson Edition)

> Before I got my eye put out
> I liked as well to see
> As other Creatures, that have
> Eyes
> And know no other way
>
> But were it told to me-Today
> That I might have the sky
> For mine-I tell you that my
> heart
> Would split, for size of me
>
> The Meadows-mine-

The Mountains-mine-
All Forests-Stintless Stars-
As much of Noon as I could
take
Between my finite eyes-

The Motions of the Dipping
birds
The Morning's Amber Road-
for mine-to look at when I
liked-
The News would strike me dead-

So safer-guess-with must my
soul
Upon the Window pane-
Where other Creatures put their eyes-
Incautious-of the Sun-

16. Hacker, op cit. 18-19. Gotanda spoke of these issues at a seminar "Reconstructing Whiteness: Color Blindness, Asian Americans, and the New Ethnicity," at California State University, Fullerton, April 16, 1996.
17. We first saw this quote from Adrienne Rich in a paper by Renato Rosaldo, entitled "Symbolic Violence: a Battle Raging in Academe," Phoenix, Arizona, American Anthropological Association Annual Meeting, 1988.
18. The Feminist Classroom, 167-170. Everyone was European American except for one African American student.
19. Neil Gotanda, "A Critique of 'Our Constitution is Color-Blind'," Stanford Law Review, 44, 1991, p.1.
20. Toni Morrison, Sula, 52 (1974).
21. Elizabeth Spelman, Inessential Woman: Problems of Exclusion in Feminist Thought, 1988.
22. Martha Mahoney, Whiteness and Women, in Practice and Theory: A Reply to Catharine MacKinnon, 5 Yale Journal of Law and Feminism, (1993).
23. Elizabeth Ellsworth, "Double Binds of Whiteness," 260-261.
24. The Feminist Classroom, 239.
25. Interview with Mona Phillips, April 1993.
26. Elizabeth Ellsworth, "Working Difference, in Education," Curriculum Inquiry, 14, forthcoming.

CHAPTER ELEVEN

Constructing a Pedagogy of Whiteness
for Angry White Students
Joe L. Kincheloe and Shirley R. Steinberg

In the emerging subdiscipline of whiteness studies, scholars seem better equipped to explain white privilege than to define whiteness itself. Such a dilemma is understandable: the concept is slippery and elusive. Even though no one at this point really knows what whiteness is, most observers agree that it is intimately involved with issues of power and power differences between white and nonwhite people. Whiteness cannot be separated from hegemony and is profoundly influenced by demographic changes, political realignments, and economic cycles. Situationally specific, whiteness is always shifting, always reinscribing itself around changing meanings of race in the larger society. As with race in general, whiteness holds material/economic implications—indeed, white supremacy has its financial rewards. The Federal Housing Administration, for example, has traditionally favored housing loans for white suburbs instead of "ethnic" inner cities. Banks have ensured that Blacks have severely limited access to property ownership and capital acquisition compared to Whites. Unions over the decades following World War II ignored the struggle for full employment and universal medical care, opting for contracts that provided private medical coverage, pensions, and job security to predominantly white organized workers in mass production industries. Undoubtedly, there continues to be unearned wages of whiteness. Indeed, critical multiculturalists understand that questions of whiteness permeate almost every major issue facing Westerners at the end of the twentieth century, from affirmative action, and intelligence testing to the deterioration of public space and the growing disparity of wealth. In this context the study of whiteness becomes a central feature of any critical pedagogy or multicultural education for the twenty-first century. The effort to define and reinvent the amorphous concept becomes the "prime directive" of what is referred to here as a critical pedagogy of whiteness (Keating, 1995; Nakayama and Krizek, 1995; Fiske, 1994; Gallagher, 1994; Yudice, 1995).

In the context of multicultural education a critical pedagogy of whiteness theoretically grounds a form of teaching that engages students in an examination of the social, political, and psychological dimensions of membership in a racial group. The critical imperative demands that such an examination be considered in relation to power and the ideological dynamics of white supremacy. A critical pedagogy of whiteness is possible only if we understand in great specificity the multiple meanings of whiteness and their effects on the way white consciousness is historically structured and socially inscribed. Without such appreciations and the meta-consciousness they ground, awareness of the privilege and dominance of white Northern European vantage points are buried in the cemetery of power evasion. Neither our understanding that race is not biological but social or that racial classifications have inflicted pain and suffering on non-Whites should move us to reject the necessity of new forms of racial analysis.

The white privilege of universalizing its characteristics as the "proper ways to be" has continuously undermined the efforts of non-Whites in a variety of spheres. At times such universal norms have produced self-loathing among individual members of minority groups, as they internalize the shibboleths of the white tradition—"I wish my eyes were blue and my hair blond and silky." Invisible white norms in these cases alienate non-Whites to the point that they sometimes come to live "outside themselves." A pedagogy of whiteness reveals such power-related processes to both Whites and non-Whites alike, exposing how members of both these groups are stripped of self-knowledge. As Whites, white students in particular, come to see themselves through the eyes of Blacks, Latinos, Asians, and indigenous peoples, they begin to move away from the conservative constructions of the dominant culture. Such an encounter with minority perspectives moves many white individuals to rethink their tendency to dismiss the continued existence of racism and embrace the belief that racial inequality results from unequal abilities among racial groups. The effects of a critical pedagogy of whiteness can be powerfully emancipatory (Tatum, 1994; Frankenberg, 1993; Alcoff, 1995; Sleeter, 1995).

What's White? Whiteness as a Social Construction

As with any racial category, whiteness is a social construction in that it can be invented, lived, analyzed, modified, and discarded. While Western reason is a crucial dynamic associated with whiteness over the last three centuries, there are many other social forces that sometimes work to construct its meaning. Whiteness, thus, is not an unchanging, fixed, biological category impervious to its cultural, economic, political, and psychological context. There are many ways to be white, as whiteness interacts with class, gender, and a range of other race-related and cultural dynamics. The ephemeral nature of whiteness as a social construction begins to reveal itself when we understand that the Irish, Italians, and Jews have all been viewed as nonwhite in particular places at specific moments in history. Indeed, Europeans prior to the late 1600s did not use the label "black" to refer to any race of people, Africans included. Only after the racialization of slavery by around 1680 did whiteness and blackness come to represent racial categories. Only at this historical juncture did the concept of a discrete white race begin to take shape. Slowly in the eighteenth and nineteenth centuries the association with rationality and orderliness developed, and in this context whiteness came to signify an elite racial group. Viewed as a position of power, white identity was often sought by those who did not possess it. Immigrant workers in the new American industrial workplaces of the mid-nineteenth century from southern and eastern Europe aspired to and eventually procured whiteness, viewing its status as payment for the exploitation of their labor. Such shifts in the nature and boundaries of whiteness continued into the twentieth century. One of the reasons that whiteness has become an object of analysis in the 1990s revolves around the profound shifts in the construction of whiteness, blackness, and other racial identities that have taken place in the last years of the twentieth century.

How are students and other individuals to make sense of the assertion that whiteness is a social construction? How does such a concept inform the democratic goals of a critical pedagogy? Such questions form the conceptual basis of our discussion of whiteness, our attempt to construct a pedagogy of whiteness. In order to answer them in a manner that is helpful to Whites and other racial groups, it is important to focus on the nature of the social construction process. In this context John Fiske's (1993) notion of an ever-shifting and realigning power bloc is helpful. The discourses that shape whiteness are not unified and singular but diverse and contradictory. If one is looking for logical consistency from the social construction of whiteness, he or she is not going to find it. The discursive construction of whiteness, like the work of any power bloc, aligns and dealings itself around particular issues of race. For example, the discourse of white victimization that has emerged over the last two decades appears in response to particular historical moments such as the attempt to compensate for the oppression of non-Whites through preferential hiring and admissions policies. The future of such policies will help shape the discourses that will realign to structure whiteness in the twenty-first century. These discourses, of course, hold profound material consequences for Western cultures, as they fashion and refashion power relations between differing social groups. Any pedagogy of critical multiculturalism, or of whiteness itself, involves engaging students in a rigorous tracking of this construction process. Such an operation when informed by critical notions of social justice, community, and democracy allows individuals insights into the inner workings of racialization, identity formation, and the etymology of racism—an empowering set of understandings. Armed with such concepts, they gain the ability to challenge and rethink whiteness around issues of racism and privilege. In this context questions about a white student's own identity begin to arise (Gallagher, 1994; McMillen, 1995; Keating, 1995; Nakayama and Krizek, 1995).

Such questioning and renegotiating induces us to consider whiteness in relation to other social forces—non-whiteness in particular. Stephen Haymes (1996) argues that to understand racial identity formation, we need to appreciate the way white is discursively represented as the polar opposite of black—a reflection of the Western tendency to privilege one concept in a binary opposition to another. The darkness-light, angel-devil discursive binarism—like other discursive constructions—has reproduced itself in the establishment of racial and ethnic categories. Through its relationship with blackness, whiteness configured itself as different, as not enslaved, as powerful, as aligned with destiny. In this bizarre manner, blackness or Africanness empowered whiteness to gain self-consciousness, often via the racist depiction of the other. Such representations affirm the superiority and power of whiteness—again, its rationality, productivity, and orderliness vis-à-vis the chaos, laziness, and primitiveness of Africans and other non-Whites.

Avoiding Essentialism: The Instability of Whiteness

Diversity in whiteness demands our attention. Critical scholars must carefully attend to the subtle but crucial distinction between whiteness, with its power to signify, and white people. The diversity among white people makes sweeping generalizations about them dangerous and highly counter-productive to the goals of a critical pedagogy of whiteness. Indeed, it is not contradictory to argue that whiteness is a marker of privilege but all white people are not able to take advantage of that privilege. It is difficult to convince a working-class white student of the ubiquity of white privilege when he or she is going to school, accumulating school debts, working at McDonalds for minimum wage, unable to get married because of financial stress, and holds little hope of upward socioeconomic mobility. The lived experiences and anxieties of such individuals cannot be dismissed in a pedagogy of whiteness.

How, then, in the study and teaching of whiteness do we avoid essentializing white people as privileged, rationalistic, emotionally alien-ated people? Understanding the social/discursive construction of white-ness, students of whiteness refuse to search for its essential nature or its authentic core. Instead, critical analysts study the social, historical, rhetorical, and discursive context of whiteness, mapping the ways it makes itself visible and invisible, manifests its power, and shapes larger sociopolitical structures in relation to the microdynamics of everyday life. This, of course, is no easy task—indeed, it should keep us busy for a while. Its complexity and its recognition of ambiguity are central to the project's success. Since there is no fixed essence of whiteness, different white people can debate both the meaning of whiteness in general and its meaning in their own lives. Critical multiculturalists believe that such debates should take place in the context of racial history and analyses of power asymmetries in order to gain more than a superficial acquaintance with the issues. Nevertheless, diversity in whiteness is a fact of life, as various white people negotiate their relationship to whiteness in different ways. Yet, whiteness scholarship to this point has sometimes failed to recognize that its greatest problem is the lapse into essentialism.

In its most essentialistic manifestations whiteness study has operated under the assumption that racial categories were permanent and fixed. In their attempt to deconstruct race in this context, essentialistic whiteness scholars tend to reinscribe the fixity of racial difference. The pessimism emerging here is constructed by a form of racial determinism—white people will act in white ways because they are "just that way." A critical pedagogy of whiteness understands the contingency of the connection between rationalistic modernist whiteness and the actions of people with light-colored skin. The same, of course, is true with people with dark colored skin—they may not "act black." They may even "act white." Such anti-essentialistic appreciations are central to whiteness study, as scholars historically contextualize their contemporary insights with references to the traditional confusion over racial delineations. Throughout U.S. history, for example, many federal and state agencies used only three racial categories—White, Negro, and Indian. Who fit where? How were Latinos to be classified? What about Asians? Originally, the state of California classified Mexicans as white and Chinese as Indian. Later Chinese Americans were grouped as Orientals, then Asians, then Pan Asians, and then Asian Pacific Americans. Analysis of such categorization indicates both the slipperiness of racial grouping and the American attempt to force heterogeneous racial configurations into a single category around similarities in skin tone, hair texture, and eye shape. Such biological criteria simply don't work in any logically consistent manner, thus frustrating the state's regulatory efforts to impose a rationalistic racial order (Keating, 1995; Rubin, 1994; Gallagher, 1994; Fiske, 1994).

Thus, advocates of a critical pedagogy of whiteness refuse to use race as an essentialist grounding of identity since it is not a natural category. Not only is race an unnatural category, but its cultural boundaries are constantly negotiated and transgressed as individuals engage the forces and discourses that shape them. If we are not careful when using race as a social category, we can reify the perceived differences between black and white and lose sight of the cultural hybridity we all share. When teaching about whiteness we need always to view the concept in historical context, keeping in mind the situationally specific nature of the term. Our emphasis should continuously revolve around rewriting racial identity, as we point out the inaccuracies embedded in present racial configurations. Such an emphasis undermines fixed notions of racial identity that separate peoples from various racial and ethnic backgrounds. Identity politics grounded on such fixed positions have often supported a form of authority garnered from membership in subordinated groups. This privilege derived from oppression assumes that particular forms of analysis can be spoken only by individuals who share a specific identity. In this essentialist cosmos it is inappropriate for a white man to ever criticize a black man, a Jew to ever disagree with a lesbian Latina. Such politics quickly destroy any solidarity among individuals from a variety of groups who want to pursue an egalitarian, democratic vision.

If we are unable to get beyond these fixed definitions of black and white identity, a pedagogy of whiteness in particular and multicultural education in general may construct impressions that racism is an inevitable feature of the human condition. Thus, the question emerges: can the multicultural analysis of racialized identities such as whiteness serve a democratic outcome? Critical multiculturalists take the question seriously, even though they strongly believe that such analysis is necessary in a multiracial, multicultural society. They take the question seriously because they have too often seen the divisive outcomes of essentialist forms of identity politics. The question induces us carefully to scan the cultural landscape for the negative consequences of multicultural analysis, learning in the process to recognize and anticipate the unexpected problems such activities may help create. The meaning of whiteness in late twentieth century societies is volatile. As such, a pedagogy of whiteness must walk a Wallenda tightrope between racial essentialism on one side and a liberal colorblindness on the other. Proponents of a critical pedagogy of whiteness understand that the only antidote to racial essentialism is not a fatuous embrace of racial erasure. They embrace a middle ground position that first, explores the socially constructed, artificial, ephemeral nature of racial identities and second, carefully traces the all-too-real effects of such identities.

As such a pedagogy separates whiteness from white people, it understands the changing meaning of whiteness for young working-class Whites. In this context it analyzes such individuals' view of themselves as racial victims and their resulting efforts to build an emotional community around their whiteness. Here critical multiculturalists explore the sobering consequences such tendencies may hold for twenty-first century race relations. Ever aware of the ambiguities of whiteness, a critical pedagogy of whiteness appreciates the plight and pain of the young white working class while concurrently exposing the ways whiteness developed in such a context works to hide racial forms of sociopolitical and economic inequality. In the global culture of hyperreality with its increasingly dynamic forms of hybrid identities, the critical work of tracing these constructions of self vis-à-vis group becomes progressively more difficult. As hope of finding discrete bounded notions of self fade, so too do traditional sociological and educational methodologies of inquiry with their antiquated identity. In the postmodern condition individuals must wear several identities, as they travel in and out of multiple cultural locales. Gone is the memory of "genuine cultures" who pass along their mores and folkways unchanged to the next generation. In this configuration the Scots would still wear kilts and the Sioux their warbonnets. In this new, more complex world critical analysts understand the need to refigure racial analysis and identity formation after the crutch and safety of essentialism is removed (Luke, 1994; Keating, 1995; Thompson, 1996; Gallagher, 1994; Wellman, 1996).

White Mutations in the 1990s: Whiteness Visible

Contradictory articulations of what it means to "feel white" at the end of the century when coupled with a panoply of socioeconomic and political forces have undermined any stable notions of white identity. The identity politics of the last thirty years have generated a widespread angst about the meaning of whiteness and induced many Whites to confront for the first time their own ethnicity. Realizing they may not constitute a majority of the population for long, understanding that they have been racialized, recognizing challenges to white supremacy, watching themselves being labeled as oppressors in the eyes of the world, white people face an unprecedented crisis of whiteness. Any pedagogy of whiteness must understand the nuances and effects of this sociocultural phenomenon if it is to speak to white people in the post-Civil Rights era. It must not simply dismiss the paradoxical concerns many white people express about pride in white culture in light of the fact that "everyone else" (meaning non-Whites) is talking about pride in theirs. Make no mistake there is a new consciousness about race in contemporary Western societies (Gallagher, 1994; Winant, 1994; Rubin, 1994).

This new consciousness induces Whites to ask "who are we?" Living in a racially charged environment where the traditionally marginalized have gained a good deal of media exposure, white students now know Whites occupy a racial category. When bell hooks argued in 1992 that Whites could assume their racial invisibility, she did not realize how quickly that invisibility would disappear. The crisis of whiteness has ended the notion of white racial invisibility, substituting in its place questions about how Whites, young Whites in particular, will construct a new white identity in this new racial world. Critical multiculturalists appreciate the necessity of carefully monitoring the political and ideological dynamics that will be drawn upon in the (re)construction of whiteness. Ruth Frankenberg's assertion, formulated in 1993, that the erasure of race and whiteness was the dominant form of racial thinking among Whites seems passé only a few years later. Her category of race cognizance among white people involves an awareness of racial inequity and an appreciation of subordinated cultures. In the racial awareness of the late 1990s, does Frankenberg's sanguine delineation of white racial consciousness account for all the ways Whites might express such awareness? Though she certainly understood the complexity of the way whiteness might be positioned in a racial consciousness that understood inequality and valorized difference, Frankenberg was unprepared for the intensity of the struggle for white identity that would follow the publication of her book (hooks, 1992; Frankenberg, 1993).

Young, White, Victimized, and Angry

In the context of this repositioning of end-of-century whiteness, many Whites, white youth in particular, have defined themselves around the denial of the benefits of whiteness. Employing a belief in a just world with equal opportunity, many white students have claimed victim status in the new racial configurations of the late twentieth century. Advocates of a critical pedagogy of whiteness must understand the social context that constructs the denial of white privilege, while at the same time appreciating the ways of seeing of white students who genuinely feel victimized. Critical teachers, thus, will not be surprised when they encounter white students who vehemently resent multicultural requirements as antiwhite restrictions that subject them to charges of racism merely because they are white. Some white students see such curriculums as burdens and enter the classes with attitudes shaped accordingly. Multiculturalists teaching about whiteness and white privilege will not succeed if they are not ready to encounter such hostility.

This perception of victimization from every direction among many white students shapes the way they interpret the canon wars, the public conversation about political correctness, feminism, and affirmative action. The multicultural effort to construct an academic curriculum grounded on the values of inclusivity and social justice has been seen as not a battle between competing ideologies and pedagogical philosophies but as a simple punitive attack on white people. The economic decline of the last twenty years has been viewed similarly by many white people: because of liberal concern with racial injustice, our (White) job possibilities are narrowing and our future looks dim. In such a context affirmative action can be portrayed as a monster, as the embodiment of an evil designed to punish white people. Thus, one hears (especially if one is white) a lot of white muttering in schools and workplaces about the climate of unfairness, of reverse racism. Such dominant group anger propels the engine of social regulation, as traditional victims of oppression become the causes of the society's and the dominant group's problems. White male anger intensifies in this ideological framing of the problem, as such men grow more and more threatened by privileged non-Whites and women (Sleeter, 1993; Gallagher, 1994; Willis, 1995; Appiah, 1995; Tanaka, 1996).

Such white anger and resentment have opened a new racial order to mark the beginning of the twenty-first century. The new order is grounded on a new white consciousness emerging from the chaos of the white identity crisis. The emergence of such a consciousness is a serious social phenomenon and cannot be dismissed by proponents of a pedagogy of whiteness. Grounded around an admittedly naïve concept of individual equality, the new white racial consciousness of the new racial order challenges the very foundations of a critical pedagogy grounded on a recognition of the interplay of power and social justice. Understanding this dynamic, proponents of a critical pedagogy of whiteness address both the ideological and interpersonal forces at work in this dangerous context. While we do not want to abandon the study of whiteness because it is dangerous and might anger some Whites, we also want to take seriously the complex reality of white anger and address it at a number of levels. One such level, for example, would involve the examination of the construction of the belief that non-Whites are dedicated to conflict with Whites. Where is the proof of such a belief and where did it come from? How does it shape the way many Whites see the world? When Whites act on the belief they tend to behave defensively and aggressively, thus fueling a dynamic of racial conflict—a classic example of a self-fulfilling prophecy. In the new racial order built on this assumption of conflict, any advance in the socioeconomic position of non-Whites is constructed as a gain made at white expense. Thus, the flames of white anger are fanned.

Declining White Power: The Dialectics of White Privilege

The white identity crisis and the anger that accompanies it are manifestations of the growing realization that white power is declining in light of dominant demographic trends. When power declines, its wielders guard their interests more zealously. Understanding that they will no longer constitute a majority of the U.S. population in the twenty-first century, Whites appreciate the challenges such a reality will present. Indeed, with the forces of history moving against it, whiteness's traditional fear of blackness is rearticulated in more panic-stricken terms. Indeed, whiteness in decline is represented as a loss of order and civility. The horror of Africa, so central to understanding the history of the U.S., reappears in a televised postmodern guise taunting Whites with its traditional desire for/fear of dichotomy. The taunting—expressed so overtly every NFL Sunday in the fall and winter by black linemen after the sack of white quarterbacks—is from "within" on the post-Civil Rights landscape at the end of the century. It's within *our* integrated neighborhood schools with their multicultural curriculums, *our* workplaces with their affirmative action, and *our* universities with their preferential admission policies. The fear within paralyzes many Whites, as they grow even more fearful watching non-Whites become more alienated. As white men cheer defensive linemen in pursuit of quarterbacks, they re-press the haunting image of black retribution and the disadvantaged position that it portends for them. The rhetorical reversal of white victimization plays well at the subconscious level in this context.

The pain of the perception of a new psychological disprivilege within an old privilege gnaws at contemporary white people. While it must always be understood within the context of a material privilege, this psychological disprivilege of whiteness must be appreciated by those intent on teaching a pedagogy of whiteness. The new disprivilege emerges from the increasingly valued concept of difference and Whites' lack of it. White people can claim little "oppression capital" in a world where representations of one's or one's group's oppression seem—especially to white observers—to mean so much. Such an absence looms large in the minds of the white working class who are the Whites who gain the least from white privilege and who perceive that they lose the most from the non-white exploitation of oppression capital. But is there really a disadvantage to being white in hyperreality? Is there a devaluation of whiteness that permeates the end-of-century social landscape? What are the implications of this new dialectic of whiteness, this yin-yang of whiteness for a pedagogy of such? How do we explore the damage of racism on those who have held it without diminishing the centrality of the ways such racism has harmed its victims? Answering such questions moves a pedagogy of whiteness to a dangerous terrain where its intentions can be challenged from a variety of directions. Questions such as "why do you want to demean white people" may be followed by inquiries including "why do you want to protect white people."

Nothing will come easy in a pedagogy of whiteness (Winant, 1994; Merelman, 1986, 1995; Hacker, 1992; Fiske, 1993, 1994; Giroux, 1995; Haymes, 1996; Du Plessis, 1995; Yudice, 1995).

Right-wing Answers to the Questions of Whiteness:Recovering White Supremacy

The right wing has answered questions about whiteness consistently over the last couple of decades. Any pedagogy of whiteness needs to understand the right-wing response to the white identity crisis as basically an insidious effort to reestablish white hegemony. As Gresson (1995) has pointed out, such recovery efforts have been largely successful and work to dismantle the gains of struggles for social justice. Under the ideological guise of arguments such as "America must learn to live with inequality," right-wing proponents rally around cries of reverse racism. In this new discursive universe, work against racism can always be represented as a form of neo-racism *against* Whites. Since Blacks and Latinos, the narrative continues, have made so much progress in recent years—at the expense of Whites—racism is not much of a problem anymore. Evidence for such non-White progress is found in the positive media images of Blacks, Latinos, and indigenous peoples found scattered throughout the mediascape. Such images have allowed many Whites to disavow the reality of racism at the end of the twentieth century. The white audience of *The Cosby Show*, for example, often interpreted the program as evidence that racism had been cured. Buying into such popular social readings, many white students express great anger when Black, Latino, and indigenous students keep bringing up historical racism. Just because some distant relative was a slave, they maintain, provides individuals with no reason to harbor resentment in the 1990s. In this context white students often express intense anger about having to take classes on race. They have accepted the right-wing answers to questions about race and whiteness: when pushed they may admit that some racism may still exist but only within the Klan and neo-Nazi organizations.

Such answers are plausible only in a society stricken with amnesia, a culture whose dangerous memories have been erased by power. In the U.S., Ronald Reagan and his handlers adeptly rearticulated old ideologies in a way that reinscribed a racism that camouflaged its racist character. The old ideologies of social Darwinism and Manifest Destiny reassured Whites shaken by the identity crisis that they were the inheritors of the moral capital of the Puritan's "city on the hill"—Reagan invoked the reference frequently during his presidential speeches. The amnesia allows right-wing spokespeople the opportunity to answer any challenge to their efforts to reestablish white hegemony with charges of political correctness. We are victims of political correctness, they have maintained, in the process reversing the rhetoric of racial oppression to the point that non-White victims become the new oppressors of white people. Of course, in this rhetorical cosmos, affirmative action becomes the ultimate expression of racism, as undeserving individuals drawing upon a distant past of oppression gain advantages in schools and workplaces at the expense of Whites. Adeptly deploying the strategy of Whites as victims, conservatives painted an appealing vision of life in America before liberal permissivism of the 1960s destroyed the nation's greatness (Gresson, 1995; King, 1996; Herrnstein and Murray, 1994; Kamin, 1995; Hacker, 1992; Yudice, 1995; Gallagher, 1994; McMillen, 1995; Lind, 1995).

The right-wing answers to questions about whiteness and education followed the rhetorical formula. Exploiting public amnesia yet again, right-wing leaders portrayed a pre-1960s, pre-egalitarian educational reform America where educational standards were high, American education was viewed as the best in the world, and because of such educational excellence U.S. economic supremacy was beyond question. Indeed, the *Nation at Risk* report issued in the spring of 1983 can be viewed as a recovery document outlining the impossibility of seeking educational quality and equality simultaneously. Racial difference in this context becomes a destructive force intent on destroying our (white) values and standards—racial difference in education, as manifested in the racial desegregation of schools, destroyed the quality of American education. Declines in test scores and increasing illiteracy, right-wing leaders proclaimed, were the direct result of misguided progressives' quixotic quest for equality and democracy. It's high time, they concluded in the spirit of the recovery of white supremacy, that we go *back* to the basics, to that *Little House on the Prairie* school with its drill, repetition, and focus on traditional values. In education, the recovery of whiteness meant a return to the little red schoolhouse.

A similar theme can be found in popular culture. Aaron Gresson (1995), for example, identifies the recovery theme in the five *Rocky* movies (1976, 1979, 1982, 1985, 1990), as Sylvester Stallone's character (the great white hope) wins the respect of the uppity black champion, Apollo Creed, by fighting him to a draw. In *Rocky II* Stallone defeats Creed and wins his support and affection as he fights Mr. T. In later sequels Rocky defeats a threatening Russian and mentors a young white boxer to carry the flag of whiteness after he retires. In *Soul Man* (1986) a white student (C. Thomas Howell) denied entry to Harvard reinvents himself as an African American and gains admission through affirmative action. Tom Berenger stars in *The Substitute* (1996) as a covert operations soldier who comes home to his girlfriend, a high school teacher in inner-city (non-white) Miami. After unruly Latino and black students hire a Seminole Indian to "kneecap" her with a baseball bat, Berenger's character poses as a substitute teacher in his girlfriend's classes to find the perpetrators. In the process Berenger and his buddies from the special forces not only find the guilty kids but uncover a Latino/black gang-related drug ring run by the high school principal (an African American) from the basement of the school. Faced with this non-White corruption, Berenger and his men exhibit their answer to school reform: they kill them all and heroically *take back* the school. In all of these movies a similar message is conveyed: white privilege is under attack from barbaric non-Whites and we (white males) must recover it by acts of heroism.

Contrary to many white people's perceptions, the recovery of white supremacy has been catalyzed by mass media such as TV and movies. When we speak of these racial dynamics to predominantly white groups we often encounter tremendous resistance and disbelief. "You've got it wrong," they tell us, "Blacks and Latinos are heavily represented in the media." Compared to thirty years ago, there indeed are more non-Whites on TV and in the movies. The question not asked, however, involves the nature of the roles non-Whites can obtain in the entertainment industry. Even when TV and movies dramatize real-life events involving African Americans, Latinos, and other non-Whites, the stars and main characters still tend to be white. For example, the NBC made-for-TV movie about the Howard Beach case, where white youths beat three African American men and chased another one to his death, focused attention on Charles Hynes, the white special prosecutor portrayed by Daniel Travanti. The promos for the movie give a sense of its perspective: as the camera focused for a close-up on Travanti, the voice-over announced that "only one man can unravel the mystery and bring the guilty to justice." In *Cry Freedom* (1987), the same theme prevails as a movie about the black South African struggle against apartheid focuses its attention on Donald Woods (Kevin Kline), the white journalist who wrote the biography of heroic freedom fighter Steve Biko. One might ask in this context if Biko was the brave figure who led the resistance, underwent torture, and died for the cause, why was Woods the star/hero of the movie. The same theme dominates *A Dry White Season* (1989), *Mississippi Burning* (1988), and a plethora of other movies too numerous to mention here (McCarthy, 1995).

The themes identified in these movies are not simply interesting readings of a trivial entertainment media; in hyperreality, TV, and movies are a central location for the production of knowledge and the generation of ideological currents that engage a diverse audience. The racial themes generated in these examples connect with rearticulations of whiteness in a neo-Manifest Destiny and White Man's Burden guise. Such an ideological dynamic reannoints whiteness, as it reawakens its messianic racial role around the fears produced by right-wing analysis. In this context, right wing representations of racial contamination via growing numbers of non-white immigrants and high birth rates strike a responsive chord with the white chorus. Using this dysgenesis as an excuse, right wing leaders shield whiteness from any blame for the socioeconomic conditions non-Whites must face. In their response to the white identity crisis many young Whites embrace dysgenesis and its concurrent refusal of white complicity in the degradation of non-Whites. "Leave me alone," they insist, "I've had absolutely nothing to do with racism or racial persecution." Black, Latino, and Native American poverty, unemployment, disenfranchisement are not white problems, they argue, they're non-white problems. Such pervasive white acceptance of right-wing responses to the racial questions of the late twentieth century has allowed white civic elites to distance themselves from issues of black and Latino poverty. In this context the disparity of wealth between White and non-White continues to grow without anyone seeming to care (Tanaka, 1996; Gresson, 1995; Hacker, 1992; Gallagher, 1994; Giroux, 1995; Stafford, 1992).

Listening, Learning, Changing

Simply put, a key feature of a pedagogy of whiteness involves inducing white people as a key aspect of their analysis of their subjectivity to listen to non-Whites as they explain the issues we have discussed. Such a process will be difficult in Western societies where the dominant culture has encouraged speaking over listening and has rewarded domination over sensitivity to the position of others, especially subordinated others. Such listening will involve both taking seriously those who have been silenced out of fear and developing an empathetic imagination that sees from the perspective of the other. It is not very difficult to understand that if Whites don't develop these abilities, the possibility for intensifying racial violence will grow—individuals become more combative the more they are ignored. Thus, it is no exaggeration to maintain that racial peace in the twenty-first century will depend on Whites developing the willingness to listen and make meaning from what they hear. The meaning-making process in which Whites must engage will require that for the first time they will assimilate to the presence of non-White culture. Having no tradition of adapting to what they have historically deemed inferior cultures, Whites will find this process difficult. Given the right-wing redefinition of whiteness and the recovery process it supports, the white effort to assimilate becomes even more formidable.

A pedagogy of whiteness encourages a form of listening that intensely attends to different ways of knowing and their implications for the restructuring of identity. Here white individuals study the insights of Blacks, Latinos, Asians, and indigenous peoples not only into racism and forms of oppression but into others' ways of being, experiencing, and living in the world. A pedagogy of whiteness asks, for example, what are the alternatives to Western modernist rationalism with its emphasis on scientific procedure, the regulation of consciousness, and the division of the world into smaller and smaller categories. Progressive Whites value these alternatives and use them to help extend their imagination beyond a confining monoculturalism. For example, right-wing constructions of whiteness have persuasively represented African Americans as dependent on the government for welfare and social services. In this representation of black dependency, Whites are portrayed as independent and self-sufficient. Such a popular construction does not hold up to examination, as even affluent Whites also depend on government to patrol and contain poor black neighborhoods, to construct highways and subways that steer clear of such neighborhoods, and to process home owners' mortgage deduction refunds. Understanding the inaccuracy and poisonous effects of this skewed way of seeing, Whites learn to empathize with Blacks deemed unworthy of opportunity. Such Whites learn ways of acting that interrupt the vicious cycle such racist representations set into motion (Fiske, 1993, 1994; Tatum, 1994; Merelman, 1995).

The implementation of a pedagogy of whiteness that induces Whites to listen, learn, and change is a delicate operation. In an era where young Whites face an identity crisis that has elicited angry responses to efforts to pursue social justice, a critical pedagogy of whiteness must balance a serious critique of whiteness and white power with a narrative that refuses to demonize white people. Teachers and cultural workers must not only negotiate this task but also induce students to form multicultural/racial coalitions that work for structural change. As Whites begin to take seriously the ways non-Whites see them, they concurrently learn to address social, political, and economic structures that perpetuate the cycle of racism. In this process they find that the structures in question are the province of whiteness, emphasizing once again the importance of studying the social center as well as multiculturalism's traditional concern with the margins. In this context, the coalitions for social transformation do not simply go to black and Latino neighborhoods and Indian reservations to do their work; in addition they work with Whites and white institutions to develop antiracist policies and progressive ways of being white.

References

Alcoff, L. (1995). Mestizo identity. In N. Zack (Ed.), *American mixed race: The culture of microdiversity.* Lanham, MD: Rowman and Littlefield.

Appiah, K. (1995). Straightening out The Bell Curve. In R. Jacoby and N. Glauberman (Eds.), *The bell curve debate: History, documents, and opinion.* New York: Random House.

Du Plessis, R. (1995). HOO, HOO, HOO: Some episodes in the construction of modern whiteness. *American Literature, 67* (4), 667-700.

Fiske, J. (1993). *Power plays, power works.* New York: Verso.

Fiske, J. (1994). *Media matters: Everyday culture and political change.* Minneapolis: University of Minnesota Press.

Frankenberg, R. (1993). *The social construction of whiteness: White women, race matters.* Minneapolis: University of Minnesota Press.

Gallagher, C. (1994). White reconstruction in the university. *Socialist Review, 24* (1-2), 165-87.

Giroux, H. (1995). White panic. In C. Berlet (Ed.), *Eyes right: Challenging the right-wing backlash.* Boston: South End Press.

Gresson, A. (1995). *The recovery of race in America.* Minneapolis: University of Minnesota Press.

Hacker, A. (1992). *Two nations: Black and white, separate, hostile, unequal.* New York: Ballantine Books.

Haymes, S. (1996). Race, repression, and the politics of crime and punishment in The Bell Curve. In J. Kincheloe, S. Steinberg and A. Gresson (Eds.), *Measured lies: The Bell Curve examined.* New York: St. Martin's Press.

Herrnstein, R., & Murray, C. (1994). *The Bell Curve: Intelligence and class structure in American life.* New York: The Free Press.

hooks, b. (1992). *Black looks: Race and representation.* Boston: Beacon Press.

Kamin, L. (1995). Lies, damned lies, and statistics. In R. Jacoby and N. Glauberman (Eds.), *The Bell Curve debate: History, documents, and opinion.* New York: Random House.

Keating, A. (1995). Interrogating "whiteness," (de) constructing race. *College English, 57* (8), 901-18.

King, J. (1996). Bad luck, bad blood, bad faith: Ideological hegemony and the oppressive language of hoodoo social science. In J. Kincheloe, S. Steinberg, and A Gresson (Eds.), *Measured lies: The Bell Curve examined.* New York: St. Martin's Press.

Lind, M. (1995). Brave new right. In S. Fraser (Ed.), *The bell curve wars: Race, intelligence, and the future of America*. New York: Basic Books.

Luke, C. (1994). White women in interracial families: Reflections on hybridization, feminine identities, and racialized othering. *Feminist Issues, 14* (2), 49-72.

McCarthy, S. (1995). *Why are the heroes always white?* Kansas City: Andrews and McMeel.

McMillen, L. (1995, September). Lifting the veil from whiteness: Growing body of scholarship challenges a racial norm. *The Chronicle of Higher Education*, p. A23.

Merelman, R. (1986). Domination, self-justification, and self-doubt: Some social psychological considerations. *Journal of Politics, 48,* 276-99.

Merelman, R. (1995). *Representing black culture: Racial conflict and cultural politics in the United States*. New York: Routledge.

Nakayama, T., & Krizek, R. (1995). Whiteness: A strategic rhetoric. *Quarterly Journal of Speech, 81,* 291-309.

Rubin, L. (1994). *Families on the faultline: America's working class speaks about the family, the economy, race, and ethnicity*. New York: Harper Collins.

Sleeter, C. (1993). How white teachers construct race. In C. McCarthy and W. Crichlow (Eds.), *Race, identity, and reproduction in education*. New York: Routledge.

Sleeter, C. (1995). Reflections on my use of multicultural and critical pedagogy when students are white. In C. Sleeter and P. McLaren (Eds.), *Multicultural education, critical pedagogy, and the politics of difference*. Albany, NY: State University of New York Press.

Stafford, W. (1992). Whither the great neo-conservative experiment in New York City. In J. Jennings (Ed.), *Race, politics, and economic development: Community perspectives*. New York: Verso.

Tanaka, G. (1996). Dysgenesis and white culture. In J. Kincheloe, S. Steinberg and A. Gresson (Eds.), *Measured lies: The Bell Curve examined*. New York: St. Martin's Press.

Tatum, B. (1994). Teaching white students about racism: The search for white allies and the restoration of hope. *Teachers College Record, 95* (4), 462-75.

Thompson, B. (1996). Time traveling and border crossing: Reflections on white identity. In B. Thompson and S. Tyagi (Eds.), *Names we call home: Autobiography on racial identity*. New York: Routledge.

Wellman, D. (1996). Red and black in white America: Discovering cross-border identities and other subversive activities. In B. Thompson and S. Tyagi (Eds.), *Names we call home: Autobiography on racial identity.* New York: Routledge.

Willis, E. (1995). The median is the message. In R. Jacoby and N. Glauberman (Eds.), *The bell curve debate: History, documents, and opinion.* New York: Random House.

Winant, H. (1994). Racial formation and hegemony: Global and local developments. In A. Rattansi and S. Westwood (Eds.), *Racism, modernity, and identity on the western front.* Cambridge, MA: Polity Press.

Yudice, G. (1995). Neither impugning nor disavowing whiteness does a viable politics make: The limits of identity politics. In C. Newfield and R. Strickland (Eds.), *After political correctness.* Boulder, CO: Westview.

Afterword

Glenn A. Doston

Dismantling White Privilege: Pedagogy, Poltics, and Whiteness is a welcome arrival for all concerned with multicultural issues and inclusiveness in the United States. In many instances in the academy, white privilege continues to be the missing link in courses concerned with social justice. The editors and contributors of *Dismantling White Privilege* provide a sophisticated, yet crystal clear framework, which enables readers to understand some of the most important political and intellectual issues facing our society around the issue of whiteness.

Numerous scholars have argued, most notably Peggy McIntosh, that "white privilege" is "an invisible package of unearned assets" and whites are conditioned not to recognize these advantages and that such an acknowledgement would challenge the notion of a meritocracy in the United States. This volume will guide teachers, scholars, and students to engage in substantive reflection about "white privilege" and its consequences to all in our society.

I find this book extremely timely in that I believe democracy is at risk in our society because of increasing nativistic tendencies in the 1990's. Cultural change and confusion in the United States have resulted in scapegoating those who are "different" and numerous scholars and citizens alike are in stronger denial of the existence of "white privilege." The irrational behavior on the part of the government, educational bureaucracies, and the society in general, reaffirms my belief that a critical analysis of the content of whiteness and its concomitant dismantling is crucial for this nation to remain "democratic."

Previous study in the analysis of race has meant examining only "people of color." This volume challenges this notion, by arguing that whiteness has "content" and that it is necessary to produce "pedagogies of whiteness." This powerful text will help our efforts to critically examine, and expand the true meaning of democracy. The editors and contributors understand education as a critical activity and believe that "whiteness" can be lived "progressively."

About the Editors and Contributors

Roymieco A. Carter is a graphic designer, art director, and instructor of graphic design and education.

Vicky K. Carter is an Instructional Designer in the Jack P. Royer Center for Learning and Academic Technologies at the Pennsylvania State University in State College, Pennsylvania. She is also a doctoral candidate in Adult Education focusing her dissertation work and research on the sociocultural practices surrounding workplace learning as seen through a critical lens.

Glenn A. Doston is Associate Dean and Associate Professor of Education at Ohio University in Athens. He is also a founding member of the National Association for Multicultural Education (NAME). He conducts research in the areas of teacher education, urban and multicultural education.

Laurie Fuller is Assistant Professor and Women's Studies Coordinator at Northeastern Illinios University in Chicago, Illinois.

San Juanita Garza is currently struggling to survive in New Mexico, economically the 47th state in the nation, 50th in education. As desperate as her situation may be, after being the token Hispanic in a predominantly white department, at a predominantly white campus for three years, she needed to find kinship--and she has.

Robin Good is a doctoral candidate in Education, Theory and Policy Department at the Pennsylvania State University in State College, Pennsylvania.

Aaron D. Gresson III is Associate Professor of Education in the Department of Educational Policy Studies at the Pennsylvania State University. A former community clinical psychologist and special educator, his research interests include aging policy, alcoholism and special populations, the psychology of political symbols, and intergroup communications and conflict management. His most recent book is *The Recovery of Race in America.*

Helen Harper taught English/Language Arts in a small rural high school in central Alberta, Canada for a number of years. She is now employed in the Faculty of Education at the University of Western Ontorio. Her current research and teaching concern the discursive formation of school identity with a focus on adolescent girls and more recently on white women teachers employed in Northern First Nations communities in Canada.

Joe L. Kincheloe is the Belle Zeller Chair of Public policy and Administration at CUNY Brooklyn College and a Professor of Cultural studies and Education at Pennsylvania State University. He is author of numerous books and articles, including *Teachers as Researchers: Qualitative Paths to Empowerment; Toil and Trouble: Good Work, Smart Workers and the Integration of Academic and Vocational Education; and Changing Multiculturalism* with Shirley Steinberg. His latest books include *How Do We Tell the Workers?* and *Fallen Arches: McDonald's Deconstructed,* with Allan Shelton.

Frances Maher is Professor of Education at Wheaton College, where she coordinated the college's Balanced Curriculum Project, which integrated the study of women into introductory courses. She has written articles exploring the principles and practices of feminist pedagogy. She is co-author, with Mary Kay Thompson Tetreault, of *The Feminist Classroom: An Inside Look at How Professors and Students are Transforming Higher Education for a Diverse Society.*

Ernest M. Mayes is currently living in Atlanta and working in the advertising industry.

Peter McLaren is an educational activist and Professor of Urban Schooling, Graduate School of Education and Information Studies, University of California, Los Angeles. He is author of numerous books on the politics of education, critical pedagogy, and the sociology of education. Among his recent books are *Critical Pedagogy and Predatory Culture* and *Revolutionary Multiculturalism.*

Nelson M. Rodriguez is an Assistant Professor of Cultural Studies in Education at Ohio University in Athens, Ohio. He is the editor, with Joe L. Kincheloe, Shirley R. Steinberg, and Ronald E. Chennault, of *White Reign: Deploying Whiteness in America.* He has also published on queer theory and education.

Shirley R. Steinberg is an Assistant Professor of Education at Adelphi University in New York. She is an educational consultant and a drama director. Among the numerous books she has written and edited with Joe L. Kincheloe are *Measured Lies: The Bell Curve Examined; Thirteen Questions: Reframing Education's Conversation; Kinderculture: The Corporate Constructions of Childhood; Unauthorized Methods: Critical Strategies for Teaching;* and *Students as Researchers.* She is the Senior Editor of the electronic journal *Taboo: The Journal of Culture and Education* and co-edits four book series dealing with issues of critical pedagogy, popular culture, and children.

Mary Kay Thompson Tetreault is acting Vice President for Academic Affairs at California State University, Fullerton. She is the author of *Women in America: Half of History.* She is the 1984 recepient of Women Educators' Research Award of the American Educational Research Association for her study of the treatment of women in high school textbooks on U.S. history. She is the co-author, with Frances A. Maher, of *The Feminist Classroom: An Inside Look at How Professors and Students are Transforming Higher Education for a Diverse Society.*

Leila E. Villaverde is an Assistant Professor of Curriculum Studies at DePaul University in Chicago, Illinois. She is the editor of *Rethinking Intelligence,* with Joe L. Kincheloe and Shirley R. Steinberg. She has also written on the arts in education, students as researchers, and bilingual education.

Index

Studies in the Postmodern Theory of Education

General Editors
Joe L. Kincheloe & Shirley R. Steinberg

Counterpoints publishes the most compelling and imaginative books being written in education today. Grounded on the theoretical advances in criticalism, feminism, and postmodernism in the last two decades of the twentieth century, Counterpoints engages the meaning of these innovations in various forms of educational expression. Committed to the proposition that theoretical literature should be accessible to a variety of audiences, the series insists that its authors avoid esoteric and jargonistic languages that transform educational scholarship into an elite discourse for the initiated. Scholarly work matters only to the degree it affects consciousness and practice at multiple sites. Counterpoints' editorial policy is based on these principles and the ability of scholars to break new ground, to open new conversations, to go where educators have never gone before.

For additional information about this series or for the submission of manuscripts, please contact:

> Joe L. Kincheloe & Shirley R. Steinberg
> 637 West Foster Avenue
> State College, PA 16801

To order other books in this series, please contact our Customer Service Department:

> (800) 770-LANG (within the U.S.)
> (212) 647-7706 (outside the U.S.)
> (212) 647-7707 FAX

Or browse online by series:

> www.peterlang.com